Russian Voices of the [
Volume III

Alexey Yermolov

MEMOIRS OF

THE NAPOLEONIC WARS

Translated and Edited

by Alexander Mikaberidze

Tbilisi, Georgia

2011

Second Edition
Published 2011 by the Napoleonic Society of Georgia

First edition by Ravenhall Books,
an imprint of Linden Publishing Limited
© Alexander Mikaberidze, 2005

All rights reserved. No part of this publication may be reproduced,
stored in a retrieval
system, or transmitted in any form or by any means, electrical,
mechanical or otherwise without
the written permission of the publisher.

Alexey Petrovich Yermolov

Russian Voices of the Napoleonic Wars

Volume I: Pavel Pushin, *Diaries of the 1812-1814 Campaigns.*

Volume II: Ilya Radozhitskii, *Campaign Memoirs of the Artilleryman, 1812-1814. Part I: 1812.*

Volume III: Alexey Yermolov, *Memoirs of the Napoleonic Wars.*

TABLE OF CONTENTS

Introduction — *1*

Chapter One
My Adolescence — *27*

Chapter Two
1801-1805 — *33*

Chapter Three
The Campaigns in Poland, 1806-1807 — *65*

Chapter Four
Peacetime, 1808-1811 — *113*

Chapter Five
The Patriotic War of 1812,
June-August 1812 — *121*

Chapter Six
The Patriotic War of 1812,
September-November 1812 — *176*

Chapter Seven
The Patriotic War of 1812,
 November-December 1812 — *227*

EDITOR'S NOTE

This is the second, paperback, edition of Alexey Yermolov's memoirs, which has been originally published by the Ravenhall Press in 2005. This title has been revised to conform to the series' style and focus; thus, chapter four, which was not included in the first edition, has been included and chapters on post-Napoleonic service have been removed.

Dates in original Russian documents are given under the Julian calendar, which was effective in the Russian Empire at the time. Thus, the Russian anniversary of Borodino was marked (and often still is) on 26 August, and not 7 September as it was done in France. For this book, I converted dates into Gregorian calendar. Similarly, Russian sources often cited old measurements (sazhen, pud, versta, etc.), which I converted to modern measurements.

The reader should not be surprised to see various numbers attached to the Russian names. There were often several officers with same last names serving in the Russian army, i.e. twelve Ilovaiskys, eighteen Grekovs, and four Tuchkovs and Ditterix. Therefore, numbers were attached to their last names to distinguish them, i.e Tuchkov IV, Ditterix III, Ilovaisky X, Grekov XVIII.

To distinguish between the uhlan (especially Polish) regiments in the Allied and Russian armies, I decided to use 'lancer' for units in the Grand Armée and 'uhlan' for those in the Russian service.

INTRODUCTION

General Alexey Yermolov is a true legend in Russia. A man who overcame imperial disgrace and exile to command armies and conquer provinces, he was the epitome of the military man of action. His career spanned decades as he served in the Russian army against Napoleon and then expanded Russian territory into the Caucasus.

Shrewd, perceptive and often sarcastic, Yermolov had just as many friends as enemies. His sharp and unforgiving observations rendered many apprehensive of him. Once, when asked how a certain general had acted in combat, he mockingly commented, '[He is] shy.'[1] After Czar Alexander asked what request he might like to make as a reward for his services, Yermolov, thinking of the many influential foreigners at Alexander's court, replied, 'Make me a German for then I shall be able to get all I want.' Indeed, He was a nationalist of the highest degree – proudly declaring, 'The feeling of being Russian never leaves me!'– but he was not so blinded by his patriotic feeling that he could not criticize Russian society and its army. During his retirement, Yermolov hung a large portrait of Napoleon on the wall behind his chair in his study. When a friend of his, General Golev, visited him, Yermolov asked him, 'Do you know why I have Napoleon's portrait behind my back? Because, while alive, he was accustomed to only seeing our backs.'[2] To some of his detractors, he was a byword for brutality and his actions in Chechnya were, and still are, often cited as an example of his vicious and imperialistic attitudes towards local populations. But Yermolov also left a positive legacy in the Caucasus, greatly contributing to the economic and cultural development of the region. Above all he was a Russian officer, well- educated, experienced and professional.

---

[1] Paul Vyazemsky, "Staraia zapisnaia knizhka," in *Polnoe sobranie sochinenii* (St Petersburg, 1883), VIII, p. 383. Vyazemsky collected hundreds of real stories about various prominent personalities, which were later published in a separate volume

[2] *Russkii literaturnii anekdot XVIII – nachala XIX veka*, (Moscow, 1990), p. 209; *Russkaia Starina*, (1881), XXX, p. 889.

Throughout the Napoleonic wars, he kept a detailed diary, which later served as the basis for his recollections. His brilliant and engaging memoirs capture the spirit of his times, while his acidic wit, acute powers of observation and grasp of drama make him a unique source on the Napoleonic conflict.

Alexey Petrovich Yermolov (often spelled as Ermolov) was born to a Russian noble family in Moscow on 4 June 1772. His father, Peter Alexeyevich, belonged to the nobility of the Orlov province and had enjoyed a relatively successful military career before retiring and serving in various civil positions.[3] Young Alexey was initially educated at home before attending the boarding school of Moscow University from 1784–1791. Throughout the eighteenth century, the nobility exploited loopholes in the enlistment system by enlisting their children at the time of their birth or infancy so that by the time the child grew up, they had already obtained the rank of officer without any experience or training. Yermolov was no exception and, at the age of twelve, he was enlisted as kaptenarmus[4] in the Life Guard Preobrazhensk Regiment on 16 January 1787 and promoted to sergeant in 1788 and to lieutenant in 1791. That same year, Yermolov decided to give up his Guard rank to participate in the military operations against the Ottoman Empire. His request was granted and he transferred to the Nizhegorod Dragoons with the rank of captain. However, by the time Yermolov reached his regiment in Moldavia, the war was over. The following year, Peter Yermolov made sure his son was not stuck in the provinces. Young Yermolov was recalled to St Petersburg, where he was appointed adjutant to General Prosecutor A. Samoilov. This was no accident as his father was the head of Samoilov's chancellery. By this time, Yermolov had already made up his mind to join the artillery. In March 1793, he procured an appointment as the quartermaster of the

2nd Bombardier Battalion and began studying for the exams at the prestigious Artillery and Engineer Cadet Corps. In August of the same year, he passed the tests, received the rank of captain of

---

[3] He died in June 1836. He was married to Maria Denisovna Davidova, the aunt of the famous guerilla leader Denis Davidov and had been previously married to Mikhail Kakhovskii. Peter and Maria had two children, Alexey and Anna (1778-1846).

[4] Kaptenarmus originated from French capitaine d'armes. It was a non-commissioned officer in charge of ammunition wagons.

artillery and entered the Cadet Corps. While studying here, he met the young captain Alexey Arakcheyev, who had already distinguishing himself in the household (Gatchina) troops of Grand Duke Paul.

In 1794, Yermolov again requested a transfer to the regular army. This time, he wished to get a place in the Russian army under the legendary General Alexander Suvorov, who was marching against the Polish insurgents. Yermolov's request was granted and he joined General Derfelden's staff, distingusing himself on the River Bug in October 1794 and then in the assault on Praga, a suburb of Warsaw. For his actions, he was decorated with the Order of St George (4th class, 12 January 1795). Returning to St Petersburg, Yermolov was instructed to accompany a Russian diplomatic mission to Italy and took advantage of this opportunity to travel extensively throughout that region. Furthermore, he volunteered for service in the Austrian Army and took part in the operations against the French in the Alps in the summer of 1795.

In late 1795, Yermolov heard rumours of an impending war against Persia, whose armies were ravaging the eastern Georgian principalities of Kartli- Kakheti, Russian allies. He immediately returned to St Petersburg and secured an appointment to the Russian expeditionary force of Prince Valerian Zubov; Yermolov was assigned to Major Bogdanov, a prominent artillery officer who had just organized the first Russian horse artillery company. In the course of the expedition, the Russian corps advanced along the Caspian coastline and Yermolov proved himself an able and courageous officer; he distinguished himself in the crossing of the Tabassaran mountain range and commanded a battery during the siege of Derbent in May 1796, for which he was awarded the Order of St Vladimir (4th class with ribbon).

However, the expedition was soon recalled because of the death of Czarina Catherine II. Returning to St Petersburg, Yermolov joined Ivanov's artillery battalion, becoming a major on 12 January 1797. Serving under Ivanov must have been an interesting experience for Yermolov. As he later told Denis Davidov, his superior was 'a thorough alcoholic', who whilst drilling 'had the habit of having a servant standing behind him with a flask of vodka; on the command of "zelena", he was given a flask which he immediately gulped down.' Furthermore, on one occasion, after his soldiers had been mistreated by the residents of the nearby city of Pinsk, Ivanov 'deployed 24 guns outside the city and ordered the bombardment of it; fortunately, thanks to the prudence of an officer called Zherebtsov, the cannonballs were hastily removed from the cartridges and the city did not suffer from the ensuing blank rounds. The drunken Ivanov did not notice this, soon halted the bombardment and triumphantly entered the city; unfortunately, he saw Policemeister Lawdon in the window of one of the houses and had him thrown out of the window.'[5]

On 31 January 1797, Yermolov transferred again, this time to Lieutenant General Eyler's battalion, where he continued his service for the next two years. Promoted to lieutenant colonel on 12 February 1798, he received the command of an artillery company in Nesvizh on the western border of Russia.

At this period, Yermolov was decisively influenced by the ideas of the Enlightenment as well as by the Russian liberals (A. Radischev, N. Novikov, etc) and helped his half-brother Alexander Mikhailovich Kakhovskii establish a political group called the 'Smolensk Free Thinkers'. The group promoted the ideas of the Enlightenment and criticized Czar Paul's policies. The secret police soon raided Kakhovskii's village of Smolevich in late 1798 and arrested Kakhovskii and his followers, including Yermolov. Investigations revealed that some members even had plans for a *coup d'état* to remove Paul. Kakhovskii was stripped of his nobility, had his property confiscated and was imprisoned at the Dumanud Fortress, where he remained until 1811. Yermolov was arrested in Nesvizh on 10 December 1798. Eight days later, he was transported under strict security to a court-martial in Kaluga, where Paul initially pardoned him. However, General Lindener, who presided over the investigation, personally questioned him about the group.[6] Lindener then told Yermolov that his personal papers, seized during his arrest, had been sent to Smolensk. Yermolov travelled to Smolensk and then rejoined his company in Nesvizh. Two weeks later he was told to make his way to St Petersburg, where he was then arrested for a second time. General Lindener believed him to be one of the

---

[5] Denis Davidov, *Voennye zapiski*, (Moscow, 1982), p. 313.
[6] According to Davidov, Lindener profited from the arrest of Kakhovskii and Yermolov; the former's estate and property were sold and Lindener pocketed 20,000 rubles.

ringleaders of the conspiracy and thought it better to have him arrested.

Yermolov spent almost three years in exile in Kostroma province, where he met and befriended Ataman Platov. The latter was exiled for a bizarre, if not absurd, reason. Czar Paul was dissatisfied with some officers and sentenced Platov, Prince Alexey Gorchakov and others to *hauptwache*, or house arrest, for three months. Davidov recalled an interesting story Platov told him,

> While detained, Platov had a dream that left a strong impression on him. He dreamed that he was fishing on the Neva and, after casting his net, he found it burdened with his own sabre, which was already rusty. Soon, Platov was visited by Adjutant General Ratkov (that same Ratkov, who as a poor staff officer arrived at St Petersburg the very moment the czarina [Catherine] died; he was first to learn the news and galloped to Gatchina, found Czar Paul half way to it and congratulated him on the accession to the throne; a sash of the Order of St Anna, the rank of adjutant general and 1,000 serfs comprised the award for his devotion.) In any case, Ratkov now had imperial orders to return Platov his sabre; Platov immediately unsheathed it, wiped it on his uniform and, remembering his dream, he exclaimed, 'It is not rusted yet so now it will exonerate me...' However, Ratkov thought Platov's words meant he intended to lead the Cossacks against the government and decided to take advantage of this opportunity to denounce him to the Czar, who ordered him to be exiled to Kostroma.[7]

Yermolov took full advantage of exile to educate himself, voraciously reading books on history and learning the Latin language; every morning, he awoke the local priest Yegor Gruzdev with the words, 'Father, its time to wake up, Titus Livy is awaiting us.'[8]

Yermolov was very disappointed that he could not participate in the 1799 campaign in Italy, where a generation of Russian

---
[7] Davidov, pp. 316-17.
[8] Ibid., p. 317.

officers made careers under the command of Suvorov. In a letter to a fellow officer, Ogranovich, Yermolov complained, 'I wish I could share your labours, participate in your glory but yet, there is no opportunity and all possibilities are frustrated.'[9] Fortunately for him, Czar Paul died in March 1801 and was succeeded by Alexander I, who immediately rehabilitated those persecuted by his father. Among the pardoned was Yermolov, who was allowed to quit his exile later the same month.[10] He was then fortunate to secure a position as a lieutenant colonel in the 8th Artillery Regiment in June 1801 and, later that summer, he was given command of a horse artillery company in the remote Vilna province.

This was a difficult, disheartening, period for Yermolov. An ambitious young officer, he certainly resented the fact that many of his peers had passed him in rank whilst he was in exile. Yermolov constantly tried to find ways to excel and earn promotion. In a letter to a close friend, he revealed his feelings, 'It is already the third week that I constantly see in my dreams that it would not be so bad to get into the Cossack horse artillery in the guise of a worthy officer who was needed to improve it, and then it would be easy to get another two companies... my ambition forces me to desire becoming a *feldzugmeister* of these units. A great idea indeed! Don Ataman [Platov] is a friend of mine from the time we spent in exile; so if there should be a commander, I am more deserving than anyone else. I am burning with desire to experience all branches of service, find fortune at every step... Perhaps, all my plans are meaningless, but they are not impossible...'[11]

While serving in Vilna, Yermolov encountered his old acquaintance, Alexey Arakcheyev, who had now become the powerful Inspector of All Artillery. Grim Arakcheyev disliked Yermolov's brash character and reviewed his company more often than those of other officers. In early 1805, after one such unnecessary review, Yermolov made an insulting remark to his superior and Arakcheyev never forgave him. In April 1805,

---

[9] Yermolov to Ogranovich, 11 July 1800, cited in Kavtaradze, *General A.P. Yermolov*, p. 20.
[10] For details see, D. Ryabini, "Ssilnie pri Pavle," in *Russkii Arkhiv*, (1876): I, pp. 379-383.
[11] Alexander Yermolov, *Alexey P. Yermolov: Biograficheskii Ocherk* (St Petersburg, 1912), p. 19.

Yermolov complained, 'I have either to retire or wait for war where I will be able to gain with my sword everything which I have lost.'[12]

In 1805, Russia joined the Third Coalition and mobilized its forces against Napoleonic France. During the campaign in Moravia, Yermolov commanded a horse artillery company in the rearguard and vanguard and distinguished himself at the combat at Amstetten and minor actions during the ensuing retreat as well as at the decisive battle of Austerlitz. For his actions in this campaign, he was awarded the Order of St Anna (2nd class) and promoted to colonel on 16 July 1806. Returning to Russia, he was initially assigned to the 3rd Division of Lieutenant General Osten-Sacken and later took command of artillery brigade in the 4th Division of General Dmitri Dokhturov on 7 September 1806.

In late 1806, Yermolov participated in the campaign against Napoleon in Poland, distinguishing himself at Golymin, for which he was awarded a golden sword with the inscription 'For Courage'. The following year, he served in Prince Bagration's vanguard participating in numerous actions. Paul Grabbe, who served in Yermolov's unit, recalled, 'At Friedland, our Guard artillery, enduring the brunt of Marshal Ney's decisive attack, performed poorly ... Yermolov tried in vain to rally the fleeing battery of the Guard artillery and had an unpleasant encounter with Eyler over his performance. However, when this incident became known after the battle and Yermolov was ordered to submit a report on it, he gallantly responded that he simply carried out his duty and had no desire to tell tales on others.'[13] For his actions in the 1807 campaign, Yermolov was decorated with the Order of St George (3rd class) and the diamonds of the Order of St Anna (2nd class).

On his way back to Russia, Yermolov's path again crossed that of Arakcheyev. In late August 1807, Arakcheyev reviewed the returning Russian troops and, recalling Yermolov's earlier criticisms, he ordered him to remain in camp until October while the other units returned to their quarters in September. Insulted by such treatment, Yermolov even considered leaving the service. To his surprise, Arakcheyev personally called upon him, offered Yermolov leave in order to rest and to visit him in St Petersburg. Yermolov

---

[12] Yermolov to Kazadaev, 18 April 1805, ibid., p. 22.
[13] Iz pamiatnikh zapisok Grada Pavla Khristoforovicha Grabbe (Moscow, 1873), pp. 70-71.

was then assigned to the 9th Division of Lieutenant General Arkadii Suvorov, the son of the great Suvorov, in the Volhynia.

Serving in the western provinves, Yermolov earned promotion to major general on 28 March 1808 and was then appointed inspector of the horse artillery companies. In early 1809, he went on an inspection tour of the artillery of the Army of the Danube and, as he wrote later, 'travelled through Bender and Odessa to the Crimea, visiting ancient ruins, enjoying the beautiful afternoon seashore…'. Yermolov was approaching the prime years of his life. One of his adjutants described him:

His appearance carried certain power and impressed at first sight. He was tall, with a Roman profile, small grey eyes with a quick and perceptive glance. A pleasant and unusually flattering voice; endowed with a rare talent of eloquence, desire to charm everyone around him, sometimes too obvious… This last trait, which he greatly developed, bonded him with many but distanced others more deserving of his attention. Because of this, he was later given an acerbic nickname, *c'est le héros des enseignes*. This was true, but he was a hero not only for ensigns. The influence of a man like him on surrounding people had one negative aspect. He disliked Count Alexey Arakcheyev and Prince Iashvili so we all hated them with the intensity of young men and I, more close to him than others, loathed them more than anyone else. This was a major mistake that later caused much harm to me.[14]

Although his division took part in the 1809 campaign against Austria, Yermolov commanded the reserves in the Volhynia and Podolsk provinces; after the war, his troops were deployed throughout the Kiev, Poltava and Chernigov provinces, while Yermolov's headquarters was set up in Kiev,[15] where he remained for the next two years. On 22 May 1811, he assumed command of the Guard Artillery Brigade and, after July of the same year, he also commanded the Guard Infantry Brigade comprised of the Life Guard Lithuanian and Izmailovsk regiments, but he could not assume his new position in time because he fractured his hand in two places and had to recuperate until late 1811. In the spring of

---

[14] Grabbe, pp. 70-71.
[15] Ibid., pp. 76-77.

1812, Yermolov was also given the command of the Guard Infantry Division consisting of Russia's elite units.

During the 1812 campaign, Yermolov was appointed chief of staff to the 1st Western Army on 13 July 1812; Yermolov was initially reluctant to accept this position and asked Alexander to reverse it. Although Czar Alexander disliked Yermolov's independent and arrogant character, he appreciated his abilities and confirmed his decree, allowing Yermolov to keep his earlier command of the Guard Infantry Division as well. Yermolov then took part in the retreat to Smolensk and played an important role in the quarrel between generals Barclay de Tolly and Bagration.

The discord between these two was not just a quarrel between two prominent generals, it stemmed from a deeper discord between the old Russian aristocracy and the foreigners, whom the Russians often referred to derisively as 'Germans'. The immediate cause of tension was the difference in views on strategy. Barclay de Tolly[16] was surrounded by the 'German party', who supported his defensive strategy. Opposing them was the 'Russian party', composed of many Russian officers, including Grand Duke Constantine, generals Yermolov, Rayevskii, Dokhturov, Platov, Vasilchikov, Tuckov, Paul Tuchkov and Alexander Tuchkov, Konovnitsyn, Shuvalov and others. It is noteworthy that the most vocal in the party was Prince Bagration, a Georgian in origin. These officers sincerely believed that Barclay de Tolly's strategy would lead to disaster and argued that it was possible to defeat Napoleon by a vigorous offensive. Yermolov became known for his quip when, upon returning from Barclay's headquarters, he commented, 'All of them are Germans, pure blood Germans, there. I found only one Russian and even he was [Senator] Bezrodnii.'[17]

Yermolov and Barclay de Tolly did not like each other. The latter thought his new chief of staff was arrogant and ambitious and some contemporaries noted that Barclay de Tolly 'mistrusted [Yermolov], never got close to him and was reluctant to consult him.'[18] Shrewd and perceptive, Yermolov played a dangerous game

---

[16] Barclay de Tolly himself was a third generation Russian from Livonia, where his Scottish ancestors settled in the seventeenth century. For further details see the short biographies at the end of this volume.
[17] Bezrodnii literally means bastard. *Russkii literaturnii anekdot XVIII – nachala XIX veka* (Moscow, 1990), p. 211.
[18] *Russkaia Starina*, 151(1912), p. 324.

involving his superior and his friend Bagration. On 28 July, he wrote to the czar that, 'We need one commander-in-chief for all the armies. The junction of the armies will be implemented much faster and their actions will be coordinated better.' Eleven days later he again repeated, 'We need a unified command!'[19] After the successful actions at Mir, Romanovo, Ostrovno, Saltanovka and Klyastitsy, Russian senior officers, especially Bagration, commander of the 2nd Western Army, became convinced that the Russians were able to contain Napoleon's forces. Bagration's conviction was further reinforced by the letters he received from Yermolov, who constantly urged him to oppose Barclay and assume command of the armies. In response, Bagration complained to Yermolov, 'One feels ashamed to wear the uniform. I feel sick.... What a fool.... The minister [Barclay de Tolly] is running away himself, yet he orders me to defend all of Russia.'[20]

The two commanders finally met in Smolensk in early August and publicly reconciled; Bagration, though senior in rank, gallantly agreed to subordinate himself to Barclay. However, anti-Barclay sentiments remained strong among many senior officers, and they continued to intrigue for his removal from command. Yermolov even appealed (without Bagration knowing) to Alexander requesting that Barclay be replaced by Bagration.[21] A group of misguided officers tried to induce Bagration to oppose Barclay publicly. General Vasilchikov recalled, 'Yermolov encouraged Bagration to oppose him, not to subordinate himself to the junior in rank, to this German, and to assume the overall command. It is obvious what disastrous results these intrigues could bring at the time when the fate of Russia was at stake and everything depended on good relations between commanders.'[22] Yermolov kept urging Bagration to write directly to the czar and boldly suggest that he be named supreme commander of the Russian armies. 'Please write to His Majesty. You must fulfil your duty.... I am young and no one will believe me. People will start talking, portray me as one of the discontented, who criticizes everything new, and they will bring

---

[19] Kavtaradze, *General A.P. Yermolov*, p. 33.
[20] Bagration to Yermolov, 27 June 1812, Tarle, *Napoleon's Invasion of Russia*, p. 91.
[21] Yermolov to Alexander, 7 August 1812, *General Staff Archives*, XIV, pp. 259-61.
[22] Pogodin, *A.P. Yermolov: Materiali dlia ego biografii, sobrannie Pogodinim* (Moscow, 1864), pp. 445-46.

shame on me and then discard me! Believe me, I am not afraid of this. When everything is perishing, when the fatherland is threatened with ignominy, there is no danger too high, there are no longer any private concerns…'.[23]

To his credit, Bagration rejected such treasonous suggestions. He told Yermolov, 'I will not write to the czar asking for the command, because this would be attributed to my ambition and vanity, not my merit and abilities.'[24]

However, Barclay's refusal to fully commit to the Russian offensive at Smolensk and the subsequent loss of the city further revived radical sentiments in the army. The British commissioner to the Russian Army, Sir Robert Wilson, recalled, 'The spirit of the army was affected by a sense of mortification and all ranks loudly and boldly complained; discontent was general and discipline relaxing. The nobles, the merchants and the population at large, were indignant at seeing city after city, government after government abandoned, until the enemy's guns were almost heard at Moscow and St Petersburg doubted of its safety. The removal [of Barclay]… had become a universal demand.'[25]

Events at Smolensk played a crucial role in this conflict. Most Russian generals and senior officers opposed the surrender of the city. According to a contemporary, 'the soldiers were disappointed, looking downcast…. Everybody was concerned about the future of the army'.[26] The artillery officer Ilya Radozhitskii noted, 'I have to admit that after the battle for Smolensk our soldiers were downcast. Blood shed on the ruins of Smolensk, despite all our stubborn efforts at defence, and our retreat along the Moscow road into the heart of Russia, manifestly made everyone feel our impotence in the face of the frightful conqueror.'[27] The soldiers grumbled, 'If we were defeated, that would be different. But now we are just surrendering Russia without a fight.'[28] Many officers publicly

---

[23] Yermolov to Bagration, 1 August 1812, op. cit., p. 178; also see Yermolov to Bagration, 31 July 1812, Ibid., p. 177; Fabry, *Campagne de Russie*, IV, p. 320, p. 356; Muravyeov, p. 96.
[24] Fabry, op. cit., IV, pp. 358-59.
[25] Sir Robert Wilson, *Narrative of events…* (London, 1860), p. 130.
[26] Ilya Radozhitskii, *Pokhodnie zapiski artilerista s 1812 po 1816* (Moscow, 1835), I, p. 125, 129.
[27] Ibid., 97-98.
[28] N. Mitarevskii, *Nashetsvie nepriatelia na Rossiu* (Moscow, 1878), p. 53.

11

slandered Barclay. The Grand Duke Constantine was among the most vocal detractors, telling the ordinary soldiers, 'We can do nothing... there is not a single drop of the Russian blood in our commander-in-chief's veins.'[29] In Dorogobuzh, Constantine insulted Barclay in the presence of aides- de-camp and staff officers, 'You are a German, traitor, vermin, and you are betraying Russia!'[30] General Dokhturov considered Barclay a 'stupid and loathsome person';[31] Platov declared that he would not wear the Russian uniform since Barclay disgraced it.[32] Relations between Bagration and Barclay also rapidly deteriorated. Yermolov later recalled that, on one occasion, the two commanders had a passionate argument with Bagration yelling at Barclay, 'You are German and do not care for Russia', and Barclay replying, 'You are a fool and do not even understand why you call yourself Russian.' Yermolov stood nearby and told some officers and troops passing by that 'the commanders are simply having a discussion.'[33]

After the Russian armies united on 2 August, Yermolov fought at Smolensk and Lubino (Valutina Gora) for which he was promoted to lieutenant general on 12 November 1812 with seniority dating from 16 August 1812. He continued writing letters to Alexander; such as that of 22 August, describing widespread discontent in the army, 'The retreat continuing for such a long time and the arduous marches cause discontent among the troops, who lose trust in their superiors. A soldier, although fighting like a lion, is always certain that his efforts will be in vain and retreat would continue.... Moscow is not far now and we have to fight! Every Russian knows how to die!'[34] The same day, he also wrote a letter to Bagration, 'We finally stopped [at Dorogobuzh]. Even a defeat

---

[29] Ivan Zhirkevich, "Zapiski," in *Russkaia Starina*, 8 (1874), p. 648.
[30] A. Muraviyev, "Avtografiobicheskie zapiski," in *Dekabristi: Novie materialy*, (Moscow, 1955), p. 187.
[31] Dokhturov wrote to his wife – 'You can not imagine, my friend, what a stupid and loathsome person Barclay is: he is irresolute, sluggish and not capable of commanding a platoon, least of all an army. The devil knows what got into him... leaving so many wounded in the hands of the enemy. My heart bleeds when I think of it.' 9 September 1812, Russkii arkhiv, 1 (1874): pp.1099-1100. The date is not correct because Dokhturov wrote the letter the day after Smolensk.
[32] Wilson, *Narrative of events*, pp. 114-15.
[33] Zhirkevich, p. 650.
[34] Yermolov to Alexander, 22 August 1812, in Kavtaradze, p. 34.

should not take our hopes from us; we should continue fighting until the last minutes of our existence.' In a letter to Peter Pahlen, Yermolov noted, 'God forbid the enemy reaches Moscow! But if fate, envying our happiness, allows this to happen, this would not end the conflict since we would continue fighting to the last extreme. The scoundrels would be deceived and the war would continue, destroying any of Napoleon's hopes to end the war before winter, and the lack of supplies and other hardships would reduce his forces until the other nations, now still under a delusion, would no longer find any benefit for themselves and would ... break away...'[35]

In late August, Alexander, taking note of public discontent, appointed General Mikhail Kutuzov as commander-in-chief of the Russian armies. As his memoirs reveal, Yermolov was not particularly thrilled by Kutuzov's appointment. He understood Kutuzov's cunning personality and often duplicitous actions. Still, under Kutuzov's command, Yermolov distinguished himself at Borodino, where he was lightly wounded leading a counterattack that recaptured the Great Redoubt. For his courage, he received the Order of St Anna (1st class). During the rest of the campaign, he served as duty officer in the headquarters of the main Russian army and was often assigned to the vanguard under Miloradovich. He took part in the battles at Maloyaroslavets, Vyazma and Krasnyi. In late November, he commanded one of the detachments in the vanguard under General Rosen, witnessing the horrors of the scenes on banks of the Berezina. On 3 December 1812, Yermolov was recalled to the main headquarters where he initially became the chief of staff of the Russian army, before being appointed commander of the artillery of the Russian armies in late December.

Unfortunately, Yermolov's memoirs end with the 1812 campaign. One of his biographers, M. Pogodin, did claim that he has seen Yermolov's diary for 1813-1814 but they were never located and are believed lost.

In the spring of 1813, Yermolov reorganized the Russian artillery and fought at Lützen, where Count Wittgenstein tried to turn him into a scapegoat for Allied defeat and unjustly accused him of failing to supply the artillery with sufficient ammunition. Yermolov was transferred to the lesser position of commander of

---

[35] Kavtaradze, op. cit., p. 39.

the 2nd Guard Division.[36] After the battle, Yermolov wrote the following letter to Arakcheyev to justify his actions:

> During my stay in Dresden, Your Excellency calculated the means to furnish the artillery with men, horses and ammunition and set five days to complete everything. When the men, horses and Park No.1 arrived at Dresden, this allowed me to fulfil your orders prior to the deadline and so all the parks that I had at my disposal joined the army by 2 May. On 7th, I submitted a detailed report on the preparations to the commander of artillery Lieutenant General Prince Iashvili.
>
> I present this letter and report on all the arrangements that depended on me and on the means that were at my disposal and humbly request Your Excellency to bring them to the czar's attention.
>
> Having served for a long time under Your Excellency's command, I could not have concealed my service from you and do not doubt that Your Excellency is aware that I never intrigued in order to achieve my goal… Common belief accuses me for the lack of artillery ammunition. I had everything with the army that was at my disposal and could not have had more than I was given in the first place. My reports will explain in detail the condition of the artillery. If I missed anything due to negligence or lack of enterprise, I request only one last favour – military court, which I do not fear and perceive it as the only means for exoneration.[37]

Yermolov then distinguished himself at Bautzen, where he played a crucial role in stabilizing the Russian centre and commanded the Russian rearguard during the retreat, 'firmly resisting the enemy and defending defiles and gardens before

---

[36] The division comprised the Life Guard Jäger Regiment, the Pernov and Kexholm grenadier regiments, the Glukhov Cuirassier Regiment, the Guard ekipazh and a horse artillery company.
[37] Yermolov to Arakcheyev, 29 May 1813, in *Yermolov: Biograficheskii Ocherk*, p. 69.

retreating in excellent order… and demonstrating throughout the battle his great skills as a commander, and the examplary courage and gallantry that inspried his subordinates in the midst of danger.' In August, Yermolov took part in the battle of Kulm, where he persuaded the Russian high command to retreat to Kulm to isolate Vandamme's corps and later took over general command after General Osterman-Tolstoy was seriously wounded. In his report, Osterman-Tolstoy wrote, 'I cannot overlook the actions of Lieutenant General Yermolov: everything was organized in the best possible way… Having lost my left arm, I had to leave the battlefield and entrusted my troops to Lieutenant General Yermolov, whose dedication and activity I constantly witnessed.'[38] For his actions, Yermolov was decorated with the Prussian Iron Cross; when Osterman-Tolstoy received the Order of St George (2nd class), he noted, 'This order does not belong to me, but Yermolov, who played a crucial role in the battle and ended it with such glory.'[39]

Between 16 and 19 October, Yermolov distinguished himself in the battle of Leipzig. A Russian officer, Muromtsev, left an interesting account of the battle:

> The entire army proceeded to one point, Leipzig. Napoleon, trying to prevent our concentration, attacked the Russian, Austrian and part of the Prussian armies on 4 [16] October. The French attack was swift and vigorous and an intense fight began at all points. In the middle, there was the village of Gossa, which we all called 'red roof'. The Prussian troops were constantly sent against it during the day, but were repulsed with heavy casualties because the French were deployed as tirailleurs. In the afternoon, Yermolov was ordered to seize this village by assault. The French were fortified behind its stonewalls and it was very difficult to dislodge them. Yermolov then commanded the Russian and Prussian Guards. He deployed the regiments in columns on both flanks and in the centre and marched with a drumbeat, having scattered the Guard Jägers as skirmishers in front of him.

---

[38] Osterman-Tolstoy to Barclay de Tolly, Ibid., p. 58.
[39] Pogodin, *Alexey Petrovich Yermolov*, pp. 179-180.

Observing our flanking columns, the French had to retreat pursued by the Jägers. There was a large stone house (it was the 'red roof') in the middle of the village and, as the Jägers rushed in, fierce fighting broke out; all the windows and mirrors were smashed to pieces. The French were finally driven out of the village. Corpses were taken out of the house and several of us, aides-de-camp, occupied it with out general [Yermolov].

There were many interesting incidents on that memorable day of 4 [16] October] and I want to describe some of them. Before noon, while our corps commanded by General Yermolov was still idle, our general decided to observe the actions on the left flank, where General Rayevskii's troops were under heavy attack and could barely hold their ground. He took me with him and we rode there, about half a verst away. Having witnessed the action and talked to courageous Rayevskii, we turned back to our positions. The Guard cavalry was moving to the left of us, by threes to the right, and presented a long but thin line. The French, meanwhile, were deployed in squadron columns. Yermolov noted our mistake and told me, 'Look, the French will soon charge and rout them.' He had hardly finished when the French cavalry indeed charged. The entire Russian line shook and then fled. Thus, we found ourselves in the middle of our fleeing cavalry and the pursuing French, but were a bit to the left and so had some open space in front of us. We soon saw several French cavalrymen, who noticed us too and galloped in our direction. We immediately spurred our horses and, thanks to their agility, quickly outdistanced them. It is well known that the French horses moved awkwardly. The general had his hat blown off by the wind and I managed to dismount, pick it up and then ride away. We soon reached a small dam on the creek, which separated us from the czar and his entire suite, and encountered the Life Guard Cossacks, the czar's escort, that were dispatched to support our cavalry. These good lads routed the French at once and our cavalry recovered.[40]

During the 1814 campaign in France, Yermolov also temporarily commanded the Prussian and Baden Guard units, distinguishing himself in the battles around Paris for which he was awarded the Order of St George on 7 April 1814. He took part in the negotiations leading to the capitulation of Paris and personally wrote an imperial manisfesto proclaiming its capture.[41] In May 1814, Yermolov was given command of reserve army forces on the Austrian borders and established his headquarters in Krakow.

In March 1815, he learned about Napoleon's escape from Elba and, writing to a fellow general, he noted, 'I am afraid Napoleon will isolate the Allies and attack Wellington in Flanders... Is it really more magnanimous to sacrifice thousands of innocent lives instead of taking the life of the villain?'[42] The Russian troops arrived too late to engage Napoleon, who was defeated by the Anglo-Prussian army at Waterloo on 18 June 1815. Yermolov lamented, 'My happiness about the defeat of the haughty enemy is bitter sweet since the Russians took no part in the victory.'[43]

Still, the Russian army triumphantly entered Paris and Yermolov wrote to his half-brother Kakhovskii, 'Our troops are in an incredible condition. Troops from all over Europe are here but none of them can be compared to the Russian soldier!'[44]

Yermolov later recalled an interesting incident that clearly shows his independent character. As the Russian army triumphantrly entered Paris, some soldiers from the 3rd Grenadier Division of Yermolov's corps stumbled on parade. Czar Alexander was infuriated and ordered the arrest of several regimental commanders. According to Mikhailovskii-Danilevskii, who attended Alexander at the time, 'many Russian senior officers protested against this decision... The Prussian king invited some officers of the St Petersburg Grenadier Regiment to his lunch, where the czar continuously lambasted the abovementioned colonels and even drove General Roth, the commander of that division, to tears.'[45]

---

[40] *Russkii Arkhiv*, 1890, I, pp. 377-380.
[41] Pogodin, p. 466.
[42] Kavtaradze, p. 62.
[43] Pogodin, p. 188.
[44] Kavtaradze, p. 63.
[45] Mikhailovskii-Danilevskii, "Journal of the 1815 Campaign," in Nikolay Shilder, *Imperator Alexander I: Ego zizn i tsarstvovanie* (St Petersburg, 1897), III, p.

That day, British troops took over guard duty at Alexander's palace. Yermolov recalled, 'The czar ordered me to send two regimental commanders to be confined in the British hauptwache [guardhouse] for this mistake. However, I told him, "Your Majesty, both these colonels are excellent officers, please consider their previous service and especially do not detain them in a foreign hauptwache: we have Siberia and our own prisons for this purpose."'[46] Yet, Alexander shouted at him, 'Obey your duty at once. They must be kept under English guard for greater shame.' Yermolov did not respond and decided not to arrest the colonels thinking that the czar's rage would soon fade away. Furthermore, in the evening, he met the grand dukes Constantine and Nicholas at the theatre and openly expressed his disgruntlement, 'Do Your Excellencies really believe that Russian officers serve only the czar, not their fatherland? They came to Paris to defend Russia, not for parades.'[47] Both grand dukes were astonished to hear such an audacious comment; one of Yermolov's biographers argued, quite plausibly, that Yermolov's words offended Grand Duke Nicholas, a future czar, who therefore mistrusted Yermolov for the rest of his life.[48]

According to Yermolov, 'Had the czar inquired about the colonels, I was prepared to tell him that they had already marched with their regiments to their quarters in the colony settlements. Later that day, the czar asked Prince Volkonsky whether the colonels had been arrested or not and threatened to have him detained as well. Volkonsky was so frightened that he sent his adjutants to search for me all over Paris; they found me in the theatre. One of the adjutants begged me in the name of Our Lord Jesus Christ to sign a receipt that I had received Volkonsky's note. I had to go to the lobby where I signed for delivery.

The following day, I again tried to appeal to the czar, but was rejected. I was given the orders again and had to place our colonels under arrest at the English hauptwache.'[49] However, Yermolov's

---

336.
[46] "Zapiski Nikolaya Nikolayevicha Muravyeva," *Russkii Arkhiv* (1886), III, p. 299.
[47] Mikhailovskii-Danilevskii, op. cit., III, p. 336. Also see, Kavtaradze, Yermolov, p. 64. Kavtaradze used an archival document that has a somewhat different account of Yermolov's conversation with the grand dukes.
[48] Kavtaradze p. 64.
[49] Shilder, *Imperator Alexander*, III, pp. 336-338.

actions impressed Alexander, who soon ordered the officers to be transferred to a special room in his palace.

Yermolov remained in Paris for several months and, although his corps was soon dispatched back to Russia, he stayed behind at imperial orders to study the British artillery, living with his adjutants at a house on 100 Fauburg St Honouré. The Duke of Wellington, showed him two artillery companies and allowed one of Yermolov's officers to make a sketch of ammunition caissons and limbers.[50] In November 1815, Yermolov went on leave, transferring command of the corps to General Ivan Paskevich and returning to his family estate at Lukyanchikov in the Orel province.

Yermolov enjoyed the tranquility of rural life for only a couple of months. He was appointed commander-in-chief of the Russian forces in Georgia and commander of the Independent Georgian Corps on 21 April 1816. In addition, he was also nominated as Russian ambassador to Persia. On 24 July 1783, King Erekle II of Kartli-Kakheti (eastern Georgia) had concluded the Treaty of Georgievsk with Catherine II, whereby Russia guaranteed Georgia's independence and territorial integrity in return for Erekle's acceptance of Russian suzerainty. Despite this agreement, Kartli-Kakheti was annexed in

1800 by Paul I, the 1,000 year-old Bagrationi royal dynasty was deposed and replaced by Russian military governors who deported the surviving members of the royal house and provoked several popular uprisings. The western Georgian principalities opposed Russian dominance, but were soon subdued. The Kingdom of Imereti was annexed in 1810, followed by the principalities of Guria and Mingrelia. The local population, which had previously felt that the Orthodox Russians would save Georgia from Muslim enemies, now realized how similar Russian domination would be compared to Turkish or Persian. Therefore, anti-Russian sentiments gradually became widespread, especially in western Georgia, where King Solomon II continued his resistance to Russian expansion and appealed to Napoleon for support.[51]

---

[50] Ibid., p. 79.
[51] David Lang, *The Last Years of the Georgian Monarchy, 1658-1832*, (New York, 1957), pp. 266-275; *Utverzhdenie russkogo vladichistva na Kavkaze*, 1801-1901: *K stoletiu prisoedineniia Gruzii k Rossii*, edited by V. Potto and N. Beliavskii (Tbilisi, 1901), pp. 104-116.

In addition to Georgian resistance, Russian authorities faced the daunting problem of dealing with the north Caucasian mountaineers. The mountaineers soon allied themselves with the Ottomans and attacked Russian interests during the Russo-Turkish wars of 1787–1791 and 1806–1812. Russia was not able to direct the necessary resources to deal with the problems in the Caucasus. However, by 1815, the Napoleonic wars were over and Alexander chose General Yermolov to extend and secure Russian influence both in the north Caucasus and in Transcaucasia.

Yermolov arrived in Tiflis, ancient capital of Georgia, in October 1816 and spent almost six months studying the region. Between April and October 1817, he travelled to Persia to negotiate with Fath Ali Shah and succeeded in confirming the Russian conquests recognized by the Treaty of Gulistan of 1813, for which he received promotion to general of infantry on 4 March 1818.[52] Returning back to Tiflis, Yermolov now felt prepared to take on the Caucasian tribes of Chechnya and Daghestan, whose resistance undermined Russian efforts to introduce imperial administration in the region. Unlike his predecessors, Yermolov rejected the notion of indirect rule and instead adopted a strategy of systematic subjugation and expansion. He proudly declared, 'I believe that having taken the responsibility of protecting this land... we must reign by force, not by appeal.'[53] He firmly believed that 'only executions can save the lives of hundreds of Russians and keep thousands of Muslims from betraying us.'[54] In a letter to Vorontsov, he commented, 'I am tormented by all these khanates that disgrace us with their way of life. The government of khans is a clear example of primordial society... absurd, villainous autocracy and other abuses that haunt humanity.'[55]

In 1817, Yermolov began the construction of a new line of Russian fortifications near the foothills of the Caucasian mountains and launched the systematic destruction of the forests to prevent raids and ambushes. He was most active against the Chechens, whom he drove across the River Sunzha in 1818. Yermolov then

---

[52] Because Yermolov was in retirement in 1827-1831, his seniority in rank was changed to 1 February 1822.
[53] Yermolov to Zakrevskii, 24 February 1817, in Sbornik imperatorskogo russkogo voenno- istoricheskogo obschestva (1890), LXXIII, p. 218.
[54] Kavtaradze p. 76.
[55] Ibid, p. 75.

built two fortified camps Pregradnii and Narzanovskoe and a fortress at Groznyi,[56] and connected them by means of a series of fortified lines to Vladikavkaz, the main Russian city in the north Caucasus. Yermolov then turned to Daghestan, where he established the fortress of Vnezapnii in the main pass into Daghestan and connected it with fortifications to Groznyi. It is noteworthy that the names of fortresses had particular meanings – Groznyi (Terrible), Pregradnii (Protective), Vnezapnii (Surprise), etc. When Alexander criticized his methods of conquest, Yermolov replied, 'I desire that the terror of my name shall guard our frontiers more potently than chains or fortresses.' One of the greatest Russian poets, Alexander Pushkin, soon wrote, 'Humble thyself O Caucasus, for Yermolov is coming!'

In 1818, Yermolov faced a widespread uprising in the northeastern Caucasus and responded with ruthless reprisals. By late 1819, he had succeeded in subduing northern Daghestan and destroying the Kazikum Khanate. To secure his communications with Transcaucasia, Yermolov began the construction of a new road in the Terek valley, which later became the famous Georgian military road. His decisive actions soon pacified the region, but he faced an uphill struggle in the western part of the mountains, where powerful Circassians, supported by the Ottomans, refused to acknowledge Russian sovereignty despite Yermolov's incessant campaigning in 1821–1824.

Meanwhile, Europe was hit by another wave of revolutions. Starting in Spain in early 1821, revolt quickly spread into Naples, where the royal family was forced to flee. Yermolov was recalled to St Petersburg and then to Laibach, where Alexander was attending a congress. He was given command of the Russian corps that was to march into Italy and support Austrian efforts to suppress revolutionary activities. However, the Austrian troops soon succeeded in capturing Naples and restoring royal authority there so Yermolov returned back to Russia and then to the Caucasus.

Yermolov served in Georgia for another six years. He supervised legal reform in Georgia and began the methodical exploration of raw materials. He used his salary as ambassador to Persia to construct a large hospital in Tiflis and facilitated the construction of several resorts at the Caucasian mineral springs in

---

[56] Groznyi later became capital of Chechnya.

the 1820s. He invited hundreds of German colonists to develop the local economy, abolished some commercial fees and reduced tariffs on European goods, oversaw the construction of a network of roads connecting the key cities throughout Transcaucasia and Daghestan, and established an effective postal service. Under his orders, the Russian Caspian flotilla was repaired and reinforced and a new harbour was established in Astrakhan. Yermolov paid particular attention to the beautification of Tiflis, where he supervised the construction of European-style buildings, an arsenal, a military hospital, caravanserai for merchants and bridges over the Kura, improved the education at local schools and facilitated the publication of newspapers.

However, times were changing. The Decembrist Uprising greatly affected Yermolov. Czar Nicholas I succeeded in subduing the rebels in St Petersburg and immediately launched an investigation. It revealed that there was a connection between the Decembrists and Yermolov. The Caucasus was often referred to as 'Warm Siberia' because of the thousands of exiled officers and punished soldiers that were sent to serve in the Separate Caucasian Corps. The Decembrists had even considered Yermolov for their Provisional Government. During the uprising itself, Yermolov, for still unexplained reasons, deliberately delayed pledging the allegiance of his troops to the new czar; rumours in St Petersburg claimed that Yermolov had joined the insurgents and was marching on Moscow. A Russian officer, A. Koshelev noted in his diary, 'Yermolov also refuses to pledge allegiance and is marching with his troops on Moscow.' In such circumstances, the official Investigation Committee naturally implicated Yermolov, but it could not uncover convincing evidence against him.

Meanwhile, relations between Russia and Persia rapidly deteriorated. In July 1826, the Persian army invaded Transcaucasia and initially achieved considerable success. Yermolov was criticized for his failure to contain the Persians and Nicholas appointed General Ivan Paskevich as deputy commander of the Russian armies, although Paskevich's actual task was to replace Yermolov. The two commanders quickly quarrelled; Paskevich being an associate of Nicholas who even called him 'Father General', and openly defied Yermolov. In February 1827, chief of staff General Diebitch was dispatched to the Caucasus to reconcile the two generals, but he instead supported Paskevich and coerced Yermolov into resigning. Yermolov did write a letter of resignation on 15 March 1827, but it was too late since Nicholas had already signed the order dismissing him. Yermolov was officially removed from command on 9 April 1827 and then discharged from military service on 7 December 1827 with a full pension.

Disgraced and unemployed, Yermolov returned to his estate in Orel. Two years later, the famous Russian poet Alexander Pushkin visited him there and the two had a pleasant discussion. Pushkin wrote, 'Yermolov received me with his usual kindheartedness. At first glance, I found no resemblance to his portraits, which were usually in profile. He had a round face, fierce grey eyes, grey spiky hair. A tiger's head on Hercules' torso. His smile was unpleasant because it was not genuine. But when he thought and frowned, he became very handsome and closely resembled that poetic painting by [George] Dowe.'[57]

In 1831, Yermolov moved to Moscow, where he bought a small house. The following year added anguish to his heartache when his father died. Still, the old general enjoyed life in the capital, where his house gradually became a centre for opposition to autocracy. The famous Russian philosopher Alexander Hertzen recalled, 'His military experience, opposition to Nicholas' military officialdom and, finally, his exile thrust enormous popularity on Yermolov.' Paul Grabbe, who had served under Yermolov during the Napoleonic wars, visited him at this period and left an interesting description of the ageing general:

> Returning to Moscow, I visited Alexey Petrovich Yermolov at his village estate. In my youth, I served as his adjutant and his caring and fatherly treatment attached me to him like a son. Yet, I had not seen him since 1815 when I had received command of a horse artillery company ... Rarely was anyone endowed by such a gift of being able to fascinate both masses and individuals with his appearance and the power of his words. The loyalty that he instilled in me was limitless.

> Yet, now I found only an old man, white as the moon; his enormous head was covered with thick grey hair and

---

[57] See Alexander Pushkin, *Puteshestvie v Arzrum vo vremia pokhoda 1829 goda* (Tiflis, 1899).

perched on wide, firm shoulders. His face was healthy but somewhat rough, small grey eyes sparkled in deep hollows and an enormous permanent wrinkle ran across his powerful forehead just above his grey bushy eyebrows. An old Russian genius. From 9 pm to 5 am we had not even moved in our chairs, forgetting about sleep and fatigue. I could not get enough of looking at him, carefully studying him and listening to his words. What unfortunate circumstances could have removed such a man from serving his fatherland, especially under such a czar! Without a doubt, he had made some mistakes. But is this the only measure of talent?

His house was in a mess. His study had not a single ornament; his large table had no cover and there were a few chairs of ordinary white wood, all dirty. Books and maps were scattered everywhere as well as small pots with glue, paper and tools. His favourite pastime was to bind books and paste maps. He was dressed in a dirty blue coat of thick cloth that was closed with hooks. The chaotic and confused life of a remarkable man![58]

Destitute but proud, Yermolov refused to appeal to Nicholas and suffered in silence. Nicholas, meanwhile, changed his mind and decided to employ this experienced general. In November 1831, he was restored to service[59] and, the following month, he was appointed to the State Council. Over the next two decades, he lived quietly in Moscow, collecting books for his library which eventually contained over 9,000 volumes. He later sold his library to the University of Moscow, where it is still preserved.

Yermolov often attended Czar Nicholas I at various parades, fetes and manoeuvres. On one such military exercise near Voznesensk, the Russian forces were divided into two groups, one under Nicholas, advised by Yermolov, and the second under Adjutant General Count Witt. General Witt suddenly began withdrawing. Nicholas was surprised and asked 'Why is Witt

---

[58] Grabbe, Iz pamiatnikh zapisok, pp. 17-19.
[59] Yermolov's rank of general of infantry was confirmed in 1833 and his seniority in rank was changed to 1 February 1822.

retreating when he is in much better position than I am?' Yermolov, with his usual sarcasm, responded, 'Your Majesty, probably because Count Witt thinks this is a real battle.'[60]

During the Crimean War, Yermolov was actively involved in the war effort and when Nicholas issued a call for militia in January 1855, Yermolov was elected head of the militias of seven provinces. Yermolov was critical of the Russian high command and its actions against the Allies. Prince Menshikov once visited him in Moscow and greeted Yermolov with 'We have not seen each other for so long! Many waters had passed!', Yermolov replied, 'Indeed, Prince, many waters had passed! Even the Danube has floated away from us!' Naturally, his dissenting views soon clashed with the imperial court and, four months after his election, Yermolov resigned. Yermolov then fell ill when the fever he had contracted in the Caucasus suddenly returned. In March 1856, his condition worsened when he learned about the fall of Sebastopol and took it so close to heart that he suffered paralysis and partial loss of vision. He lived for another five years, but those were years of misery and declining health.

General Yermolov breathed his last on the morning of 23 April 1861 in Moscow. His funeral was the largest seen in decades. On 30 April, his body was buried at the Trinity Church in Orel. Yermolov was never officially married but had three temporary marriages that were allowed under local Caucasian traditions and produced five sons and one daughter.[61] He recognized all of them and enrolled his sons in the artillery schools setting them onto a military career.

Yermolov was a complex character of Spartan habits, careless of his personal safety and comfort but a man who cared for his troops. A man of many faces, he was 'the modern sphinx' to Griboedov while Pushkin, another admirer, was often baffled by him, describing as 'the great charlatan'. Emperor Nicholas' Chief of the Secret Police left an interesting portrait of Yermolov:

---

[60] *Russkii literaturnii anekdot XVIII – nachala XIX veka*, p. 209.
[61] Yermolov's wives Suida, Totai and Sultanum-Bamat-Kazi stayed in the Caucasus and remarried after Yermolov left. Yermolov's sons were Bakhtiar (Victor), 1820-1892; Omar (Claudius), 1823-1895; Allah-Yar (Sever), 1824-1892, Isfendiar and Peter, and his daughter was Satiat (Sofia Khanum), 1825-1870.

Nothing has any influence on Yermolov except his vanity. He sometimes permits certain of his admirers to speak the truth to him, but he never follows their advice. The more intelligent the man beside him, the less influence he has. Yermolov has the unusual gift of binding to himself – unconditionally, like slaves – the people near to him... Officers and men truly love him for quite trifling things: on active service, he allows the soldiers, even when off duty, to wear loose trousers and jackets, and the officers to go about in forage-caps and to dress how they please... In time of need, he shares his last crust. Yermolov's great virtue is that he is not greedy for gain and despises wealth.[62]

Alexander Mikaberidze
2005-2011

---

[62] M. Medvedeva, "Novoe o Griboedove i dekabristakh," in *Literaturnoe nasledstvo* (Moscow, 1956) LX/1, pp. 485-486.

CHAPTER I
MY ADOLESCENCE[63]

I[64] owed everything to the mercy of the czar [Paul I]. Inquiring into circumstances related to my brother, which were unknown to me and, in some cases, were untrue, I had received only negative responses. General L.[65] invited an officer[66] to accompany me and told him that he was free to go if I decided to return alone. After a warm farewell, he told me that an officer, dispatched to meet me, had been ordered to deliver documents to the commandant of Smolensk, Major General Prince Dolgorukov. He also told me that the papers which had been returned were missing a journal and a few plans that were drafted during my stay with the Austrian army in the Alps[67] and which the czar had decided to examine. On my way back through Smolensk, I received these documents and delivered an order to the battalion commander in Nesvizh.

Two weeks later, filled with appreciation and praising the generosity of the monarch, I was called in to my commander[68] and ordered to leave for St Petersburg with a courier sent specifically for this purpose. I was neither discharged from service nor arrested but simply told that the czar wanted to see me. I was given two days to prepare for the journey: no one spied on me prior to my departure

---

[63] These recollections were found after Yermolov's death and were part of a larger volume of memoirs written by Yermolov on his early life and career. However, a large part of the volume was lost over time and the remaining pages published by the Russkii Arkhiv in 1867.

[64] In the opening paragraphs, Yermolov spoke of himself in third person and later changed to a first-person narrative. We have adjusted this to first-person throughout.

[65] 'General L.' was Fedor Ivanovich Lindener; born Lipinskii, he changed his name to a more German sounded Lindener to help his career.

[66] This officer was Sub Lieutenant I. Ogranovich, who was earlier given secret instructions to transport Yermolov under strict security.

[67] Yermolov served in the Austrian army in Lombardy in 1795.

[68] Chef in the original [shef, colonel proprietor] was a senior officer in the regiment responsible for maintenance and service of the unit.

and, after bidding farewell to my friends in Nesvizh, I left, carefree, for St Petersburg.

Throughout my life, I have lacked foresight, but, at 22, with a passionate character and imagination, honoured by imperial attention and invited at the request of the sovereign and feeling complete devotion towards the czar, I allowed myself to enjoy the most flattering of dreams and envisioned the brightest of futures for myself. I had seen the rapid elevation of other people, though some of them later proved their insignificance, and hope carried me away!

On the journey, the courier was very courteous to me; however, at the last station before St Petersburg, which we reached before lunch, he advised me to wait until evening, telling me that some of my acquaintances might see me and that it might lead to unfortunate conclusions. Suddenly, I realized the truth of my position. In St Petersburg, I was taken directly to the house of the governor, General Peter Vasilievich Lopukhin. After a long interrogation in his office, the courier was ordered to take me to the head of the Secret Police. From there, I was sent to the Petersburg Fortress[69] and placed in a cell in the Alekseyev Ravelin.[70]

During the two months I was there,[71] I was summoned once by the General Prosecutor: the head of the Secret Police questioned me and wrote down my answers; to my surprise, the head of the Secret Police was Makarov, a most noble and magnanimous person, who had served with Count Samoilov, knew me well from adolescence and from my service as his adjutant. He knew about the initial amnesty given to me but learned about my second arrest

---

[69] The proper title of this fortification was Petropavlovsk Fortress.

[70] Alekseyevskii Ravelin was a small fort inside the Petropavlovsk fortress. In 1797, Paul I established a prison for political criminals. It operated until 1884 and was destroyed in 1895.

[71] Many years later, Yermolov told Denis Davidov a few details on his arrest. Davidov recorded,

'Yermolov's cell was six steps wide and had a small stove, which was unpleasant when heated; a sole candle end illuminated the cell… and the walls were covered with mould … The prisoner was guarded by Staff Captain Iglin of the Senate Regiment and two sentries, who constantly remained in the cell. Often, when he tried to speak to one of them, the most compassionate, Yermolov was told, "Would you stop talking; we are strictly prohibited to talk; my comrade could hear us and immediately report to the superiors.' Davidov, Stories About Yermolov, pp. 315-316.

only after inquiring about the missing courier who had been dispatched and the reason for his absence was cloaked with secrecy. I presented my explanation on paper and Makarov corrected it, criticizing my style, coloured as it was by a feeling of righteousness, unfair persecution and imprisonment. I rewrote it and returned to my cell.

Some time later a courier[72] was sent to take the prisoner from cell No.9 and accompany him on a designated route. I was told to take warm clothes for the journey.[73] After staying in that vicious prison, I would have welcomed even exile to Siberia. Although nothing comparable to the horrors of the Inquisition ever took place in the Ravelin, certainly much had been borrowed from that beneficial and philanthropic establishment. Tranquility was ousted by a sepulchral stillness, augmented by the complete silence of two, always vigilant and inseparable, guards. Health care consisted of a constant concern not to overburden a prisoner's stomach with good quality food nor with food in quantity. Cells were illuminated with an inextinguishable tallow candle, lowered into a sheet metal tube filled with water. Different drumbeats for the morning and evening helped to determine time; but when they were not sufficiently distinct, one could judge the passage of time from the corridor, which was sometimes illuminated by a sunshine otherwise unknown in this tomb.

During the journey, my escort told me that he had to deliver me to the governor of Kostroma [N. Kochetov] and that some unhappy prisoners were often ordered further east and even into Siberia.

On our arrival at Kostroma, I was informed that I had to remain in the province for life because of a crime known only to the czar himself. Luckily, the governor's son was a friend of mine. On his own accord, he reported to the General Prosecutor that he found it necessary to leave me under his personal supervision for the strictest surveillance of my behaviour, and so I was told to live in Kostroma.

---

[72] The courier was a Turk, who initially refused to respond to Yermolov's questions about the destination of their trip. Davidov, Stories About Yermolov, p. 316.
[73] Yermolov was given his old clothes, washed linen and 180 rubles. Ibid., p. 316.

For a while, I lived in the house of Provincial Prosecutor Novikov, a very kind and noble man, but then I moved in with Major General of the Don Cossack Host Platov, later a well known Cossack ataman, who was also exiled to Kostroma on the czar's orders. I stayed here for a year and a half; the local inhabitants treated me very generously, finding nothing incriminating in my character and behaviour. I turned to the study of Latin, translating the best Latin authors, and time passed slowly, almost unnoticeably, and barely saddened my gaiety. Fate, so unfavourable to me then, caused me to complain only once when I recalled that an artillery battalion I served in was now deployed in Suvorov's army in Italy and that my comrades were participating in the remarkable exploits of our invincible army. At 22 years of age, I had been a lieutenant colonel in the reign of Catherine, wearing the orders of St George and St Vladimir. Suvorov launched so many careers that year: could it have been possible that he would not have noticed my ability, and intense and passionate steadfastness that knew no danger?

Whilst in Kostroma, I received a message from one of my best friends and comrades,[74] who was related, through his marriage, to the czar's favourite, Count Kutaisov. He had directed Kutaisov's attention to my despondent situation and was told to let me know that if I write him a letter with the most touching expressions, he hoped to obtain a pardon for me. Certainly, my resolution not to respond to this letter could be called imprudence but I would not have valued freedom gained through such means.[75]

Shortly before Paul's demise, a courier delivered an order to Platov to come to Petersburg. The czar met him very graciously, restored him in the service, granted an order and appointed him to command the troops dispatched to conquer Bukharin [Bukhara]. I was saddened by Platov's departure but did not envy his luck since

---

[74] The friend was Kazadaev, who was married to the daughter of General Rezvy. Count Kutaisov was married to another daughter of Rezvy. Davidov, *Stories About Yermolov*, p. 318.

[75] Later Yermolov noted, '[Kutaisov] could have easily done it but I had to write him a letter describing my situation in most pathetic terms. He told me that he would choose a favourable moment to report about me and could already congratulate me with freedom. My youthful ignorance interpreted this offer as disgraceful and I did not even answer my friend. So I spent another year in Kostroma until the czar died.'

it belonged to a person noted for his outstanding gallantry and abilities.

Czar Paul soon passed away,[76] and the following day after his accession to the throne, Alexander I freed both Kakhovskii and myself, together with other alleged accomplices of that fictitious crime. He was well aware of the punishment we had suffered. Thus, I arrived at St Petersburg amid many other thousands of people seeking employment after their hateful designation of dismissed from service was substituted with discharged.

The War College was then headed by General Lamb,[77] who, during the reign of Catherine, had been a major general and the governor of Kostroma. On his departure from Kostroma, he left his two daughters there, whose families accepted me very well during my exile. Meeting their father, they touched him by describing my lot as a young exile, and this noble old man wanted to show me his sympathy. So, my petition went unnoticed only for a brief moment before he finally called me into the office and, after showing a pre-prepared report, he told me: 'I did not hurry [to report your case] since I want you be restored with the rank [of colonel] at which you were unfairly deprived.' However, he soon told me that he had failed in this attempt and that I had been accepted in the artillery with my previous rank of lieutenant colonel. I remained unoccupied only for a brief period before getting command of a horse artillery company: this was a flattering appointment for a young officer because, at that moment in Russia, there was only one horse artillery battalion comprised of five companies. My appointment was facilitated by that friend of mine, who had tried to release me through Count Kutaisov.

When Count Arakcheyev was appointed Inspector of All Artillery, he persecuted me without any apparent reason. He would create impediments to my promotion and when I was to receive a rank based on my seniority, he brought in others from retirement and placed them ahead of me for promotion. I then considered leaving the service and would certainly have had no difficulty in doing this, but to highlight my resignation and be able to explain the reasons forcing me to submit it, I resorted to a strange tactic:

---

[76] Paul was murdered by conspirators on the night of 23-24 March 1801.
[77] General of Infantry Ivan Varfolomeyevich Lamb was vice-president of the War College.

during the inspection of my company by the Horse Artillery Inspector, Major General Bogdanov, I presented him with a report that my father, being of elderly years and having only one son and his estate disordered, desired me to join him. I also told him that in violation of existing procedures, I not only refused to receive a higher rank at the time of discharge, but, despite serving seven years as a lieutenant colonel, I wished to be discharged with a major's rank. The inspector, a good friend of mine, urged me to take my report back, correctly calling it fictitious, but I disagreed and he had to present my petition to Count Arakcheyev. My company was then located in Vilna, where the Military Governor Baron Bennigsen also served as the head of the Lithuanian Inspection, to which I belonged. Knowing me from my childhood, he often showed me his especial benevolence and I was confident in his favourable opinion, if he was asked to verify my sanity. Count Arakcheyev, however, wrote a very favourable letter to me, expressing his desire for me to remain in service. I complied with his will and [later] had many reasons to regret this decision.

CHAPTER II
1801–1805

1801

With the death of Paul I, many unhappy souls found an end to their miseries and I was among those who received their freedom. I can frankly call this period a rebirth since I had already been detained as a criminal, found innocent and returned to the service by an Imperial decree, only to be detained for a second time a couple of weeks later. I had then been removed from the list of serving officers as deceased, sent to the St Petersburg fortress and later exiled to the Kostroma province, where I was told to remain for life. But the omnipotent Lord, in his kindness, determines the lives of both the worldly kings and the rest of us and I was destined to enjoy freedom again.

My happiness silenced all other feelings; there was only one idea in my mind: to dedicate my life to the service of the sovereign and nothing could equal my commitment. I arrived in St Petersburg and spent almost two months wandering around the War College, boring secretaries and clerks to death. Finally, the report on my case was presented to the sovereign and I was restored to service. Yet, I was denied my promotion, though it belonged to me;[78] naturally, I was also unreasonably denied seniority in rank. Despite his support, the President of the War College General Lamb, who was well respected by the czar, could not help me in this matter. Only with difficulty did I receive command of a horse artillery company since many hesitated giving it to an officer unknown among the new generation.[79] I had previously earned the orders of St George and of St Vladimir, had taken part in the campaigns in Poland[80] and against Persia, served in the Austrian army in the Alps in late 1795. Yet, none of this was of any use to me since I was unknown in

---

[78] It is unclear why General Arakcheyev denied Yermolov his rank.
[79] Yermolov was appointed to the 8th Artillery Regiment on 13 May 1801; he then transferred to the horse artillery company on 21 June 1801.
[80] Yermolov refers to Suvorov's campaign in Poland in 1794 and to General Valerian Zubov's expedition against Persia in 1796.

exertzhauses[81] or on the Smolensk Field[82] that benefited so many famous people of our time.

I arrived in Vilna where my company was deployed. The town was pleasant, with many residents; lots of people, who had fled during the previous reign, were now returning to enjoy the benevolent rule of Alexander I; everyone blessed his name and the people's love towards him was boundless! My army life proceeded blissfully, service flattered my ambition and constituted my main aspiration; all other passions were subordinated to it! I turned twenty-four years old; full of dedication and good will, as well as good health! The only thing missing was a war. Lady Luck never smiled on me!

1803

Peaceful times prolonged my stay in Vilna till late 1804. A life of idleness led to certain habits and, my dear beautiful ladies, I fully experienced the power of your charms; I owe you many of the most pleasant moments of my life![83]

1804

I received an order to leave Vilna. Callous superiors were persecuting me and soon sent me off to Libava, Vindav, Birzha, Grdono and Kremenetz in Volhynia; I led a nomadic life and, with my abstinence and thrift, I took measures to make ends meet. My company was in good condition, officers were excellent and they respected me; because of this, I tolerated everything and considered my duty as my only benefit.

---

[81] Exertzhauses – barracks where soldiers were drilled.
[82] The army held its parades on the Smolensk Field.
[83] While in Vilna, Yermolov's dedicated service attracted the attention of Alexander. In a letter to his friend on 16 June 1804, Yermolov described Alexander's visit to Vilna. He wrote, 'Reviewing the troops, Kaptsevich's legion and my cohort, the czar personally expressed his goodwill to me, spoke to me and even repeated twice, "I am very satisfied with how fast your company's firing is as well as with the speed of its maneouvres." Major General Markov, of the Pskov Regiment, was granted a ring. According to everyone, he was displeased with Kaptsevich's battalion; while he watched me for hour and half, he did not spend even quarter of an hour [with Kaptsevich] and, even then, half of that time he was speaking to me...' N. Dubrovin, A.P. Yermolov pri naznachenii ego na Kavkaz, Voennii Sbornik (1869): LXX/11, pp. 31-32.

1805

While coming from Birzha, the Inspector of All Artillery Count Arakcheyev reviewed my company in Vilna and I recklessly and arrogantly objected to one of his remarks;[84] as a result, I only amplified the disfavour in my powerful superior and would later feel it many times. The year before, I had already appealed to another inspector for a discharge and had agreed to go with the rank of major, although I had already served as a lieutenant colonel for seven years. I believe there was never a similar report filed and a physician should have examined my health for sanity!

Campaign against the French in Austria

Russia's tranquility was interrupted by involvement in the war against the French in Austria. Since 1799 and Suvorov's brilliant victories in Italy, Russia had avoided all wars originated by the turbulent governments of France. Finally, our armies advanced against those infringers of common peace. General Kutuzov marched in support of Austria; his army was to amount to some 50,000 men. Troops under General Michelson entered Polish territories acquired by Prussia. Forces commanded by Lieutenant General Count Tolstoy were dispatched to Hanover; Prussia was to assist us.[85]

General Kutuzov was to unite with the Austrian army led by General Mack, then deployed in Bavaria. However, Austria, hoping for the friendly disposition of the Bavarian kurfurst[86] who was

---

[84] In early 1805, Yermolov had to undertake a long march to Vilna. The company arrived only to find Arakcheyev, who immediately reviewed it and found in good order. However, he ordered Yermolov to deploy his exhausted company on some nearby heights. He then reviewed it again and criticized Yermolov for having weary horses, noting that artillery officer's reputation depended on horses. Yermolov bluntly responded, 'It is pity indeed that the reputation of officers in the Russian artillery very often depends on beasts.' Arakcheyev never forgave him for this phrase. See Davidov, Stories About Yermolov, pp. 318-319.

[85] In early 1805, Yermolov had to undertake a long march to Vilna. The company arrived only to find Arakcheyev, who immediately reviewed it and found in good order. However, he ordered Yermolov to deploy his exhausted company on some nearby heights. He then reviewed it again and criticized Yermolov for having weary horses, noting that artillery officer's reputation depended on horses. Yermolov bluntly responded, 'It is pity indeed that the reputation of officers in the Russian artillery very often depends on beasts.' Arakcheyev never forgave him for this phrase. See Davidov, Stories About Yermolov, pp. 318-319.

meantime misleading her by establishing large magazines in his realms, and planned to take the war as far from her territory as possible. Archduke Charles led another army in Italy. The Austrians awaited our army and the military operations were not yet initiated.

General Kutuzov was still in St Petersburg, when Adjutant General Baron [Ferdinand] Winzegorode was instructed to lead the army to Austria and make all necessary arrangements for the march.[87] Under new orders, generals, even senior in ranks, had to obey him and this alone was sufficient to spread discontent; however, General Winzegorode added to this his haughtiness and arrogant demeanour which widely spread indignation. The troops complained that, after the regiments began march, he had ordered that wagons be left behind, surplus possessions sold and artels[88] abolished. Everything was sold for a penny and without any regard for the soldiers. There are only a few examples of Germans not acting in a calculated way so it is natural that the baron had no time for artels. Fortunately, Kutuzov immediately revoked these orders upon his arrival and it is impossible to describe the joy experienced by the troops on this occasion!

Having arrived at Radziwill with my company, I did not find our army there and had to march to catch up with it. Therefore, I was still en route when I encountered General Kutuzov, who was travelling from St Petersburg. He reviewed my company, which had been on the move for two months already, found it to be in good order, encouraged the officers and soldiers, inquired about my

---

[86] Maximilian Joseph had been Elector since 1799 and Napoleon elevated him to royal status in 1806.

[87] The Army of Podolsk was the first of the Russian armies to march to support the Austrians with 56,713 men. By early August, Kutuzov had made several organizational changes and divided the army into two corps comprised of six columns: 1st Column (Major General Peter Bagraton), 2nd Column (Lieutenant General Essen II), 3rd Column (Lieutenant General Dokhturov), 4th Column (Lieutenant General Shepelen), 5th Column, (Lieutenant General Baron Maltitz) and the 6th Column (Lieutenant General Baron Rosen). The Russian vanguard comprised of 12,879 men, the 1st Corps included 24,852 men., the 2nd - 18,982. The Podolsk Army also had 88 field cannon and 24 horse artillery guns. The 6th Column (Rosen) was detached from the army soon after the campaign began and reinforcements were late to join the army. As a result, the numbers for the Russian army at the opening of campaign vary between 45,000 and 57,000 men.

[88] Artels were unions established by permission of regimental commanders. Artel members shared their possessions and provisions.

previous service and was surprised that despite my two decorations from the time of Catherine II and rapid promotions during the previous reign, I was still a lieutenant colonel. He told me that he would take note of me and ordered me to move along and join the army.

Meanwhile, our troops passed through Austrian Galicia, being well fed and in complete order, and were not far from Braunau.[89]

On the commander-in-chief's order, additional wagons were distributed to the troops and workshops established to replace carriages.[90] Every day troops made progress as some of the infantry were transported on wagons[91] and farm horses drew the artillery. The army proceeded in five columns, each one march from the next.[92]

Thus, our army concentrated in the vicinity of Braunau, where our main headquarters was established; our vanguard was in Bavaria on the thirteenth hour of march.[93]

---

[89] The distance from Radziwill to Teschen was approximately 450 miles, and the Russian army covered it in 28 days.

[90] The Russian army advanced on 26 August but was slowed down by heavy rains. Furthermore, the Russian artillery consisted of the new guns of General Alexey Arakcheyev's 1805 ordnance system that were too heavy for the horses to pull. Kutuzov wrote, 'As for the artillery, despite my desire to comply with the requests of the Austrian court, it is impossible to move [the guns] as fast as the infantry; the horses are worn out... and it would do the service no good to see this important element of the army exhausted on the way.'

[91] A contemporary recalled that, 'We moved at normal speed to Teschen, but from that point we were moved on the wagons and at triple speed, sometimes up to 60 versts (39 miles) a day. The movement was well organized: twelve men, with their entire outfit, usually sat on the wagon which also carried ammunition and the backpacks of another twelve soldiers. Ten versts later there was a change: those walking replaced the soldiers on the wagons, who now walked with their muskets.' I. Butovskii, *Feldmarshal kniaz Kutuzov pri kontse i nachale svoego boevogo poprischa* (St Petersburg, 1858), p. 14.

[92] Kutuzov ordered most of the baggage to be left behind. From Teschen, the Russian army made 30 miles a day, marching the first half of the day, and then moving on the wagons. However, the Austrians still urged Kutuzov to hurry and only rest the troops every four days. Kutuzov refused and kept his previous marching order.

[93] It is unclear what Yermolov meant by this. The Russian vanguard reached Braunau on 12 October, covering 300 miles in sixteen days. However, it lost 79 men due to fatigue and some troops were barefoot.

It was known that the French army was concentrating near the Austrians so our troops received instructions en route to Ulm and we prepared for an offensive.

Then, General Kutuzov was introduced to an elderly man, who had important news for him. How could Kutuzov expect that it was General Mack himself with the news of the complete destruction of the Austrian army?[94]

Napoleon had attacked the Austrian army at Ulm. Mack, poorly informed about enemy movements, was not sufficiently cautious, his forces were scattered and could not regroup. The surprise attack caused such confusion among the Austrians that their army, which was sufficiently strong and in good order, was annihilated piecemeal and without offering resistance. A large part of it was captured by the French together with its entire artillery and transport. Only some minor forces under Archduke Ferdinand, generals Kienmayer and Merfeld managed to escape destruction. Even Mack could not avoid captivity; but having promised not to serve against the French, he was released and sent to his estates. A white bandage on his head raised doubts that he would retain any memory of his exploit. But he explained that he had suffered more from the clumsiness of a coachman than from the enemy. His carriage had overturned and he had suffered a blow to the head, although in such a manner that his head was preserved to serve his benign motherland.

When a staff officer, Mack had distinguished himself as an enterprising and courageous officer at Belgrade during the wars against the Turks. Since then, he became famous, found strong patronage at the court and cleared his path to promotion through intrigue. Based on his absurd plans, the Austrian troops under Prince Coburg had undertaken a campaign against the French Republic in Belgium. Mack enjoyed particular goodwill from the empress, the first wife of Francis II.

Learning about the incident, General Kutuzov thanked Mack for the news and departed. General Mack then distinguished

---

[94] Kutuzov was misinformed about the situation. Despite meeting Francis of Austria in early October, Kutuzov returned to the army unaware of the actual situation around Ulm. Kutuzov also received news of alleged Austrian victory in vicinity of Ulm, that further confused him.

himself by travelling faster than the news of Ulm. The Austrian army did not have a more efficient fugitive.

General Kutuzov found it necessary to change his earlier orders, his situation worsening by the hour. The enemy had advanced with speed and was already close to us. A hasty retreat was the only means of survival but we had heavy artillery, hospitals and transports. To lighten the troops as much as possible, he ordered all heavy transport to turn back; meanwhile Kutuzov remained at Braunau, awaiting the Austrians that had survived the defeat at Ulm.

Eventually, we left Braunau and began the famous withdrawal that amazed even our enemy.[95] It was late autumn and heavy rain hindered us so that on the third day from Braunau our troops caught up with heavy transports and our speed significantly decreased. Our army amounted to some 27,000 men, because most of our cavalry remained far behind due to our rapid advance from Braunau, and Lieutenant General Shepelev's strong column, which had earlier returned to Russia, was ordered to return but had not yet joined us.[96]

At Lambach, our army halted for one day to allow the heavy transports to move forward. It was here that the enemy vanguard caught up with us[97] and we engaged the French for the first time during the reign of Alexander I. We occupied favourable terrain,

---

[95] The Russian army left Braunau on the night of 26 October, marching via Reid and Lambach to Wels. The bridges over the River Inn were promptly destroyed. At Wels, Kutuzov met Emperor Francis and discussed plans. It was agreed that the Allied army would put up a series of delaying actions behind the tributaries of the Danube and then deploy in the vicinity of Vienna.

[96] A contemporary wrote, 'Supplies were scarce. The troops looked for bread and potatoes in the villages; we were ordered to take provisions, but not to pillage the residents.' Austerlitz: Vospominania suvorovskogo soldata (Moscow, 1901), p. 8. Another witness recalled, 'We arrived at Lambach late in the evening of 29 October, and stayed there for two days. In three days of forced marching, we covered over 100 versts [66 miles]... Our troops were starving, could not find supplies, except for small quantities of hay and wood.' Butovskii, Field Marshal Prince Kutuzov, p. 18.

[97] Having destroyed the Austrians, Napoleon began preparations for the pursuit of the Russians. He formed three columns with Marshal Lannes leading the left flank, Soult, Davout, and the Imperial Guard in the centre and Bernadotte, Marmont and the Bavarian corps on the right. Murat with his cavalry was moved to the vanguard. After marching in continuous rain, Oudinot's troops of 5th Corps reached Braunau on 29 October.

our rearguard fought with spirit and our losses were light; the 8th Jäger Regiment distinguished itself, but its leader, Colonel Golovkin, died of his wounds. We lost one gun of the horse artillery company of Colonel Ignatiev because the axle of the carriage broke because of Ignatiev's saving on lubricant. The authorities did not learn the real reason for the loss as he thought it better to claim that enemy fire destroyed his gun. The French vanguard was not strong because its troops had no provisions and had spread out along the road to pillage.[98]

During the retreat from Lambach our troops were deployed in the following order: the rearguard remained under the command of Major General Prince Bagration. Major General Miloradovich commanded a special detachment, designated as a separate brigade to support the rearguard and keep close at hand. Other forces were divided into two divisions under lieutenant generals Dokhturov and Maltitz. My horse artillery company, in addition to two other field artillery companies, were assigned as reserve artillery under the commander-in-chief's orders. As a result, I was attached to the main headquarters and was the last to get supplies for my troops and horses, especially when supplies were insufficient and hard to come by.[99] I was often denied any provisions and, suffering from hunger, I asked that my company be attached to some unit. My request was denied. The Austrian General Kienmayer, having no horse artillery in his forces, requested that my company be assigned to him but the commander-in-chief turned him down, and I must say I was happy about it because if I had to endure hardship I would rather have done so with my comrades in arms.

While we marched from Lambach, the residents of Zaltzburg, fleeing from the French, informed us that they occupied the town

---

[98] The combat at Lambach occurred on 30 October, when Marshal Davout's troops attacked four Austrian infantry battalions. The Austrian commander appealed to Bagration for help. The Allied troops succeeded in halting the French for over five hours and then disengaged to follow the main army. Bagration reported 100 killed, 44 wounded and 1 gun lost, while Austrian casualties amounted to 210 men. The French losses were light, though General Bisson was wounded.

[99] Kutuzov wrote to Alexander, 'Since we left Braunau, the troops bivouac without tents and with provisions for a day only. Sometimes they do not have any food at all because there is no time to receive it. Artillery horses are extremely exhausted ...'.

and had advanced towards Vienna. The enemy must have known about our inferior numbers and the lack of Austrian defence because it weakened itself by taking this direction. Prior to arriving at Wels, our rearguard was constantly engaged in fighting which always started early in the morning since we usually marched during the night and broke from the enemy. We tried to reduce skirmishes that, due to our small numbers, caused considerable loss to us.

Later on, we continued the retreat through the town of Linz and found favourable defensive positions covered by the River Traun near Ebersburg, and our army was rested for one day. At Ebersburg, a strange incident occurred: the cavalry patrols were ordered to cross the river in the wake of the heavy transports. However, bored by the prolonged movement of the wagons, they spread the rumour of an enemy attack on the bridge. Suddenly everything fell into confusion: the carriages were quickly abandoned, many fell off the bridge and musket fire broke out in the camp, although not a single enemy soul was on our side of the river. The commander-in-chief was unable to stop the disorder and the agitators were never found.

The enemy had occupied Linz. Marshal Mortier with 11,000 men crossed to the left bank of the Danube with the intention of beating us to Krems, seizing a bridge over the Danube and forcing us to proceed to Vienna, since there were no other bridges in the vicinity. Pursued at every step, we would have been unable to attempt a safe crossing. Meanwhile, another French column was dispatched through Zaltzburg to beat us to Vienna.

Our commander-in-chief was initially unaware of Mortier's movement and this further complicated the situation. There were also frightful deficiencies in supplies, which caused an outbreak of plunder, disorder and insubordination among our troops. Regiments had abandoned numerous stragglers behind, whom we called marauders: this was the first word borrowed from the French. They usually gathered in a group and were relatively well organized since a squadron of hussars that was sent to prevent pillage found one of the groups ready to repel their charge.

The Austrian emperor arrived to see our retreating troops at Wels and then turned back. He was accompanied everywhere by despair and the complaints of the local inhabitants, whom we were leaving destitute even before the French arrived. He witnessed the devastation of his land and was unable to provide any assistance.

He counselled the residents of Wels to count on Napoleon and hope to find mercy in his generosity. Seeing our inferior forces, the Austrian emperor could have no doubt that his capital would soon be the enemy's prize.

At Enns, our army crossed the river, while the rearguard halted close to the town. The enemy was deployed nearby and remained idle; however, it was ascertained that a strong enemy detachment had been dispatched to St Florian's monastery to halt our army's progress or at least to slow it down. The commander-in-chief, informed about this, tried to forestall the enemy's movement and Major General Strick's detachment arrived at the monastery, covering the army's march. Yet, a bitter engagement took place there and, although we suffered considerable casualties because of enemy superiority, our army still continued its march uninterrupted. I do not know why the commander-in-chief criticized General Strick, but he was very upset by the whole event.

Meanwhile, our rearguard, threatened with being cut off, retreated hurriedly across the Enns; it delayed the enemy for some time and then slowly began withdrawing.[100] The artillery and other heavy transports meanwhile pushed on. The wounded were dispatched down the Danube towards Krems.

The commander-in-chief hurried to cross over the Danube; it was impossible to delay the enemy with the forces available and even if we had achieved success in battle, our losses would have completely weakened us. In addition, General of Infantry Buxhöwden was marching with strong reinforcements from Michelson's army while Grand Duke Constantine[101] was leading the Guard from St Petersburg and Lieutenant General Shepelev's column was approaching our army. The slightest delay could have been disastrous for us; only speed and union with the reinforcements would have saved us from this dangerous situation.

---

[100] The Russian army crossed the Enns on 4 November, covered by Prince Bagration. The Russian rearguard reached the bridge over the Enns only minutes ahead of the French, who tried to seize the crossing. Bagration deployed batteries and arranged infantry to repulse any enemy attacks. He sent the dismounted Pavlograd Hussars under Joseph O'Rourke, who destroyed the bridge under enemy fire. The French tried to cross the river on boats, but the Russians contained their attempts until darkness.

[101] Grand Duke Constantine (1779-1831) was the brother of Czar Alexander I. In 1805, he led the Guard units to Moravia.

Protected by the Danube, we could finally give our exhausted troops a much-needed break.

The enemy had every reason to desire a decisive engagement with us and prevent us from receiving reinforcements. The French knew about our small numbers and it is probable that obliging Germans provided them with accurate information about us. Moreover, the Austrian army under Archduke Charles achieved a victory over Marshal Massena in Italy and was rushing to Vienna after hearing about the defeat of Mack. Archduke Charles, being a generalissimo and having previous experience in command, chose the most gallant regiments and the best generals and officers for his army.

On 22 October [3 November], superior enemy forces attacked Prince Bagration's rearguard near Amstetten.[102] Despite the courageous resistance of the Kiev and Malorossiisk grenadier and the 6th Jäger Regiment, and regardless of Prince Bagration's efforts, our troops could not resist the impetus of a superior enemy and were thrown into disorder, sustaining heavy casualties. The artillery was forced from its positions and the troops massed in ragged groups along the road. However, the woods concealed Major General Miloradovich's forces and when the French decided to pursue the beaten rearguard, they encountered fresh forces resolutely awaiting them. This abrupt turn of events slightly confused the enemy and Miloradovich skillfully exploited this. He ordered the cavalry to charge the hesitant enemy and Lieutenant Colonel Igelstrom, an officer of exceptional courage, led the charge of two squadrons of the Mariupol Hussar Regiment, swiftly falling on the French infantry and driving the enemy back, the hussars almost capturing a battery. Yet one canister shot – and our army lost another gallant officer! Following Igelstrom's death, his squadrons scattered and the enemy rallied; two days before we, as good friends, had promised to support each other in need and, as soon as I learned about the order for him to attack, I rushed forwards with my horse company to support him; Yet, I found him already dead and, having halted the enemy movement, helped his squadrons to rally and hold their ground. I continued the cannonade and, meanwhile, the grenadier battalions of the

---

[102] Prince Bagration had approximately 6,000 infantry and 1,900 cavalry. He was supported by Austrians under Count Nostitz.

Apsheron and Smolensk regiments prepared for a bayonet attack led by Miloradovich himself. Encouraged by the presence of their commander, the grenadiers attacked vigorously and the enemy, driven back, retreated into the woods and did not dare appear again. Some French forces, which were deployed nearby, took no part in the action and retreated as well; others continued useless musket fire, accompanied by harmless artillery fire; however, in the evening all the French forces withdrew and we spent the night on the battlefield. At dawn, we resumed our retreat and the enemy soon came into view, but did not pursue us with their previous audacity.[103] From this time, Miloradovich's separate brigade formed the rearguard, replacing Prince Bagration's troops for, in all justice, they needed some time to rest.

At Amstetten, I engaged the French for the first time in my life and led my horse artillery in action for the first time as well, knowing about its command as little as anyone else. Its manoeuvrability allowed me to hasten everywhere and that is why I found myself with the hussars. Then again, I anticipated the enemy's moves and, having taken the heights, prevented the deployment of an enemy battery that could have inflicted heavy losses on us.

General Miloradovich was very grateful to me, but of course not for having carried out his orders since this successful action

---

[103] Yermolov's account of the battle contains a few errors that require explanation. The road from Enns ran through a dense forest with a few clearings where troops could be deployed. Bagration made a fighting retreat along this road to Amstetten pursued by superior French forces. He made a stand near Amstetten, where the forest receded and allowed him to arrange his troops in two lines on both sides of the road while the artillery was set up on the road itself, protected by the cavalry. As the French cavalry attacked, Allied cavalry overwhelmed them. It was at this moment that two guns, which Lieutenant Octave Levasseur deployed in the middle of the road, opened fire, disorganizing the Allied cavalry. The French received reinforcements and counterattacked, penetrating the first line of Bagration's defence and engaging the second. Bagration appealed to Kutuzov for reinforcements and received Miloradovich's brigade. Bagration then withdrew part of his fatigued troops while Miloradovich counterattacked with his fresh forces. The fighting continued for the rest of the day and was notable for its savageness. According to Russian sources, the Allied forces suffered around 1,800 losses. Bagration reported that his detachment alone suffered 232 dead, 174 missing, 240 lightly wounded and 130 seriously wounded, who were left at Amstetten. His cavalry lost 77 horses, 17 artillery horses and another 83 horses were wounded.

happened by chance and I suspect it was not easy for him to acknowledge that he could not have ordered things better. Nevertheless, for me, still an unknown officer, it was pleasing to hear my superior's praise.

Approaching the monastery at Melk on the banks of the Danube, the rearguard observed a column of troops moving along the opposite shore. We were unable to identify them because of the distance and thought that they were Austrians fleeing from the French; however, near the monastery, the Danube narrows and the road is right next to the water so we easily realized that it was an enemy column moving in substantial numbers: it was Marshal Mortier, who, as mentioned above, had crossed to the left bank at Linz.[104]

The commander-in-chief could not receive this news indifferently as our situation was now extremely dangerous. On our side, rocky hills on the bank of the Danube diverted the road from the river towards the town of St Pölten and forced us to make a lengthy detour. We could only hope to beat the enemy and establish a crossing by a quick dash to Krems. Fortunately, the French faced an arduous road on the left bank.

The Austrian generals Merfeld and Nostitz were in our army together with their cavalry which had survived the defeat at Ulm. Until now, they believed that the commander-in-chief would defend Vienna and give battle in its vicinity. Probably Kutuzov did not want to clarify their misunderstanding and, with his famed shrewdness, Merfeld failed to perceive Kutuzov's exact intentions. At St Pölten, the road divided into two routes, the first leading towards Vienna and the second to Krems only four German miles away. It was here that Kutuzov announced his decision to cross the Danube to join the reinforcements coming from Russia, and the army turned to Krems, hurriedly crossing to the left bank of the Danube.[105]

---

[104] On 6 November, Marshal Mortier moved his 8th Corps by forced marches from Linz to Spitz on the north bank. He hurried General Gazan's division to Durrenstein. Meanwhile, Murat lost contact with the Russians and, after some hesitation, decided to move towards Vienna. Mortier was left to face the entire Allied army. Kutuzov realized that he had a chance to destroy Mortier's isolated corps.

[105] Kutuzov marched from St Polten to Krems and crossed the river on 7-8 November before destroying the bridge.

The Austrian generals were visibly exasperated but their anger was unfounded since it was impossible to beat the French at Vienna. It was well known that the Austrian generals were as devious as their troops were cowardly.[106] It happened so that General Nostitz, who with the Hungarian hussars served in Prince Bagration's rearguard, had removed the outposts and left the rearguard without informing Bagration after a French general deceived him about a truce. Prince Bagration was in danger, but Major General Ulanius, who was close to the rearguard, spotted this in time and joined the rearguard.[107]

During the army's retreat to Krems, General Miloradovich's rearguard remained on the road to prevent the enemy from detecting the direction of our army. Miloradovich was reinforced by cavalry and Bagration was instructed to stay close to him. Our outposts of Hungarian hussars were deployed far in front and occupied a favourable position between some forests; the enemy could discern neither our small numbers nor our deployment. The outposts soon reported that a French negotiator delivered an offer from the French vanguard to parley with General Miloradovich. However, arriving at the place, General Miloradovich did not find the French general, who, after a long wait, had departed and left his captains with instructions. Following a rambling discussion and numerous inappropriate greetings, the French captain suggested we remove our outposts and promised that they would not undertake

---

[106] The Russians despised the Austrian troops, whom, they claimed, had lost every battle in the campaign. Thus, General Dokhturov wrote to his wife, 'As for the Germans [Austrians], you cannot imagine what horrors they commit and what a misfortune it is to be with these scoundrels. The French, like us, hate them and treat them as rascals. But the French are afraid of us and the butts of our muskets'.

[107] Yermolov refers to an incident at Hollabrunn on 14 November, when Murat tricked Nostitz into believing that a truce was concluded between France and Austria. Nostitz withdrew part of his forces but several Austrian units still remained with Bagration; thus, on 18 November, Prince Hohenlohe wrote to Francis, 'The Russian Imperial General Pankration [sic] was pleased with the actions of the Hessen-Homburg Hussars in this battle.' On 15 November Kutuzov wrote, 'During the engagement today, the Austrian General Count Nostitz, who is attached with his cavalry to my rearguard, received a letter from the commander of the French vanguard, who assured him of an armistice between the Emperor of Austria and France. So, Nostitz refused to commit his troops to the battle and informed Bagration of his [decision].'

any action that day. The negotiator's disgusting appearance should have shaped the extent of our trust in his words. However, Miloradovich was filled with ideals of chivalrous times, when strangers used to make eternal vows of friendship and the slightest doubt was considered a crime; so Miloradovich did not dare to offend this knight by mistrusting his words and, without even asking his name, he ordered the removal of our outposts. I witnessed this meeting and suspected that it would have been more advantageous for us to have dealt with King Francois I instead of Napoleon.

Approaching our camp, we received news that while leaving their positions, our outposts had been attacked and pursued by superior enemy forces followed by a considerable number of enemy troops.

The enemy soon appeared and occupied the nearby heights, threatening our retreat. I do not know who persuaded Miloradovich to cancel his order and send reinforcements to the retreating hussars because this order would have led to a battle, which would have been unsuccessful for us because of our disadvantageous positions. So, without leaving our camp, we deployed and prepared for the enemy attack. The French moved strong infantry forces against our right flank which was exposed on unfavourable terrain and forced us to direct our forces and attention in this direction, while their large cavalry detachment reconnoitered on our left flank and observed that we had no reinforcements besides Prince Bagration's troops. Fortunately, the enemy could not complete its reconnaissance before dark because the short cut through the woods passed in front of our batteries and the French cavalry had to make a long detour. So, the evening prevented them from taking any drastic action and Miloradovich escaped retribution for an inexcusable mistake that would have had to be corrected by sacrificing many lives. Probably, the enemy would not have found a head on Miloradovich's shoulders as he, despite his fearlessness, had completely lost it. At midnight, having set huge bonfires, we retreated without any interference and I must confess I was as happy as anyone else; I do not know if our knight [Miloradovich] would take advantage of such lessons from beneficial Fortune.

Marching all night, the rearguard crossed the Danube at 10:00 am on the following day; only a few cavalry posts were left on the right bank. The enemy arrived in the late afternoon and, having recalled our last forces, we burnt that gorgeous bridge over the Danube.

Leaving the Danube between us and the enemy, the commander-in-chief could now for the first time hope to link up with the reinforcements from Russia; he did not know about Marshal Mortier's crossing at Linz and had we not detected the French troops in the vicinity of Melk monastery, Kutuzov might have ordered that we proceed at normal speed to shield the weary soldiers from bad weather and difficult retreat and the French might have captured the bridge at Krems.

Having saved the army from destruction, the commander-in-chief enjoyed the full confidence of the troops. Commanders were discontent with his severity but saw it was necessary and respected him for it. I happened to see him when he was instructing generals and how tolerant and lenient he was when others misunderstood him. He once noted, 'Gentlemen, I feel I talk Arabic to you'. And indeed, one could notice that some, despite his efforts, retained the ability to completely misunderstand him. Lieutenant General Dokhturov and major generals Prince Bagration and Miloradovich enjoyed his particular trust. The last two officers were the only ones engaged at the moment and they suffered great hardships; in short, they were entrusted with the protection of the army.

The day after we arrived at Krems, our rearguard occupied the town of Stein. Marshal Mortier, having occupied some vineyards on the steep hills above the town, approached the town gates with part of his troops; intense musket fire followed.

The commander-in-chief had intended to rest his troops since they needed to repair clothes and boots damaged by rain and, for this purpose, an enemy force so close could not have been tolerated.

General Miloradovich received the order to attack and only his fearless and enterprising character could succeed in such a mission.[108] Our regiments had to assault steep cliffs, where the enemy was protected by stonewalls and defensive lines, and would fiercely defend them. Facing terrible obstacles at every step, our troops were driven back many times and suffered many casualties while the

---

[108] Kutuzov ordered Miloradovich to attack the French along the riverbank, while Dokhturov and Schmitt made a flanking march across the hills to assault Mortier's positions from behind.

artillery, unable to deploy, could not support them for long. At last, they managed to drive the enemy from one point and captured part of its camp. Cannon then went into action and restored the balance in the battle, but the enemy, being able to safely retire, resumed its resistance and we achieved minor success only through major sacrifice. Our losses were heavy, especially among the officers.

The commander-in-chief had initially wanted to outflank the enemy but it was impossible to move along the road on the bank of the Danube because the enemy fired on it; so we had to cross mountains to attack the French left flank. The Austrian Quartermaster General Schmitt, a man of excellent abilities whom the Austrian emperor had recalled to service after a long retirement, offered to carry out this attack. Being a native of Krems, he knew the area well and led a column commanded by General Dokhturov. Our troops followed a secret path towards the enemy and they did not notice us until we turned their left flank and advanced into the rear. This movement gave us victory. The French made a weak attempt at resistance, and unable to thwart widespread confusion, they abandoned all positions and fled. We captured General Gren d'Aurge, five artillery pieces, colours and over 40 staff and junior officers.

Marshal Mortier escaped into the mountains with a small number of men. Some of his troops looked for boats to steer down the Danube but they were either decimated by our batteries on the banks or were taken by the current to the burnt bridge and begged for mercy. Unfortunately, among our numerous casualties was Quartermaster General Schmitt, who was killed by one of the first shots from an enemy battery.[109] Because of the terrain, artillery was but little used in action and therefore I spent most of battle with General Miloradovich and can testify that it was one of the most savage combats with our troops demonstrating all the gallantry they could.

Although the skilful movement of troops under General Dokhturov brought a decisive outcome to this battle, General Miloradovich, in all fairness, should be credited with an important contribution since he succeeded in driving the enemy from heights

---

[109] The death of Schmitt was consequential. He was replaced by Franz Ritter Weyrother, who drafted the disastrous Allied battle plan at Austerlitz.

around the town despite the apparent impregnability of the enemy position.

It was here that Dokhturov laid the foundations of his military reputation; but I cannot conceal one strange incident that did not attract attention at the time. When he flanked the enemy and was certain of success, Dokhturov deployed his troops in such a manner that a battalion of the Vyatka Musketeer Regiment and a colour were lost to the enemy.

The French prisoners told us that Mortier had between 7–8,000 men and because of their rapid marches from Linz, he had up to 4,000 sick and stragglers left along the road. The number of troops assigned to him proved that his orders were only to destroy a bridge and probably to prevent our crossing if we tried to use boats, but to avoid any decisive battle with us. Only a few of the German generals would ever turn down an offer of a truce, and therefore they might not have rejected a similar proposal from the French. Marshal Lannes deceived some Austrian sentries and a French column ran to capture a bridge.[110]

The Imperial family left for Hungary and the French in Vienna consoled themselves for this loss by levying a heavy contribution and seizing a large arsenal, plenty of provisions and many other supplies necessary for troops.

After capturing a bridge on the Danube, the enemy had an open road to Brunn and, had our commander-in-chief delayed for a few days, the French could have beaten us on our march from Krems. Now, leaving part of their troops in Vienna, the French advanced with the remaining forces against our lines of communication.

Once again, the only means to survive was by moving at extraordinary speed. But we could not hope for a well-organized retreat since the road to Brunn was a very filthy and muddy path that we had already marched down once.[111]

We suffered horrible difficulties even without an enemy presence. It was late autumn, marches were arduous and no one

---

[110] Yermolov refers to an incident in Vienna, where an Austrian detachment under Count Ausperg was protecting the Tabor Bridge. Marshals Murat and Lannes tricked Ausperg by telling him that an armistice was concluded while the French grenadiers captured bridge intact.

[111] Yermolov's note: When we marched to Gorunau, large numbers of horses were assigned to pull the artillery and carriages.

doubted that we would lose most of our artillery and transports. We had to hurry to pass a junction with the road from Vienna and the commander-in-chief ordered the troops to leave at once.

Prince Bagration was given command of the rearguard. General Miloradovich's separate brigade, worn out in the last battle, was assigned to support him. So, we departed from Krems. Unable to take our wounded with us, we left them there and one of the officers waited with a letter for an enemy commander to whose generosity we entrusted these people. A few hours prior to our march a vigorous frost had set in and, to our good fortune, the road froze and the surface hardened.

The enemy, utilizing numerous boats, quickly crossed the Danube and our rearguard was not so far from the town of Krems when the enemy appeared in pursuit. The same day, the officer, left with a letter at Krems, returned and informed us that the enemy headquarters had been established in the town and a large number of troops were concentrating there.

The commander-in-chief learned that Lieutenant General Shepelev's column, marching from Russia, would soon join him and, since it had no cavalry, he dispatched Her Majesty's Cuirassier Regiment to escort it; my horse artillery company was also sent with that regiment and, after a long march, we rejoined the column as our outposts encountered enemy cavalry moving from Vienna. The commander-in-chief accelerated the retreat and passed through Etzelsdorf, where Miloradovich soon deployed his forces. Thus, we no longer feared being cut off by troops coming from Vienna.

To avoid a battle which might have been fatal to us on account of enemy superiority, Kutuzov decided to deploy Bagration's rearguard and left it near the town of Hollabrunn.[112]

Meanwhile, the enemy forces received reinforcements at Krems and visibly multiplied, while Napoleon himself commanded the

---

[112] The Russians left Krems during the night of 14 November. Marching all night, Kutuzov arrived at Ebersbrunn on 14 November, where he received Emperor Francis' letter about the French crossing of the Danube. Kutuzov realized that the French would be first to reach Guntersdorf and cut the Russian army from Znaim. Consequently, he decided to dispatch a detachment to Hollabrunn to halt the French advance and gain time for the main army. Bagration left Ebersbrunn and arrived at Hollabrunn with his force of some 8,000 men. He found the terrain there disadvantageous for the defence so he moved his troops three miles northward to a small village of Schöngrabern.

vanguard.[113] Adjutant General Baron Winzegorode went to the French camp to negotiate and that same day a truce was concluded until 4:00 pm.[114] However, Napoleon did not want to uphold the truce and wished to destroy our rearguard that same day.[115] It is possible that he planned that his troops, moving from Vienna, would attack and pin down our army giving him enough time to arrive with his remaining forces.

Taking advantage of the armistice, Prince Bagration wanted to withdraw so that his troops were not isolated from the army. However, as his troops began to move, the French insisted that these units should return to the same positions they held at the conclusion of the armistice; failing that the French would immediately attack. We could not refuse this demand, although there was real danger.

At 4:00 pm the enemy fired a single artillery shot, signalling that the armistice was over, and the enemy columns advanced from every direction. Every minute counted and Prince Bagration immediately began to retreat.

---

[113] Yermolov is mistaken in claiming Napoleon commanded the vanguard since it was led by Marshal Murat.

[114] The French declared to Nostitz that an armistice had been concluded between the French and Austrians, citing the French crossing over the Tabor Bridge as a proof of that. Nostitz believed the French and withdrew from Hollabrunn with his detachment. Murat then tried to use the same trick with Bagration. He sent his staff officer to offer the Russians an armistice, claiming that the French and Austrians were already at peace. An experienced commander, Bagration realized that the French proposal was just a bluff. However, he decided to exploit this chance to his advantage. He agreed to the French offer and informed Kutuzov of the situation. Kutuzov was delighted by this news and immediately sent two aides-de-camp, Wintzegorode and Dolgoruky, with instructions to prolong negotiations as long as possible while the Russians marched to Znaim. The treaty was signed by Winzegorode and August Belliard, Murat's chief of staff.

[115] Napoleon did not know about the armistice until 16 November when Marshal Murat sent him a copy of the signed treaty for ratification. He was furious at Murat's unauthorized actions, declaring 'It is impossible for me to find words to express my displeasure with you. You command only my vanguard, and have no right to conclude an armistice without my order. You made me lose the fruits of a campaign. Break the armistice at once, and march upon the enemy.... March! Destroy the Russian army; you are in a position to take its baggage and artillery.... The Austrians suffered the humiliation of being duped out of the passage of the bridge of Vienna, but you have been fooled by the Russians.'

The rearguard was deployed with its right flank resting on a small gorge, protected by the 6th Jäger Regiment. The commander on this flank Major General Ulanius also had cavalry, comprised of the Pavlograd Hussar and Chernigov Dragoon regiments, with a small number of Cossacks. The centre and left flank were deployed in a valley; Major General Selikhov's brigade, comprising of the Podolsk and Azov musketeer regiments, with one light artillery company, was deployed on the left flank. Prince Bagration was in the centre with the Kiev and Malorossiisk grenadier regiments as well as all of the artillery. Three verstas behind the rearguard's positions, there was a deep ravine difficult for the troops to cross. The cavalry was ordered to cross it immediately so that it did not hinder the other troops during the retreat. Major General Ulanius, following the cavalry, covered the valley with his fire and reached the ravine without any loss. The grenadier regiments were retreating too, supported by part of our artillery that moved forward. Skirmishers from these units were engaged in fighting.

Meanwhile, complete confusion reigned on the left flank. Before the attack, Major General Selikhov made the mistake of allowing the troops to run to the nearby stream for water and to collect wood, and wasted time waiting for them. Most of these soldiers were captured and superior enemy forces isolated their units. These courageous units desperately defended themselves as the battle continued late into the night, but most of them fell while the enemy captured colours and eight guns. The remnants of these regiments escaped under the cover of darkness, carrying off four cannon. The reason for such considerable casualties was Major General Selikhov's incompetence. He did not understand that he could have saved the troops if he had decided to abandon the soldiers sent for water and wood, since they could have easily eluded the enemy. The enemy, having surrounded the left flank, intended to bar the grenadier regiments from the crossing or at least to spread confusion among them as they did so. But, Major Ekonomov, commanding the 2nd Battalion of the Kiev Grenadier Regiment, defended a village covering the crossing and met the enemy with intense fire. Ekonomov's action, which he carried out on his own initiative, disrupted the enemy plans; it was the reason for the grenadier regiments' withdrawal without loss and the escape of survivors from the left flank.[116]

The battle turned out much more successfully than anyone had anticipated and Prince Bagration earned his fame.[117] There were less than 7,000 men under his command, while the enemy had over 20,000 men and Napoleon personally commanded them. Of course, it was not Napoleon's mistakes or lack of means that prevented the French from achieving a complete victory. Only speed of movement saved our rearguard.

During the night, our rearguard passed the abovementioned junction at Etzelsdorf and, having lost contact with enemy, was out of danger.

Thus, the army was now far away from the enemy forces proceeding from Krems as well as those moving up from Vienna; the army avoided a battle that it could not have survived and that would have been unwise to accept since General Count Buxhöwden's army was already approaching.

General Miloradovich's brigade joined the rearguard and, although the enemy soon caught up with it, there were only a few minor skirmishes of no consequence.

Meanwhile, the commander-in-chief passed Brunn and joined Count Buxhöwden's troops.[118] Part of the latter's men arrived to replace us in the rearguard when we reached Wischau. Our

---

[116] The Russians suffered heavy casualties at Schöngrabern. Bagration reported that out of 6,000 men he led into action, 1,479 men were killed and missing; 931 men were wounded, but only 194 men were taken, and the rest (737 men) were left to the mercy of the French. The officer corps was hit particularly hard, losing 30 killed, 24 missing and 39 seriously wounded that were left on the battlefield. Bagration also lost eight guns whose carriages were destroyed by enemy fire. Napoleon estimated Bagration's losses as 2,000 captured, 1,500 wounded, 12 guns and 100 wagons captured. As always, the 26th Bulletin exaggerated Russian casualties, claiming 2,000 killed, 2,000 wounded, 12 cannon and 100 wagons captured. The French lost approximately 1,200 men. Bagration reported one colonel, 2 French officers and 50 privates were captured as well as the eagle and battalion flag of the 40th Line.

[117] The news of Bagration's escape caused widespread celebration in the main army. On 18 November, Kutuzov himself went to meet Bagration and told him, 'I do not ask about casualties – you are alive and that's enough for me.' Kutuzov asked Alexander to send 300 Orders of St Anna to decorate the rank-and-file who distinguished themselves at Schöngrabern.

[118] The Russian army bivouacked at Olmutz on 22 November 1805. Mikhail Kutuzov received reinforcements of some 27,000 men there and was joined by the emperors Alexander and Francis. The Allied forces now amounted to 68,500 Russians and 14,000 Austrians.

sovereign was with the Austrian emperor in the fortress of Olmutz. Grand Duke Constantine Pavlovich was to arrive soon with the Russian Guard.[119]

Thus it was that during the engagements with the enemy that took place during the retreat from Braunau to Brunn, General Kutuzov achieved success against superior enemy forces at Lambach and Amstetten and a complete victory at Krems; he saved his exhausted troops, but they were in high spirits and suffered no loss except one gun at Lambach.[120] In all fairness, this retreat should take its place among the most celebrated military events of modern times.

There was a notable difference between the newly merged armies. The troops arriving from Russia were well preserved and in better order. Our army, on the contrary, had suffered from prolonged hardship and was exhausted from lack of supplies and bad autumn weather. The soldiers' uniforms were almost completely worn-out and there were virtually no shoes. Officials in the army wore ridiculous clothes.

Czar Alexander joined the army and, considering the way he greeted many officers, it seemed that he was pleased with the performance of his courageous and loyal troops.[121] He expressed to me, among others, his gratitude for my service. He then ordered the army to rest.

After the merger, the armies were deployed near the walls of the fortress of Olmutz, where a military camp was set up and various fortifications built. Supplies were issued in an orderly manner. Measures were taken to ensure further supplies and, during the following week, our condition visibly improved.

The headquarters of both emperors was in Olmutz. A new rearguard was established under the command of Prince Bagration and deployed near Wischau.

---

[119] The Bavarian diplomat, Olry, described Grand Duke Constantine forcing his Guard units to move from St Petersburg to Olmutz. He estimated that the Guard Corps lost 2,000 men as a result.
[120] Yermolov's statement of course is an exaggeration since at Schongrabern alone Russians lost over 2,000 men and eight guns.
[121] General Alexander Langeron also described the arrival of Alexander and noted, 'I was surprised by the deep silence and sombre mood of the troops as they met the emperor'.

At Olmutz, I met Count Arakcheyev, who enjoyed the same authority as before and was still indisposed towards me despite the commander-in-chief's flattering comments about me. I hardly had any access to him and never received any commendation although he showed a lot of support to others. It was here, while seeing the benefits others enjoyed, that I realized how unbeneficial it was to be disliked by a powerful superior, especially when he believed that I was well off since he only mistreated me instead of completely ruining me!

Whilst the armies remained at Olmutz, a few skirmishes took place near Wischau. When Prince Bagration noted that the enemy had more cavalry than infantry in the town he instructed the chef of the Mariupol Hussar Regiment, Major General Count Wittgenstein, to deploy his unit on the outskirts of the town to prevent the enemy from escaping and then ordered his infantry to attack. The enemy cavalry still managed to escape and Count Wittgenstein could do little. However, Adjutant General Prince Dolgorukov, who served in the rearguard, captured some 100 enemy soldiers left in the town. The importance of the affair was greatly exaggerated, and Prince Bagration, as a shrewd man, attributed the success to Dolgorukov. This gentleman had the complete confidence of the czar and Bagration knew that he might prove useful to him. The enemy retreated to Brunn, where, as it was known, it had concentrated.[122] Everyone at our headquarters was enthralled by this victory and prepared for more to come.

Our army was ordered to advance. General Kutuzov was of the opposite opinion and there were various discussions. Many believed that the French had only retreated to entice us from our advantageous positions at Olmutz, which they did not dare attack, and so we should have remained there, awaiting Lieutenant General Essen (I) who was marching with a corps from Silesia. Others thought that if the enemy decided to attack us here, we should retreat and allow Archduke Charles's army, that was approaching Vienna, to move against the enemy rear. Perhaps, Napoleon would

---

[122] When Bagration fought the French between Wischau and Raussnitz, Alexander accompanied him and witnessed combat for the first time. He was initially thrilled by the action but soon came across the dead and wounded that shocked him and made him sick. He retired to the rear and refused to eat for the rest of the day.

not have placed himself in such a dangerous situation and he could either have retreated or left part of his troops facing us while he led the remaining forces against Archduke Charles. It is more probable that Napoleon would have chosen the latter solution since he could only retreat along the route we had used, a road so completely devastated that his army would have certainly faced starvation. Having defeated Archduke Charles, Napoleon could have had no doubts that the Austrian emperor would readily leave our alliance and that we would not risk opposing him alone. Napoleon could not retreat because he would have lost the important advantages he had achieved with his victory at Ulm, which brought immense stretches of Austrian territory into his power, forced the Austrians to withdraw from Italy and even leave the Tyrol. Many thought that if Napoleon turned against Archduke Charles, he could not leave sufficient troops to halt us and therefore we should advance and follow Napoleon, placing him between the two armies. There was also an opinion that, as we advanced, our left wing should approach Hungary, immediately establishing communications with Archduke Charles and receiving support from the Hungarians, a martial nation.... If Napoleon attacked our army and we could not give battle, Hungary, a mountainous country, favoured a defensive war; and there was always the correct assumption that Napoleon could not waste time and depended on quick and decisive action.

Because of my minor position in the army, I could not know the exact intentions of my superiors; rumours had reached me that the czar disagreed with Kutuzov's opinion and concurred with the Austrian proposal.[123]

So our army advanced. The Austrian Quartermaster General Weyrother prepared the necessary plans. We made short marches but they were so confusing that we rarely completed them before 10:00 pm or 12:00 am because the columns always crossed each other's path, in some cases as much as several times, and some columns wasted time waiting for others.[124]

---

[123] The Allied headquarters was divided over the strategy. General Kutusov and senior Russian officers emphasized the importance of not fighting Napoleon and withdrawing towards Galicia. However, Alexander and Francis objected to these arguments. According to Russian regulations, the czar assumed the command of the army when with the troops. Although Alexander officially kept Kutuzov in charge of the army, his presence limited Kutuzov's actions.

[124] Prince Adam Czartoryski recalled, '[Weyrother] was an officer of great bravery

For three days only minor enemy detachments were observed on the road to Brunn and they withdrew when our vanguard advanced.

I was attached to Adjutant General Uvarov's cavalry division with my horse artillery company. On the fourth day, in the evening, we encountered the enemy cavalry, which, after a brief skirmish, was driven away.

Darkness forced us to halt in a good position on top of the heights. The rest of the army bivouacked not far behind us.[125] In front of us, there were enemy bonfires that seemed to represent a line of outposts. There was a rumour, which everyone believed, that the enemy was retreating. Around midnight, fires were suddenly ignited along a long distance near one of the hills where our division was deployed. We saw immense bivouacs and numerous people moving that strengthened our belief that the enemy was not concealing its retreat. However, some found this incident suspicious. We later learned that the fires were meant to celebrate Napoleon and were ignited in his presence.[126]

Adjutant General Uvarov was summoned to headquarters but soon returned with orders written on several sheets of paper, crowded with difficult names of villages, lakes, streams and distances and heights; it was so confusing that we could not remember or understand anything. We were not permitted to make a copy because the plan had to be read by a good many

---

and military knowledge, but, like General Mack, he trusted too much in his combinations, which were often complicated and did not admit that they might be foiled by the skill of the enemy.' Weyrother's disposition was so complex and confusing that 'when the day [of advance] came, some of the generals had not yet sufficiently studied their dispositions.' In addition, the plan had not been translated into Russian.

[125] The Russo-Austrian army passed through Austerlitz on the morning of 1 December and slowly climbed the slope to the Pratzen plateau since the French had evacuated this position. Because of confusion, the columns became entangled. The first three columns, of Dokhturov, Langeron and Przhebishevskii, were on the Pratzen heights, but the fourth, under Kollowrath, was behind Przhebishevskii's while the fifth column of Prince Liechtenstein stopped even farther to the rear. Bagration bivouacked his forces around Posoritz on the extreme right flank of the Allied positions.

[126] During the night of 2 December, Napoleon went on reconnaissance to determine the Allied positions. However, he encountered a Cossack patrol, which prevented him from getting a clear sight of the Russian positions.

commanders and there were only a few copies available. I must confess that when I heard it read out, I understood very little of what was intended. The only thing I comprehended was we were to attack the next day.

Concerned that the enemy could retreat, the army advanced before dawn. The troops had to arrive at points assigned to them but the columns began to collide with each other or move through one another causing chaos, further amplified by the darkness. The troops scattered, intermingled, and it was certainly difficult for them to find their places in the dark. The infantry columns consisted of a large number of infantry regiments and they were unaccompanied by so much as a single cavalryman. They had no means of knowing what was going on ahead, or of finding out the location or movements of neighbouring forces supposed to cooperate with them. I myself saw how General Miloradovich begged a regimental chief for just twenty hussars to convey important messages. It must be added, that not one column possessed a vanguard. The main vanguard was on the far right, and, in fact, not far ahead of anybody else, so it did not cover anything and the army was exposed in its movement. Uvarov's division was moved far behind so that it could transfer to the right flank, where almost all the cavalry was concentrated. Thus, the columns advanced in false security. Wide gaps opened up between them, since we assumed the columns would deploy into line on the approach of the enemy.

Early in the day, as we assumed we were some distance from the enemy and thought to adjust our ranks that had become confused in the darkness, we saw the entire French army deployed in battle formation and there were less than two verstas remaining between us.

From all of this we can conclude how accurate our intelligence was on the retreating enemy and how much we owed to those baffling Austrian orders which resembled a topographic description of the Brunn region rather than directions designed to prepare an entire army for battle.

The fact that the French were completely prepared proved that they were informed about our plans since they did not bother to probe our movement and there was not a single outpost except those before their actual positions. Their troops remained idle, confused by the strange appearance of our troops since it was difficult to imagine that an army could execute such a movement in front of a prepared enemy without having some cunning plan. In addition, some broken terrain covered our forces. We crossed a marshy and muddy stream and as many of the columns entered villages located between the lakes in a valley that extended up to the heights occupied by the enemy, immense gaps separated our forces. Then terrible artillery fire began and the enemy advanced towards us, always keeping the advantage of being on higher ground. Some of our columns were attacked while still on the march and they could not deploy in lines. Others managed to deploy their regiments, but either lacked support or were surrounded and could not withstand the superior enemy numbers. In a very short time, much of our army was completely disorganized. The initial action, particularly the assumption that the enemy was far way and the troops would be able to unite, did not correspond with the facts.

The fighting soon became localized, communication between forces did not exist and there was no possibility of concentrating the troops. The gaps between us were so immense that the Guard under the Grand Duke, which was in reserve, had to move into the front line at the beginning of the battle and covered so much space that it had insufficient troops to form a second line. The left flank under General Buxhöwden, occupying the same heights where Uvarov's division was deployed earlier, held its ground for quite some time and retreated with fewer casualties; however, 24 battery guns and part of the infantry defending them were captured by the enemy. A bridge collapsed under the leading cannon and halted the others in their tracks. General Miloradovich's column in the centre was scattered after stout resistance; Lieutenant General Przhebishevskii's column recklessly advanced through a village, was surrounded and suffered heavy losses, with many captured, including the commander of this column himself. Due to the terrain, Lieutenant General Count Langeron's column's resistance was brief but it also suffered high casualties. The Life Guard regiments made several unsuccessful uncoordinated attacks and their men, inexperienced in war, were carried away by gallantry and wasted their efforts, suffering heavy casualties. The Chevalier Guard and Horse Guard regiments acted with exceptional bravery and some of the latter unit broke the French cavalry, capturing an eagle[127] but shared the common fate of being repulsed with loss.

Having achieved this success, the enemy moved against Bagration's vanguard, deployed on the extreme right, and against the cavalry of Lieutenant General Essen (II) and Adjutant General Uvarov. These were holding their ground only because the enemy had not yet turned on them, perhaps intending to destroy them later. All this cavalry was commanded by the Austrian general Prince Liechtenstein. They charged the enemy but had to retreat having met superior forces. Early in the battle, Major General Baron Müller-Zakomelsky led a brilliant attack with the Grand Duke Uhlan Regiment, scattering enemy cavalry and dispersing their infantry before a severe wound interrupted his success and left him in enemy hands just before the guns that his courage threatened to capture, while his regiment was scattered.[128] Our cavalry, like the rest of our army, acted in an uncoordinated fashion without any attempt at mutual support.

Thus, our forces were disordered, routed and pursued on both flanks. Our losses increased when the troops massed near a very muddy stream with only a few bridges across it, and it was impossible to cross except over these points. Our fleeing cavalry tried to ford the stream but many of its men and horses drowned. Abandoned by the units to which I was attached, I halted my company, intending to open fire and halt the pursuing enemy. The first guns I unlimbered managed to get off a few rounds before they were seized, their crews slaughtered and I captured. Meanwhile, Uvarov's division, massing near a bridge, realized it was being pursued by inferior enemy troops as the main enemy forces had halted on the heights. The troops pursuing us, were routed and destroyed and I was liberated close to the French lines.[129]

As I rejoined the remnants of my devastated company, I found my division in great confusion at the bottom of the hill, where the czar was. This hill was occupied by the Life Guard Grenadier

---

[127] A group of soldiers (Elie Omeltchenko, Zacharie Lazunov, Fedor Ushakov and Gavrilov) of the Horse Guard Regiment seized the eagle of the 1st battalion of the 4th Line.

[128] The Grand Duke Constantine Uhlan Regiment attacked alone and was decimated by point blank fire and left some 400 dead and wounded on the field.

[129] Yermolov's note: I owe my freedom to Colonel Vasily Ivanovich Shau of the Elisavetgrad Hussar Regiment, who rescued me with a few soldiers from the Kharkov Dragoon Regiment. He had not a single person from his unit, which indicates the level of confusion.

Regiment and a company of Guard artillery which had been in the battle but retained order. There was almost no one from the Imperial suite accompanying the czar, whose face expressed great sorrow and whose eyes were filled with tears. Fragments of the entire army concentrated here, and whilst our prudent dispositions had divided us, defeat united us. We left over 60 guns on the battlefield and the army retreated. Bagration's troops suffered fewer casualties than the others; part of his infantry was disordered by the enemy cavalry, but they had not been supported in their attacks and had paid a high price for such audacity; even so, a few artillery pieces had been lost as well. These surviving troops formed up under Prince Bagration. A detachment was deployed on the shortest route to Austerlitz; I commanded these troops, probably because no one else wanted such an unfavourable appointment.[130]

Fortunately for us, it was evening and the enemy did not pursue us after we crossed the stream. My detachment and I owed our escape to the contempt that the enemy felt towards my small force since they did not bother to add several hundred prisoners to their already complete victory. But when they needed water, they drove my outposts from the stream. I had had to listen to music, songs and joyous shouts in the enemy camp. They mocked us by yelling the Russian 'Hurrah!'. Around midnight, I received the order to withdraw; it should have come earlier but the courier had not reached me. At Austerlitz, the place which gave its name to this memorable battle, I found Bagration's rearguard and he could not believe that I had been kept six miles in front of him, and was not impressed by Uvarov's decision. Four verstas later, I rejoined the army, but not all of it was here and we had no information; there was such chaos that it seemed there were no regiments just various chaotic groups.[131] The czar did not know where Kutuzov was, while

---

[130] Yermolov's note: This detachment comprised one company of Life Guard Grenadiers, one sotnya of Leib-Cossacks, one squadron of dismounted Chernigov Dragoons, one squadron of Her Majesty's Life Guard Cuirassiers, one squadron of the Elisavetgrad Hussars and two horse artillery guns. I was ordered to set large bonfires and sing: the latter order was not carried out because we were not cheerful.

[131] Prince Czartoryski also described the utter confusion and saw General Buxhöwden, who 'had lost his hat and his clothes were in disorder; when he perceived me at a distance he cried, "They have abandoned me! They have sacrificed me!"' Buxhöwden had only 2 battalions surviving out of the 44 he had

the latter was concerned about the czar. I had to report to Uvarov, who was delighted that he could embellish the importance of a detachment he had created himself. Without waiting for stragglers, the army marched throughout the night. At dawn, our scattered troops began to concentrate and, around 10:00 am, enemy cavalry appeared, observing our retreat. That day, due to the exhaustion of the horses, we left as many cannon along the road as we had on the battlefield.[132] We soon learned that the Austrian emperor had concluded an armistice with Napoleon, pledging to begin peace negotiations; so we could not expect assistance from the Austrians.

Our army arrived at Gödding on the Hungarian border, which we had to cross en route to Russia. We were surrounded everywhere by French cavalry and our rearguard was moving close to the army so that it would not be cut off.[133]

In the armistice, concluded with the Austrians, it was mentioned that the Russians could retreat without molestation but the time and direction were indicated by what the French called à *journées d'etapes*.[134] We had no need for such patronising permission since the enemy did not risk following us into a country like Hungary in late autumn. They could not have been certain that Austria, having Archduke Charles' and Archduke Ferdinand's troops ready at Znaim, might not consider breaking the armistice, placing Napoleon in a difficult position.

---

led into action.

[132] Austerlitz was Napoleon's masterpiece. Despite numerical superiority, the Allies were decisively defeated. The French lost some 9,000 men, of whom 1,300 were killed, but the Allied army suffered around 27,000 casualties. The Russians bore most of the loss, with over 21,000 killed, wounded and captured and 133 guns lost. Some Russian regiments suffered appalling casualties: the Galicia Regiment lost 1,271 men, the Butyrsk Regiment - 1,902 men, the Narva Regiment – 1,600 men, the Arkhangelogorod Regiment lost over 1,600 men around Kruh and Holubitz, while the Old Ingermanland Regiment suffered 1,099 casualties.

[133] On 3-4 December, the Russian rearguard under Bagration fought a series of actions between Urschutz and Czeitsch. Mikhailovskii-Danilevskii noted, 'Bagration had the glory of the first meeting with the French at Lambach and now he enjoyed the honour of exchanging the last shots of this campaign.'

[134] Yermolov's note: I saw the commander-in-chief, who, as he dispatched a courier off to St Petersburg, said the following to him: 'I graciously ask the commanders of the advance forces of the main French army to give permission for our free passage.'

Thus, our army moved along bad roads in terrible weather in one of the poorest regions of Hungary, passing through Kaschau, Eperies, and, having crossed the Carpathian Mountains near Bartfeld, descending into Galicia near Dukla. Our army was met in the most friendly fashion throughout Hungary nothing being refused to rest our exhausted troops. The local nobles greeted the commander-in-chief with complete respect. Two celebrations were organized, and, to our surprise, there were many who wished to entertain themselves after so shameful a defeat almost as though the enemy had lost and been destroyed.

Looking at our troops, the Hungarians were surprised that the French could defeat them; their annoyance was visible; but they did not embarrass us with compassion. They thought the only reason for our defeat must have been the betrayal of the Austrian generals, and this alone showed how they trusted us! Not knowing that I understood Latin, they spoke openly about the Austrians and I heard praise for some of them.

During the battle of Austerlitz, Lieutenant General Essen's corps had been a short march from the battlefield and it retreated along a different route, rejoining us in Galicia. Heavy artillery, dispatched to the fortress of Olmutz, also rejoined successfully. Alexander was not with the army and left for Russia at Gödding.

I have not described the battle of Austerlitz in great detail because it was accompanied by so many strange incidents. I heard the opinions of many notable officers on this battle but none of them had a clear understanding of it and they agreed only on events they had not witnessed. Histories of this battle will certainly be written but it will be difficult to completely trust them and it will be easier to describe some local actions rather than how they related and connected to each other. It can be said about Austerlitz that each part of the army was instructed to operate separately, on condition that it would neither await nor support other elements, indeed it might have been better if we forgot that there were other Russian troops on the battlefield at that same moment.

Thus, Fate placed us, divided and without any mutual support, in front of an enemy, wary of Russians, but who dared to be a vanquisher. A Russian should never forgive the defeat at Austerlitz and the heart of each Russian should burn with a desire for vengeance!

CHAPTER III
THE CAMPAIGNS IN POLAND, 1806–1807

In mid-January, our army returned to our frontiers and established itself in Volhynia. The headquarters was at Dubno.

1806

After passing through Prussia's Polish territories, General of Cavalry Michelson's army encountered no enemy forces and returned to our frontiers. General of Cavalry Bennigsen assumed command.

We remained in Volhynia until the spring; following the arduous campaign, much-needed rest revealed hidden troubles in our reduced army. I was attached with my company to the 3rd Division of Lieutenant General Baron von der Osten-Sacken, deployed near Shavel in Volhynia.

Awards were soon distributed for the last campaign. Many received generous awards for Austerlitz alone; I was decorated with the Order of St Anna (2nd class) for the campaign, since it was impossible to award me with a lesser decoration. Finally, based on the commander-in-chief's and Uvarov's excellent recommendations, I was promoted to colonel, bypassing a more senior officer in rank. I had to consider this as a great honour, although I had already served in the same rank for over nine years.

Following the new reorganization of artillery into brigades and their attachment to infantry divisions, I was appointed commander of the 7th Brigade in Lieutenant General Dokhturov's division, deployed near Dubno in Volhynia, and also took command of a newly-organized horse artillery company. Vigorous measures, to restore the army following our losses, confirmed rumours that a new war was looming. General Baron Bennigsen's army was assigned to assist Prussia.

The War against the French

The army received fresh forces that had not participated in the last campaign and it now comprised of:

2nd Division (Major General Count Osterman-Tolstoy)
3rd Division (Lieutenant General Baron von der Osten-Sacken)
4th Division (Lieutenant General Prince [Dmitry] Golitsyn)
5th Division (Major General Sedmoratsky)

Cavalry was attached to divisions, but, according to circumstances, could serve in detachments. A few Don Cossack regiments were assigned to the army too. In early October, the army crossed the Niemen at Urburg and Olita. Another army of four divisions under Buxhöwden had taken part in the battle at Austerlitz but had been boosted by a large number of recruits. This army entered Prussia via Brest-Litovsk in late November.[135]

By then, General Bennigsen was already on the Narev and had occupied Praga, a suburb of Warsaw, with his division. A cavalry detachment was deployed along the Vistula, a 12-hour march away.

Meanwhile, Napoleon had completely destroyed the Prussians at Auerstadt. This battle was even more catastrophic than the one the Austrians had lost at Ulm. The Prussians lost almost their entire artillery and a remarkably large number of troops were captured. The remnants of the army were scattered or forced to surrender. The best fortresses in the country were captured, some of them surrendering without resistance. The enemy took Berlin and the Prussian king, with a few hastily-assembled troops, withdrew to Königsberg. The Duke of Brunswick, one of Frederick the Great's famous commanders, had led that shattered army. The previous year, Prussia had hesitated in helping us as though it was concerned that we might eclipse their glory of defeating Napoleon.

Following his success, Napoleon dispatched a special corps to subjugate Silesia, while he led his army towards Warsaw, having been informed about the approach of our troops. We also learned about his movement and both our armies were ordered to halt.

Our armies concentrated at Belostock and their commanders, having no friendship before, turned into enemies. Their actions were not coordinated and confusion reigned even over trivial orders. And in such a state of affairs, we expected the arrival of an

---

[135] Bennigsen commanded some 70,000 men with 276 guns. Buxhöwden had 55,000 men with 216 guns. In addition, General Essen's corp of 37,000 men with 132 guns was marching from the Dniestr.

enemy flushed by victory. Our cavalry detachment, previously deployed ahead of us, moved back over the Vistula.

Napoleon occupied Warsaw and captured large magazines as these had not been destroyed because we had hoped to use them afterwards too. However, Major General Sedmoratsky, the commander in Praga, should have either evacuated them or, if there was no time, set them alight to deny the enemy their use. However, he did not consider himself authorized to act and had awaited specific instructions. In addition, he did not destroy the boats that would allow the enemy to cross the river; Sedmoratsky was also concerned that he might be forced to cross the Vistula into Austrian territory close to Warsaw and, therefore, he abandoned Praga and withdrew a considerable distance, leaving cavalry patrols to observe the Vistula.[136] Our other division, deployed on the right, also had its cavalry on the Vistula, but they did not coordinate their actions; so the enemy, having boats at its disposal, used a place where the Vistula was separated by an island, and constructed a bridge to the right bank. We only noticed this when it was too late and could only deploy our troops when the enemy was already present in force.

At that moment General Field Marshal Count Kamenski arrived to assume command of both armies.[137] This experienced commander immediately realized our dangerous position, our troops being dispersed over a vast area while the enemy had concentrated and controlled the right bank of the Vistula. Kamenski ordered our troops to rally at once. However, because of the enemy's proximity, we had to pull back some distance in order to do this.

Our troops were suffering from the lack of supplies; the only provisions they had were potatoes, which had to be unearthed far away and required large parties to be detached for this purpose. The

---

[136] Yermolov's note: General Sedmoratsky belonged to a group known as the Gatchina officers and he had learned his art under Kannabich, who taught the kind of tactics someone shrewdly described as the science of rolling up your coat.

[137] Alexander was exasperated by bickering between Bennigsen and Buxhöwden. He finally chose Kamenski to lead the united Russian armies. Yet, the new commander-in-chief brought no changes to the army – he kept Bennigsen and Buxhöwden in command and gave them complete freedom of action. Kamenski was 69, in poor health and had not commanded since the death of Catherine the Great.

troops were sometimes dispatched not to the areas where circumstances required them, but rather where better supplies were hoped to be procured. Villages were devastated everywhere, late autumn and constant rain destroyed roads and there was no assistance from the locals in delivering supplies.

As it slowly retreated, our army concentrated and, although danger forced us to accelerate, some of our troops could not avoid the unequal struggle against the enemy. Major General Count Osterman-Tolstoy made a stoic stand at Czarnow and Serotsk but, despite his fearlessness and the gallantry of his troops, he suffered considerable loss, losing several guns. Major General Count Pahlen was also attacked by superior enemy forces at Lopachin. He was marching to his division's assembly point and was only one and half miles from it when attacked. How vulnerable our lines of communications were! Count Pahlen could have retreated to Golymin directly by taking advantage of a forest that prevented the enemy from deploying; in addition, he would find reinforcements at Golymin. However we must credit his prudence because he preferred to overcome greater difficulties by heading towards Chaplitz's detachment near Tsekhanov, which could have been isolated and destroyed. I was attached to this unit with three artillery companies and could easily see that our position at Tsekhanov was ineffectual and was a result of Count Buxhöwden's instructions. Field Marshal Kamenski, having learned about this, reprimanded him for thoughtlessly dividing forces and ordered our detachment to retreat immediately. However we could not return because we were exhausted after marching on extremely muddy roads.

Fortunately, General Count Pahlen's able resistance prolonged the fighting and he joined us late in the evening and the enemy was not able to prevent us from rejoining at Golymin.

When on the following day we marched there, the enemy advanced along the direct route I mentioned above, but we beat them to it by an hour. Having reached Golymin on 14 [26] December, we encountered Lieutenant General Dokhturov's 7th Division, Lieutenant General Tuchkov (I)'s 5th Division and part of Lieutenant General Prince Golitsyn's 4th Division from General Benningsen's army.

The enemy began an exchange of fire. The French had smaller forces, largely of cavalry under Prince Murat. Although the wet ground complicated the deployment of our forces, we took up positions at a road junction and the enemy had even less favourable positions covered by woods and scrub. Against their eight guns, we had up to 80; the entire 5th Division was moved into reserve, while the enemy had no other skirmishers but some dismounted chasseurs. We could have easily destroyed Prince Murat but were satisfied by a useless exchange of fire so Murat took the initiative. They were soon reinforced by artillery which could not be utilized because of the swampy terrain and impassable roads. The enemy infantry faced the same problem and it arrived in inferior numbers. Based on seniority, one might think Dokhturov should have commanded on our side, but in all fairness no one was in charge: when I dispatched a brigade adjutant for instructions, he spent over half an hour meeting at least five generals, yet still could not obtain any orders.

Meanwhile, the enemy made some probes and unexpectedly managed to turn our left flank, only because of a mistake on our part; however, some additional forces soon restored order. Major General Prince Sherbatov's gallantry should be recognized: when his Kostroma Musketeer Regiment was disorganized by heavy casualties and had to retreat, he picked up its standard and rushed forward, leading an attack that drove the enemy back. In the evening, our forces were significantly reduced and gaps in our ranks were visible. It was easy to see that it was an improper way to retreat and that the troops were withdrawing on their own initiative. For some time I did not dare retreat without orders but, seeing it was not necessary to remain, I persuaded Lieutenant Colonel Prince Zhevakhov to retreat with his two squadrons of Pavlograd Hussars; so we went in the direction in which most of our troops seemed to be heading. After passing Golymin, I turned towards Makov. At the same time, our right flank, Major General Chaplitz's detachment, noticed that our left flank had already withdrawn and did not expect that Golymin, in our centre, would be abandoned before our last troops retreated; so it carelessly approached the town only to be hit by canister fire. This incident spread confusion, further amplified by the darkness, between the troops of the Ekaterinoslav Grenadier and the Vladimir Musketeer Regiments and they lost two artillery pieces.

Thus ended a battle that brought one benefit to us since we divided the enemy forces and pinned some of them down. But how justifiable was this when we had committed forces that were three times larger than the enemy's? One can imagine what Napoleon would have done in such an encounter.

Some five verstas from Golymin, in the village of Kluchnitzy, I found several of our generals in a local noble's house; naturally, some of them were already asleep and the leftovers of their dinner testified that their nap was not induced by hunger. In such cases, the person who arrives last, usually enjoys certain privileges and rights and so those officers, who were still awake, honoured me with a bottle of port. I saw that my companion, Prince Zhevakhov, was not thrilled by this mean greeting.

Although we were neither pursued nor observed during our retreat from Golymin, we abandoned around 40 guns, most of them heavy pieces, because of the extreme fatigue of the horses and the impassibly muddy roads. It seemed my company had to share the same fate; however, I found a few horses that had been abandoned by other companies and thus avoided the shame of abandoning a gun without a shot.

A major battle took place at Pultusk on the same day. Napoleon, having concentrated his forces except for Murat's cavalry, approached Bennigsen who could not retreat without endangering his troops and so awaited the enemy. Napoleon tried every means to defeat us; his troops were encouraged by his presence and acted with vigour and courage. Our forces were hesitant since the enemy enjoyed superiority. We were driven back at some points and exhausted their forces by resistance, but fortunately the French could not match our artillery since theirs had been left behind because of bad roads; this not only prolonged the battle but also helped us to improve our position. Bennigsen was firm in his resolution and, facing a desperate situation, he called on his last resources, ordering his reserve of two infantry regiments to launch a bayonet attack. Regimental commanders were told that the safety of our troops depended solely on this last endeavour, and the regiments attacked furiously. The French retreated unable to withstand our bayonets. Their troops lost touch with each other and, being unable to check our success, they fell into a hasty retreat; thus, a part of the enemy's position was suddenly in our hands. It was evening and Napoleon could not correct this failure since he needed time to rally his forces before attempting further attacks. Hence, Bennigsen's firmness turned our desperate situation into a victory. To repulse superior enemy forces led by Napoleon himself was indeed a great feat, but to overwhelm and route them was a glorious exploit that no one had claimed before.

Had we taken advantage of Pultusk we could have liberated Warsaw and the Polish territories belonging to Prussia and driven the enemy across the Oder.

Following Pultusk and Golymin, our armies had to either advance against the enemy or, at least, bar their further progress. Buxhöwden should have been the first to do this because his troops had faced inferior enemy forces and even if he had been unable to destroy them, then at least it was unnecessary to flee before them. If he considered retreat essential, then he should have coordinated his actions with General Bennigsen. We had precise intelligence on the enemy's main forces and it would have been better to use the troops that were wasted at Golymin to reinforce Bennigsen and complete his victory. However, Buxhöwden, either because of his row with Bennigsen and desire to harm him or because of a misunderstanding, kept following the Field Marshal's instruction to retreat which had been issued to concentrate our forces, but which should have been adjusted in the light of events which now clearly showed the benefit of attacking. If one is unable to comprehend this, then one should not command an army. If the common well-being is sacrificed for personal squabbles, then punishment should be administered; in any case, the army would have been relieved of this cruel commander, whose mediocre skills it could not trust, and who was famous only for his courage which can never replace the essential skills of a commander.

On the day of the battle, Field Marshal Kamenski arrived at Golymin at 9:00 am and personally positioned the Malakhov Cossack outposts, having seen the importance of the place where he had ordered the other troops to concentrate. In order not to waste time in correspondence, he dispatched a courier to the chief of staff at Tsekhanov with instructions to return to Golymin to avoid being cut off. The Field Marshal was at Pultusk during the battle; however, after it was over, when new orders based on new circumstances were needed, he declared that he was abandoning the army on the grounds of illness and left for Grodno.[138]

---

[138] Kamenski was in bad health indeed. Four days before the battle of Pultusk, he wrote, 'I have almost completely lost my vision. I am not able to find any locations on the map and had to ask others to find them. I suffer from pain in the

He made an unforgivable mistake: his presence with the army was even more essential because he had not expected Pultusk to end successfully, so following his departure, the disagreement between the commanders could only have had disastrous consequences. The army regretted his decision because it trusted in his experience and reputation. The senior officers agreed that the bickering between commanders would bring us no good.

General Bennigsen was unable to exploit his success and had to retreat because Buxhöwden had already withdrawn and exposed our rear to the enemy; therefore Bennigsen moved towards Rozan and crossed to the left bank of the Narev at Ostrolenka.

General Buxhöwden retreated through Makov.[139] He left a rearguard under Major General Markov to cover the army while it crossed the river. This movement continued slowly until late into the night. Transports crowded on a long bridge, and the enemy appeared from the nearby forest and took up positions in superior numbers close by. It was impossible to destroy the bridge, yet there was a danger that the enemy would capture it under cover of darkness. With permission from my superior, I dispatched a company with instructions to set fire to two of the suburbs to illuminate the French should they dare attack. The French approached the river twice, probing for fords in a few places, but some 40 guns under my command beat them back. French casualties must have been considerable and we were able to destroy part of the bridge.

I was threatened with dire punishment for the harsh measure of setting the town on fire and this matter was discussed at headquarters. Of course, after a nice lunch and rest, some 20 verstas from any danger, it was very easy for them to show magnanimity. They finally accepted my explanation. The rearguard withdrew to Novales, where Dokhturov's division was deployed. The Ingermanland Dragoon Regiment, that he had sent towards Rozan, encountered an enemy cavalry detachment there, failed to halt it and instead brought it back with them to the general's headquarters in a Catholic priest's house near the camp. The general himself was sitting quietly in the window when he suddenly saw French cavalry

---

eyes and head and cannot ride a horse… I am signing [orders] without even knowing what they prescribe.' Kamenski to Alexander, 22 December 1807.
[139] Makov is located on the River Orzyc.

galloping past the fence. Fortunately, the gates to the house were closed and some movement in the camp frightened the enemy. The house owner was suspected of providing information to the French.

When Count Buxhöwden arrived at the Narev it was frozen, the bridges were destroyed and there was no communication with the other bank. We remained here for a few days and when the enemy advanced our situation became more precarious with every hour. The enemy might have known our armies were separated by the river and could not support each other. However, it seemed that confusion prevented the French from attacking since they limited their operations to reconnaissance only and Major General Pahlen's outposts kept them at some distance from us.

General Bennigsen took every measure to reestablish communications between the armies. Ropes were stretched across the river, covered with wet hay which froze and allowed our infantry to cross to the opposite bank. Bridges were soon constructed and the armies were happily united.

The czar was unhappy with the field marshal's departure from the army but was elated by the success at Pultusk. The field marshal was ordered to remain in Grodno until further instructions. Both armies were placed under command of Bennigsen while Buxhöwden was recalled to Russia.[140] The army welcomed this news since Buxhöwden had failed to gain the trust of the troops. Whilst few knew of his knowledge and limited skills, everyone felt his unbearable haughtiness and arrogance.

1807

The commander-in-chief received the order to advance into Prussia and, in late December, the army marched for Kolno, Byala, Johanesburg and beyond. Three vanguards were established and the largest of them was given to Major General Markov, while Major General Barclay de Tolly and Baggovut commanded the others. Major General Markov's vanguard, in which I commanded the artillery, was instructed to go through Aris, Rein, Rastenburg and Ressel to Heilsberg. The army was close behind.

---

[140] Buxhöwden left the army for Riga and complained to Alexander about Bennigsen's actions. When his appeals were ignored, Buxhöwden challenged Bennigsen to a duel.

There were rumours that the enemy's left flank was also moving on Prussia. Enemy cavalry soon appeared near Nikolaiken and Zeeburg, observing our movements. We also dispatched cavalry which cooperated with the locals and were very useful in a region bisected by numerous lakes. They captured several Frenchmen at Nikolaiken.

On 12 [24] January, the vanguard arrived at Elditten and learned from the residents that a French detachment lay at Liebstadt and its patrol had been inquiring about Russians just half an hour ago. We made a rather long march that day and General Markov had to call for volunteers from the less-fatigued troops. A large number volunteered but when the 5th Jäger Regiment was ordered up and the others heard that Colonel Gogel himself would lead the regiment, everyone declared that they would join him and off they marched without a break. I asked for permission to take two guns and join them to witness the action. Some two verstas from Liebstadt, the enemy caught sight of us from some heights and began deploying troops on the city walls and gates, preparing for defence. We could see, however, that there were few of them. Our Jägers occupied a cemetery adjacent to the town and engaged the enemy, while the line infantry went against the city gates that led to the main street. Colonel Yurkovskii with two squadrons of the Elisavetgrad Hussars rushed into the town from a side gate and the infantry made a bayonet attack. The enemy was routed and pushed into narrow and twisted streets, suffering heavy casualties. Those who fled from the town were pursued by the Cossacks of courageous Colonel Sisoev. Our guns did not fire a single shot. We captured 22 officers and over 300 rank and file.[141] The red hussar regiment, for some reason referred to simply as the Parisian, was almost destroyed here. Leaving some cavalry in the town, Markov returned to Elditten, where the exhausted troops found food and shelter. That day we had marched and fought for 16 hours.

The disposition of 13 [25] January instructed the vanguard to bivouac at Mohrungen so we marched at dawn. Colonel Yurkovskii led the way with the Elisavetgrad Hussars and two Cossack regiments and drove the enemy pickets back; as he climbed the nearby heights, that surrounded the vast Mohrungen valley, he

---

[141] According to Russian official reports, Markov captured 18 officers, including one colonel, and 291 soldiers.

observed large enemy forces deployed for battle. Colonel Yurkovskii made the mistake of descending into the valley and the enemy engaged him with its cavalry. Moving by forced marches, the vanguard arrived on the battlefield only to find Yurkovskii hard pressed by the enemy and falling back to a small village, the main street of which was being bombarded by enemy artillery. I immediately brought my horse artillery company up and, taking advantage of my elevated position and numbers, I drove the enemy guns back and covered our cavalry's retreat. They took up positions behind our troops while part of the Cossacks engaged the enemy. Major General Markov deployed his troops on the nearby heights. The enemy attacked our left flank; its infantry column moving against the village. To protect itself from our artillery, it went towards the frozen lake located on the right. Having captured the village, the infantry deployed in some gardens enclosed by high fences and ditches. Since the trees had no leaves, our skirmishers were easily detected and driven out and enemy musket fire caused us considerable harm. Colonel Vuich was ordered to attack with the 25th Jäger Regiment. This unit had been established just before the start of the campaign and was not accustomed to the dangers of war; it became disordered while crossing the ditch and could not hold its ground. Some courageous lads climbed the fence but were not supported and remained isolated. Six companies of the Ekaterinoslav Grenadier Regiment, led by the gallant Major Fisher, and two companies of the 5th Jägers rushed forward and, without firing a shot, broke through and exterminated virtually everyone in the gardens and the village. We captured the flag of the 9th Light Regiment, while a few survivors fled to the lake. At that moment, Don Cossack Lieutenant Colonel Malakhov brought the news that, some eight verstas away, he had detected a large body of enemy infantry and heavy artillery and discovered 1,500–2,000 men concealed three verstas away on our right flank. The latter news was particularly unpleasant because our only escape route lay in that direction.

Less than two hours later, we saw the enemy issuing from a forest on to the road to the village of Holland. Covered by cavalry, the enemy formed up for battle and advanced against our right flank. Captured flanqueurs told us that these troops belonged to Bernadotte's corps and he was in command. We could have disengaged an hour earlier, but now could not hope to escape without heavy losses. Our forces were exposed and we could not deceive the enemy in respect of our strength or force him to act cautiously. The French could see at once that they exceeded our forces by at least three to one. The enemy advanced against the heights we occupied and, although our canister fire and bayonets defeated several columns, fresh enemy forces immediately resumed the offensive, forcing us back. Several battalions on the right, not far from the road, moved towards Georgiental, which the enemy seized with skirmishers from the infantry that Malakhov had detected earlier; we could not allow them to hold this place and General Markov led our battalions as they advanced. The enemy infantry was supported by fierce artillery fire and punished the rest of our rearguard, forcing us to retreat. Our artillery fired only canister. It was already dark when we entered the forest and the enemy ceased its pursuit, probably hoping to capture us the next day. After General Markov's departure, there were no other generals left so colonels Turchaninov and Vuich and I took orders from Senior Colonel Yurkovskii. Our first goal was to find an escape route, and I was concerned about not abandoning some 20 artillery pieces; however, we encountered either deep snow or swamps throughout the forest and could not escape. Commander of Don Cossack regiment, the gallant Sisoev, finally found a place where artillery could reach the main road, but it had to pass very close to the enemy bivouac near Georgiental. Of course, this was a very unreliable way of saving our guns, but we had no other choice and decided to use it. While passing the French camp, they opened up with musket fire and we had a few wounded, but we made it through. We soon found our cavalry led by General Anrep and returned to Liebstadt.

The commander-in-chief had sent General Anrep's cavalry to our aid. Although he received this order late in the day, Anrep decided to make up for lost time and moved his cavalry at the trot. A mile and half away from the battlefield, he met General Markov, who assured him that the battle had ended, our troops were retreating and nothing else could be done. General Anrep did not accept General Markov's assurances because of the audible artillery fire and he ordered his regiments to accelerate. At Georgiental, he encountered enemy infantry and his flanqueurs opened fire: just as he was climbing a nearby hill, Anrep was killed by a bullet that hit him in the head. It might still have been possible to attempt something but it would not have helped us and therefore his reconnaissance was ultimately futile.

It is remarkable that the French did not block us as we passed their camp, which they could have done without loss and we would have lost our entire artillery.

We found Markov at Amtmann's house at Liebstadt and he was already asleep, having enjoyed a nice dinner; his companions had devoured everything as though we were not supposed to return. To console ourselves, we could have instead admired the beautiful breasts and gorgeous eyes of Amtmann's wife, but since I was a defeated hero who had just accomplished a retreat, I was not granted even a glance, which, I was told, a victor would have claimed together with her heart. Well, the vanquished have no claim to any booty! Shrewd General Markov did not look surprised to see us as though we had simply carried out his orders. We paid him back with the same indifference when an hour later Prince Bagration arrived to replace him in command of the vanguard. At Mohrungen, we suffered heavy casualties and a half company, attached to the Pskov Musketeer Regiment, lost one gun.[142] The vanguard had 5,400 men under arms, while the enemy had 19,000 men.

It must be mentioned that our troops were just three miles away from Mohrungen but yet no one came to our rescue. The sound of the guns was heard at the main headquarters as well but only Anrep moved towards us, and only because he had orders to bivouac at Georgiental. After Golitsyn's division arrived, a few squadrons were detached to investigate the gunfire. Major General Pahlen accompanied them and the sound of the guns brought them to Mohrungen just as the enemy attacked. Count Pahlen rushed into Mohrungen, seizing Marshal Bernadotte's headquarters and capturing his entire train, chancellery and the contribution he had levied on various Prussian cities.[143] A dinner ready for the

---

[142] Losses were heavy on both sides, totaling in 26 officers and 670 men killed and wounded, 400 captured for French, and 1,100 killed and wounded, 300 captured for Russians.

[143] Russian cavalry also captured some 300 French and released about 200 Russian and Prussian prisoners. The British commissioner to the Russian army, Sir Robert Wilson claimed 12,500 ducats were found in Bernadotte's personal baggage, which he had levied for himself in Elbing, as well as a quantity of plate bearing the arms of minor German states.

victorious marshal was even found. Count Pahlen had enough time to retreat before the enemy cavalry. This event shows that had more of our troops participated in the battle, it could have ended in a brilliant victory. General Markov sent several officers to headquarters but received no response or instructions, probably because the commander-in-chief had no reliable information about the enemy.

At 9:00 am on 14 [26] January, at least 50,000 men were at Liebstadt and, expecting an enemy attack, we took up strong positions on steep heights near the town; a better informed enemy, meanwhile, abandoned Mohrungen and retreated.

Prince Bagration's vanguard was ordered to move forward and we stopped for the night at Mohrungen, now vacated by the enemy.

Marching at dawn on the 15th [27 January], we caught up with the French near the village of Zonnerwald but they did not fight, limiting their resistance to just a few artillery rounds. Later, our outposts surprised Marshal Bernadotte himself whilst dining at the village of Lubeschil and, without any Gascon bravado, he could boast of his remarkable agility. The food was still warm. Following the enemy, we reached the town of Deutsch-Eylau, while our outposts marched towards Neimark, where the enemy destroyed a bridge and halted our advance. The vanguard established quarters here and rested with abundant supplies from the Elbing province. The army followed the vanguard along the same road.

Colonel Yurkovskii, who commanded our outposts, sent a captured courier to Bagration. Napoleon had sent him to Bernadotte with instructions to halt his retreat, the order stating that withdrawal had been necessary to lure us in the direction of Graudentz, while Napoleon planned to concentrate his entire army at Allenstein by 2 February [new style] and attack our extended forces.[144]

This capture was a stroke of luck because otherwise our main army would have advanced along a single road and would have been either defeated piecemeal or at least isolated and forced to retreat, abandoning its line of operations and magazines. In the

---

[144] According to Napoleon's plan, the French troops would make a sweeping attack on the right from Thorn, driving Bennigsen into the angle between the Lower Vistula and the Frisches-Haff. Napoleon had approximately 115,000 men concentrated against some 50,000 Russians.

latter case, only a small part of our troops would have survived; any remaining forces, isolated from Russia and pushed against the sea, would have suffered disaster and been forced to surrender.

Although it was a well-conceived plan, Napoleon's enterprise could have succeeded only because of our complete carelessness. We should not have attempted our movement on Deutsch-Eylau without precise intelligence on the location of the main French army. If our goal had been the destruction of Bernadotte's corps, then we had had our chance at Mohrungen, and should not have followed him afterwards.

Prince Bagration sent the captured documents to the commander-in-chief, and, since only two days were remaining before Napoleon's offensive, he retreated on his own initiative. He divided the vanguard into two columns, with one of them moving to Bergfried, while the other, under Markov, was to proceed through Osterode. I was attached to the second column with most of our artillery and, having marched for 26 hours with two three-hour breaks, we arrived at Jankovo, near Allenstein, on 1 February [new style]. The other column joined us here and we were ordered to rest until further instructions.

That same day, parts of the 8th Division commanded by Major General Count Kamenski and the 3rd Division of Major General Titov were engaged in a minor action, which turned out unsuccessfully because of the unfavourable terrain. Artillery fire was fierce on both sides.[145]

The morning of 22 January [3 February] revealed a large enemy army in front of us and we prepared for battle. The French were surprised by our preparedness because they had not expected us to be able to concentrate. They did not dare to attack and our commander ordered a retreat to move closer to our supply depots. The army began withdrawing to Landsberg that same evening.[146]

---

[145] Count Nikolai Kamenski's 8th Division, supported by the 3rd Division, was deployed at Bergfried. Napoleon directed Soult and Davout against him to cut off the Russian line of retreat. The fierce fighting continued for hours and the bridge over the Alle changed hands several times.

[146] Bennigsen's retreat was slow because of deep snow and bad roads. On 4 February, Wilson wrote, 'At present, I can only mention that I never saw a more martial army. Their discipline is good; their marching is regular; and, considering what they have gone through, their appearance is admirable. The infantry are all equal to what you saw in England. The cavalry are excellent, with truly warlike

The vanguard, reinforced by Baggovut's detachment, left at dawn. It was ordered to cover the movement of our heavy artillery guns as well as the Prussian artillery. It was a surprising order since the column closest to enemy was that of the artillery; its horses were exhausted and it slowed us down considerably.

The vanguard soon caught up with this column and had to take up positions to allow artillery to get clear. The enemy did not pursue until the afternoon but, although it attacked vigorously, our vanguard had managed to cover come distance. Baggovut had a fierce engagement at Warlak.

At dawn on 24 January [5 February], the enemy attacked us in superior numbers and we could hardly maintain order. At Wolfsdorf, the enemy struck our position and our left flank was only able to hold ground by charging with the bayonet, although that caused some casualties. The 7th Division of Lieutenant General Dokhturov, whose retreat the rearguard now covered, moved in complete disorder, its transports blocking the road and causing delay. We fell back slowly, fighting until late in to the night. Passing through forests in the dark, we became so confused that the only way to distinguish enemy from friend was by shouting. Major General Count Lambert, hoping to assemble our dispersed skirmishers, approached the French lines by mistake and was almost captured.[147]

Our artillery was under fire the entire day, and if our hussars had not captured some French horses to replace our killed animals, I would have lost a few guns. I employed my horse artillery company more than others because of its flexibility. We had to use

---

bearing and even the infantry exult in their courage. The artillery is well appointed, and draws through fosses of snow that astonish me to look at.'

[147] Another participant noted: 'Often during a night march through a wood or a defile, the troops would be obliged to file past some trifling object, which blocked the way, because no one gave the order to remove the obstacle. What would I not have given to sleep on the snow for a few hours during these marches, but even that could not be ... The weary soldier would sink instinctively to the ground, only to get up in a few minutes and do as many more paces. This went on for hours, whole nights indeed, until at last we came within sight of some broken down wagon, which had caused the jam. ... In our regiment [the Azov], which has not seen the enemy and had a full complement when it marched across the frontier, the companies are reduced to 26 or 30 men. The grenadier battalion scarcely counts 300 men, and the other two are even weaker.' The passage is cited in Lettow-Vorbeck but the author remains unknown.

it even in the dark forest where it fired in the direction of enemy shouts or drumbeats. The troops were extremely satisfied with it and Bagration praised it. We suffered considerable losses that day, at least equal to those of the enemy. Marshal Davout's corps was fighting against us. Marshal Soult's corps was pursuing Barclay de Tolly's detachment, but the fighting was mostly limited to skirmishing.

On 25 January [6 February] we resumed our retreat at dawn in order to beat the enemy to the junction where our rearguard and Barclay de Tolly's detachment were converging. After that junction, Prince Bagration's rearguard took a narrow path towards Landsberg, while Barclay de Tolly's men headed in the same direction but along the main road through Hoff. Less than an hour later, both Davout and Soult appeared. A small force was dispatched to pursue Bagration but, having proceeded for some distance, it soon disappeared and the rearguard remained undisturbed for the rest of the day, which it desperately needed following recent actions. At Landsberg, we joined the main army that was deployed in battle formations.

Meanwhile, Barclay de Tolly's detachment faced a different situation. It faced a force five times stronger but Barclay de Tolly opted to delay the enemy, taking up various positions, abandoning them, often in disorder and suffering heavy casualties. He finally reached Hoff and halted here but deployed his troops at a disadvantage. Hoff is in a valley surrounded by steep hills. As superior enemy cavalry engaged Barclay's exhausted cavalrymen, they would be forced to retreat through its narrow streets. His infantry, which should have occupied the town and enclosed gardens, was placed before the town and, because of the deep snow on the plain, would also have to fall back through the town. So, it was – the French routed our cavalry and drove it onto our infantry and batteries. One of the batteries was captured and the commander of the second, Lieutenant Markov, fired canister against our own Olioviopol Hussars, although he also halted the enemy attack and forced it back with casualties.

The Russian infantry repulsed a charge, although the enemy cavalry reached its lines. The enemy made another attempt, and this time was more successful. The Dniepr and Kostroma musketeer regiments withstood the charge, but they were exhausted and did not retain formation for long. They were routed and at least half of them were cut down. The flags and the regimental guns were captured. Those who escaped sought the safety of the gardens to join the Jäger regiments already there.

This action demonstrates how disastrous the deployment of infantry in the open can be. Barclay de Tolly had been reinforced by five battalions under Major General Prince Dolgorukov, but this force was insufficient and the new battalions were routed as well, losing many men. Our troops, retreating through Hoff, suffered from terrible artillery fire. Fearless Barclay de Tolly paid no heed to danger and appeared everywhere. However, this battle did not flatter his skill as a commander, it would not have been difficult to find a better way![148]

Night did not allow the enemy to disturb our army at Landsberg. The commander-in-chief thought it prudent to abandon this position as it was not broad enough to allow the troops to deploy. The second line was separated from the first by a stream with steep banks, which, despite the frost, had not frozen and complicated communications. The right flank was adjacent to a forest which covered part of the front, and this would have placed our skirmishers, whom the French surpass in skill, at a disadvantage. The proximity of woods also hampered the effective use of artillery and masked enemy movements. There were two roads for retreat and both were on the extreme left flank: one of them passed over a hill, which was very difficult to ascend because its steep elevation was frozen; the second road led through narrow gates into the twisting and constricted streets of Landsberg which would cause chaos and large casualties in our troops.

On the night of 26 January [7 February], General Tuchkov (I)'s division began withdrawing over the hill in some disorder, thus delaying everyone else. The columns moving through Landsberg did not bother to maintain order and became confused in the narrow streets so, despite the long winter night, some forces remained in position because the units ahead of them had not moved. It is easy to imagine the position our rearguard was in: it

---

[148] There are no official reports on the Russian losses because Barclay was wounded and many of his officers were wounded and killed at Eylau on 7 February. Estimates vary between 1,800-2,000 killed and wounded. The French losses are projected as some 1,400 men.

faced the French but could only retreat a step at a time so that the main army could withdraw to a safe distance.

Barclay's men withdrew with the main army. Bagration's rearguard was left at Landsberg. An hour after dawn, the rearguard marched through Landsberg and took up positions near the town, having left a strong infantry detachment and several guns at the gates. Some time later, a large body of French troops approached and, diverting our attention by its artillery fire, moved against our right flank. Taking advantage of the terrain, we fought back resolutely for a considerable time before quickly traversing a field that separated us from the forest. The enemy, following us, entered Landsberg and began deploying its forces on our former positions. It was obvious that we would have to engage not only the enemy vanguard but his main body as well; fortunately for us, the region between Landsberg and Preussisch Eylau is mostly covered by dense forest. Prince Bagration dispatched his cavalry and part of his artillery for greater freedom of movement. All the Jäger units were combined and the line infantry was left in reserve.

We effectively contained the French with light losses until 11:00 am; however, numerous barrels of wine, abandoned by other troops in order to lighten the transports and save more valuable goods, were soon found along the road and it was impossible to restrain the troops, who were cold and hungry, from consuming alcohol. Before long, four Jäger regiments were so drunk it was impossible to rally them. The French noticed this confusion and made vigorous attacks, trying to cut our troops off they came from all directions. Artillery had to be committed to defend the drunkards and we were slowed down considerably. Generals Pahlen and Lambert used cavalry to protect these troops; but it was impossible to rally and withdraw these drunken soldiers and we lost plenty of them killed or captured.

Approaching Preussisch Eylau, the rearguard came onto an open plain and was assigned positions covering the town behind which our army began deploying for battle. The rearguard was reinforced by several regiments from the 8th Division and cavalry units. We deployed on both sides of the road that ran through woods. I placed 24 guns on a steep plateau on the left flank. A small plain lay before this hill and the enemy would have to cross it to advance; our skirmishers were spread out there, concealed by the broken terrain. Part of the cavalry was on the right flank and the rest was moved behind our positions.

The enemy soon deployed batteries on the opposite heights and subjected us to an intense bombardment; we rarely returned fire because I did not have a single heavy artillery piece. The French columns then came down at various points but were halted by the fire of 40 of our guns, our canister fire routed some of them, inflicting considerable casualties. We maintained our position for almost two hours, but then the enemy advanced in superior numbers. Of their three columns, one marched on the main road, where we had fewer infantry, another moved against the Pskov and Sofia musketeer regiments and a third advanced against my 24-gun battery.[149] The first column moved easily and threatened to outflank our strongest point; the other columns advanced slowly because of the deep snow and they had to endure our canister fire for a prolonged time.[150] Although disordered, one of them still managed to reach our position, where it was destroyed on the bayonets of the Pskov and Sofia regiments. Simultaneously, another column scattered its corpses before my battery. Meanwhile, Colonel Degtyarev led the St Petersburg Dragoons against the column on the main road; to evade our cavalry, the French veered away and moved into deep snow. The haste of their action led to confusion and our cavalry regiment took full advantage, capturing one eagle and 500 men after enduring light enemy musket fire. At least another 500 were killed, including the general who commanded this column.[151]

I have never witnessed a more decisive cavalry attack; I was equally surprised by how the St Petersburg Regiment came down a snow-covered slope without disorder. However, our success was

---

[149] Of the three French columns, the central one was the 46th Line; the second the 18th Line and the third, marching against the Russian left, the 24th Line.

[150] One of the Russian participants described this charge, "The artillery fired canister at the masses of the attacking columns; their front ranks were mowed down in lines, but those following stepped over the corpses of their comrades and advanced forward, with remarkable heroism and impudence.' Davidov, Recollections on the Battle of Preussisch Eylau, p. 211.

[151] Several Russian dragoons fought their way to the eagle of the 2nd Battalion of the 18th Line. Dragoons Stephan Fomin, Vasilii Podvorni, Savelii Deriagin, Efim Erofeyev and trumpeter Filip Logvinov captured the eagle and were later awarded Orders of St George (4th class) for this exploit.

short lived as the enemy brought up more troops; the French increased their batteries that now covered their columns and, being unable to contain them, we were ordered to pull back. The enemy immediately occupied our positions and followed us closely. I successfully carried out my orders to cover our troops with my horse artillery as they entered Preussisch Eylau.[152] As soon as I passed the city gates, the enemy launched assaults on the town. Its defence was entrusted to Barclay de Tolly, his detachment having been reinforced by fresh troops. The unequal ratio of forces did not allow us to take full advantage of the walls and fences that ringed the town; enemy skirmishers appeared, fired in the streets and entered the nearest houses. Our infantry drove them out with bayonets on several occasions and the town was in our hands until Barclay de Tolly received a serious wound. Discouraged by this loss, his detachment abandoned the town to the enemy holding on to part of it. Major General Somov, who commanded a brigade of the 4th Division, arrived with reinforcements, stormed the houses, smashed the enemy and recaptured the town.[153]

However, Somov made the mistake of trying to rally his troops in a remote part of town and so when the drums beat the alarm the troops retired and did not have time to organize. The appearance of the enemy spread confusion, amplified by the darkness and French canister rounds. We had to abandon the town and, in addition to considerable casualties, we also lost a few artillery pieces.[154] This incident forced the commander-in-chief to change the deployment

---

[152] According to Bennigsen, Colonel Yermolov 'skilfully deployed his horse battery on the hill and opened effective fire against the French.' Bennigsen, Memoirs, Russkaya starina, (July 1899), pp. 208-209.

[153] Bagration met Bennigsen behind the town and was ordered to recapture Eylau at any cost. He was given Major General Somov's division and led the leading column in a bayonet attack. Davidov described the soldiers following him 'quietly, without noise, but, when they entered the streets, everybody howled "Hurrah", charged with bayonets - and we captured Eylau again.' In a savage combat, the Russians captured the eagle of the 2nd Battalion of the 4th Line. Lieutenant Dmitri Kaftirev of the Polotsk Regiment claimed the trophy but, in 1808, it was discovered that Vasilii Demchinsky of the same regiment had seized it.

[154] After Eylau was recaptured, the soldiers of the 4th Division were allowed to rest for the night and scattered looking for food and shelter. Somov had not specified the exact rallying point, and ordered the drums to beat at 9:30 pm in the northeast part of Eylau, close to the main Russian position.

of our army and during the night our troops shifted to different positions. Bennigsen thought this necessary because the enemy, after it captured the heights defended by our rearguard, had made a reconnaissance of our positions.

It was 27 January (8 February) and the battle of Preussisch Eylau was one of the bloodiest battles in recent times. Details of this battle can be read in various histories. I will briefly describe the advantages and disadvantages of our deployment. The main flaw was that our entire left flank faced heights on which the enemy had concentrated its artillery. The proximity of the forest to our rear further inhibited us. Preussisch Eylau would protect the enemy if he chose to approach our centre and we now had to defend it with a large battery and keep these guns constantly in position. The right flank was completely to our advantage because a vast marshy plain in front of our positions did not favour large actions there and the French pushed out only a few skirmishers in this direction. It is incredible that our quartermaster general was unaware of these swamps and committed 12,000 men here without purpose. These troops were limited to futile exchange of fire with distant enemy batteries while we were in dire need of forces at other places. I was deployed here with my two horse artillery companies and fired without any purpose until the afternoon.

The French made several futile attacks against our centre and suffered from 60 guns that were concentrated here. Their attack on our left was more successful. Neither could General Baron Sacken's reasonable orders, nor intrepid Major General Count Osterman-Tolstoy's resistance halt the French. The left flank moved back and was virtually at right angles to the rest of army. At around 11:00 am dense snowfall obscured everything and action was delayed for 15 minutes. Just then, two squadrons of French guard cuirassiers lost their direction and found themselves between our infantry and cavalry; only a few of them managed to escape.[155] The resumption

---

[155] Yermolov describes Murat's famous cavalry charge, when, at around 11:40 am, 80 squadrons of the French cavalry advanced in the one of the greatest cavalry charges in history. Davidov recalled, 'The field was engulfed in a roar and the snow, ploughed over by some 12,000 riders lifted and swirled from under them like a storm. Brilliant Murat followed by a large cavalry mass, was ablaze ahead of the onslaught with a naked sabre and flew directly into the thick of the fight. Musket and cannon fire and levelled bayonets were unable to stem the deadly tide.' The French overwhelmed the Russian cavalry, pierced through the infantry

of light revealed a column of French infantry less than 100 paces away from our 7th Division. The French stopped in bewilderment at the sudden appearance of our regiments. With a loud jeer, the Vladimir Musketeers attacked and left nobody alive in the French column to mourn the death of their comrades.[156]

Our troops met variable success but held their ground everywhere except for the left flank. Between the centre and left, seven cavalry regiments made a rapid attack and overwhelmed everything that opposed them; the enemy infantry abandoned its muskets and fled to the forest; our cavalry almost captured an enemy battery but failed in the ensuing confusion. it was shameful that it fled from inferior enemy cavalry that could have been halted by the Alexandria Hussars alone.[157]

Soon after the battle began, a distant cannonade was heard on our right flank. We learned that Marshal Ney was pursuing the Prussians of General Lestocq, who was ordered to join our army as soon as possible but failed to accomplish it.[158] When the enemy resumed its attacks around 2:00 pm, the commander-in-chief sent a dispatch requesting Lestocq to join us as soon as possible. Meanwhile, it was necessary to contain the enemy success on our left. The 8th Division was recalled to the centre; our reserves were fully committed so I was ordered to move my two horse artillery companies. Lieutenant General Count Tolstoy simply pointed to the left and I followed this direction. I did not know what my objectives were, nor under whose command I would operate.

---

line and then charged back again through the Russian positions.

[156] At around 10.00 am, Napoleon ordered Marshal Augereau to take his 9,000 men against the Russian left. Blinding snowstorm and dark clouds from artillery fire obscured the view of the marching Frenchmen. So, the French divisions strayed from their path of march and went straight towards the massed Russians batteries in the centre. Over 60 Russian guns suddenly opened canister fire at point blank range.

[157] Yermolov describes the Russian counterattack following the destruction of Augereau's corps, when some Russian units advanced as far as cemetery at Eylau and threatened Napoleon's command post. However, Napoleon's personal guard was sufficient to drive the Russians back.

[158] Yermolov is unfair in his criticism of Lestocq. The Prussian general succeeded in eluding Marshal Ney's superior corps and fought a series of delaying actions to prevent the French from reaching the battlefield. The arrival of fresh Prussian forces (5,583 men with 2 horse artillery batteries) turned the tide on the Russian left flank.

Taking another horse artillery company, I arrived at the vast plain on the extreme left flank, where the remnants of our forces were barely holding their ground against a superior enemy who had captured the nearby heights as well as a village close to the rear of our troops. I opened fire and set this village on fire, driving out the enemy infantry that harassed my guns. Then, I directed my fire against the enemy batteries and held my ground for two hours.[159]

It was then that General Lestocq's corps began to arrive, with our Kaluga and Vyborg regiments leading its column against the enemy flank. The enemy fire, directed against me, became infrequent and I observed large numbers of enemy guns being diverted against Lestocq. I moved my battery every time it was obscured by smoke and moved all the horses, including my own, and equipment to the rear, declaring to my troops that retreat would be unacceptable. I directed all my efforts on the road at the bottom of the hill by which the enemy was trying to move its infantry as it was impossible to move through the deep snow on either side. I caused heavy casualties with the canister fire of my 30 guns. In short, the enemy failed to pass and it was late to look for a different path since Lestocq, encountering inferior enemy forces, routed them, falling on the heights and batteries which the enemy abandoned. Gloomy night descended on the battlefield. The commander-in-chief, wanting to see Lestocq's actions, arrived on the left flank and was surprised to see my horses and equipment but not a single gun. Hearing my explanation, he was very pleased by my action.

Marshal Ney's corps pursued Lestocq's troops along the road to Königsberg passing behind our rear and occupying a village with a strong detachment. Prince Dolgoruky was ordered to attack them with the Tavrida Grenadiers. When, after two failed attacks, Dolgoruky persisted, the enemy withdrew unnoticed, probably because of the general retreat of the French.

---

[159] General Alexander Kutaisov is usually credited for bringing these artillery companies to the left flank but Yermolov was first to arrive with 36 guns. Kutaisov followed him with 12 more. However, after the battle Kutaisov received the prestigious Order of St George (3rd class) for his actions; the fact that he was a cousin to the chief of the Russian artillery probably played a role in the receipt of this award.

Our army marched to Königsberg that same night. Ataman Platov, who arrived with the Don Cossack Host a day before, was ordered to remain on the battlefield.

The enemy also retreated and during the night, its rearguard withdrew to Landsberg. On the next day, seeing that our army had abandoned Preussisch Eylau, the French returned to gather their guns and transports. We soon learned that special orders had been issued directing the evacuation of hospitals, the commissariat and the army treasury. And after this, Napoleon had enough impertinence to claim the battle as a victory!

The commander-in-chief initially wanted to pursue the enemy and he even told his senior commanders of his intent; however, it proved impossible to rally our troops dispersed over such a vast area. The soldiers were exhausted and weakened by heavy losses. It was known that Napoleon still had Bernadotte's corps and with such superiority of forces, our success seemed doubtful. Besides, the lack of supplies further restricted us.[160] The commander-in-chief did not escape criticism; and since detractors often have no understanding of the subjects they are discussing, so it was with the critics of Bennigsen.

Approaching Königsberg, the army bivouacked in the vicinity of the town, while the vanguard was some 12 verstas ahead of it.[161] A small number of enemy cavalry appeared on the last march to Königsberg, and, as their number rapidly increased, the French took up positions some distance from us.

Early in February, a detachment from our vanguard had destroyed some enemy troops at Mansfeld and Bochersdorf. General Lambert distinguished himself in these actions. It was obvious that the French cavalry was so exhausted that on one occasion two squadrons, forced to withdraw across a lake, fell off

---

[160] Robert Wilson described, 'The Prussians had provisions, but the Russians had no other sustenance than the frozen snow. Their wants had induced numbers during the battle to search for food in the adjoining villages and the plain was covered by foraging parties passing and repassing.' Wilson, Brief Remarks, p. 109.
[161] The Russian army arrived on 10 February 1807. Juliette de Krüdener wrote in her diary, 'The town was overflowing with wounded; it was impossible to find shelter for everybody, nor to dress the wounds immediately.' Juliette de Krüdener, Journal 1806-1808 cited in Francis Ley, Madame de Krüdener et son temps 1764-1824, (Paris, 1964), pp. 273-74.

their horses and were captured lying on the ground. Both squadrons numbered 60 men only.

The commander-in-chief dispatched Bagration to St Petersburg with a detailed description of Preussisch Eylau, which had been unjustly described to the czar because of various court intrigues. There were rumours that Count Tolstoy used his brother, who was close to the czar, to spread malicious rumours against the commander-in-chief. The general opinion was in favour of the latter.[162]

Less than two weeks after arriving at Königsberg, the army advanced again. Two marches later, the vanguard under Major General Markov arrived at Preussisch Eylau. He was supported by General Prince Golitsyn's cavalry.

I observed the battlefield with intense curiosity. I was horrified to see so many corpses lying where our lines had been. I found even more bodies where the enemy troops had been, especially where their columns massed before attacks. Local residents (who informed for us) were ordered several days ago to tip French corpses into the nearby lakes, since it was impossible to excavate the frozen soil. As an artillery officer I noticed evidence of our artillery fire and was pleased. There was not a single undamaged building in town; a suburb had burnt to the ground, and here, according to the locals, the French wounded had been gathered and consequently many of them died.

The French abandoned Preussisch Eylau upon our approach. Numerous abandoned transports, caissons and ambulances with wounded and sick indicated a hasty retreat. Soon, a thaw made roads impassable and, because the retreating side always suffers more in such conditions, the French had to discard all their ambulances at various towns and villages.

---

[162] Bennigsen claimed Eylau as a Russian victory reporting, 'I am very happy to be able to acquaint Your Majesty that the army which had been entrusted to me, has again been victorious… The enemy has been completely beaten, near 2,000 prisoners taken and 12 standards, which I lay at the feet of Your Majesty.' Instead of 12 captured French eagles mentioned in the report, only five arrived at St Petersburg. Three days later, Bennigsen offered his resignation to Alexander. Based on Bagration's report, Alexander decided to keep Bennigsen in charge of the main Russian army and sent one of his adjutants to settle the tensions at the headquarters.

Arriving at Landsberg, we found a hospital for French officers; these were surprised to receive better care from us. Some of them had had no bandages for several days. The landlord of my apartment spoke poor French and told me that he overheard the officers discussing the terrible conditions in their army when it arrived at Landsberg after the battle; they mentioned that if it had not been for Bernadotte's corps which did not participate in the battle and was left in the rearguard, there would have been no one else left to cover the French retreat since the troops were in complete disorder and the number of pillagers was impossible. Many corps lacked ammunition. The French rearguard had reached Landsberg that same evening.

Our vanguard quickly marched on Arensdorf and some troops seized Guttstadt. Ataman Platov, with his Cossacks, a battalion of hussars and a battalion of Jägers, was deployed at Benern. General Count Pahlen was at one of the crossings over the Passarge, maintaining communications with Colonel Vuich's detachment at Wormsdit. Baron Sacken's division, the closest to the vanguard, occupied Launau. The remaining forces were approaching Heilsberg and the main headquarters was at Bartenstein.

The enemy was on the other side of the Passarge and Napoleon's headquarters was at Osterode. On 18 February [2 March], the enemy concentrated his forces on the right and crossed the Passarge, while other forces appeared near Guttstadt and Arensdorf. We hastily abandoned the latter place but could join neither Ataman Platov nor General Count Pahlen. Major General Baggovut could not defend Guttstadt and the enemy drove back his 5th Jäger Regiment, capturing the village of Zechern as well. During this unexpected attack, we almost lost our guns. General Baggovut joined General Baron Sacken at Launau, where Adjutant General Uvarov also arrived with his cavalry.

The vanguard had no other means of retreat but to pass close by to the French camp at Peterswalde; all the other roads were too far off and the enemy had outposts there. To avoid confusion and disorder, the French hated to do anything important during the night so we were able to freely pass their bivouacs.

The vanguard passed through Launau and joined General Baron Sacken. Other detachments, previously isolated from each other, soon concentrated here as well.

On 19th [3 March], our forces concentrated around Launau. Marshal Ney's corps opposed us, with its headquarters located at Guttstadt. Enemy skirmishers, deployed in the direction of Peterswalde, covered the forest in front of our camp. Well positioned and defended French batteries harassed us from Zechern. General Baron Sacken also deployed skirmishers, but the French were more experienced and inflicted considerable casualties on us for two days. Therefore, General Sacken decided to launch a night-time attack on Zechern, hoping that the enemy would be driven from there and forced to abandon Peterswalde, leaving us better off. During the attack, the infantry began to shout 'Hurrah' some way from the batteries, and awoke the French, who immediately prepared themselves. We exchanged canister and musket fire; the men at the head of our column grew timid and threw themselves down, while the rear ranks continued to advance and it all became so confused that it was impossible to move them out of harm's way for a long time. We lost several officers and many rank-and-file during the fighting. It was here that I observed for the first time how cavalry covered retreating infantry in darkness. I do not know why the disordered troops were not rallied by the drummers but, instead, General Count Pahlen and his Sumsk Hussars had to round the soldiers up.

The following day, the French commander at Zechern sent a message that he would allow us to bury our corpses and mockingly noted how far these were from his guns. We had to shut our mouths; however, everyone criticized Sacken for restarting his old night-time excursions! The vanguard was reinforced by several units and Sacken was given a different assignment. Major General Markov ordered the establishment of a battery in front of Zechern, and I set to willingly since my company had suffered a lot at that spot. Having reconnoitred part of the forest defended by the enemy, I deployed six guns close to the edge of the woods and masked them with fir branches; I then waited for dawn when the enemy usually moved its infantry from the camp near Peterswalde. Early in the morning, a strong enemy column left the camp and proceeded in a carefree manner towards the woods where a small contingent was always deployed for the night. During its march, the column exposed its flank to my battery and the canister fire of my six guns at close range caused such confusion that, having abandoned many corpses, it fled towards the camp pursued by our fire. We occupied the remaining part of the forest and the enemy did not dare challenge us. We now had some six infantry regiments here. The batteries near Zechern often exchanged fire, mostly ineffective, with the French. Marshal Ney's courier was captured delivering a message to Prince Berthier with information that the Russians indeed planned to defend their position since they had constructed batteries at various points. The enemy soon abandoned Zechern and Peterswalde, and dug trenches along the edge of the forest.

General Markov occupied Zechern with two Jäger regiments, while two hussar squadrons and some rotating infantry units were at Peterswalde. There were frequent skirmishes with the French, who searched for dry wood in the village. My horse artillery company had already suffered enough and was replaced by another unit and moved back for repairs and reinforcement. However, due to the whims of the senior artillery colonels, neither of whom had held such a distinguished command, I was ordered to join my company.[163] The commander-in-chief was told that this change was made to give me some rest, and he later said the same to Bagration. Having just returned from St Petersburg, Bagration requested that he keep me and so I remained with this commander, whom we all completely trusted.

An unpleasant incident took place prior to Bagration's return. Four Jäger regiments at Peterswalde, commanded by Major General Korf, lost their commander in bizarre circumstances. Billeted in the best house in the village, which belonged to a priest, Korf was busy with his usual exercise, sipping punch, and did not trouble himself about security. He kept a hussar officer in charge of the outposts with him. Meanwhile, a few French voltigeurs, guided by the priest, entered the house via the garden and, under cover of darkness, captured the general. In the ensuing noisy struggle, our regiments were called to arms but, following a skirmish, the French escaped with their prize.[164]

---

[163] Yermolov is suggesting that the senior officers envied him his role in the vanguard and tried to remove him from command.
[164] It is unclear when Korf was released from captivity because his record of service shows him fighting at Heilsberg and Friedland, for which he received a golden sword with diamonds and the Prussian Order of the Red Eagle (1st class).

Napoleon did not miss the chance of portraying this skirmish as a victorious battle in his bulletin. They had captured a corps commander and, to exaggerate this victory, Korf's gallantry and noble character were highlighted. But I would have been surprised if the French had been able to identify their prisoner right away as the general was too drunk to even use his tongue. The French can only have thought Baron Korf a general due to the darkness and wouldn't have guessed such from his condition and appearance. Then we would not have had to learn about his merits by reading foreign newspapers.

Following this incident, there was complete inactivity on both sides for almost three months; there were no skirmish lines and not a single shot was fired, although no armistice was concluded.

A general commanding the French advance troops offered to make Peterswalde neutral because otherwise it would be a source of constant strife and the French would have to capture it. Bagration responded that he agreed with the latter contention but warned that it was easier for the French to demand this than to actually carry it out. So, French threats remained words and we retained control of Peterswalde.

The French deployed against us suffered greatly from the lack of supplies and their cavalry was sent back to refit. The 27th Dragoons was exhausted by hunger and deserted to us in numbers. Our vanguard endured similar hardships; there was no bread or salt; biscuits were completely rotten and very scarce. The soldiers ate ox hides which had earlier covered our tents for two or three weeks. In the 23rd and 24th Jäger regiments the soldiers began slaughtering horses and the latter unit had many deserters.

Prince Bagration sent me to describe our hardships to the commander-in-chief. Despite stern orders, the situation remained the same. Duty officer Major General Foch was upset about my report and I also found myself the subject of his enmity because I did not admire his mediocre abilities whilst others praised them. We were both in the artillery and had known each other for a long time.

The czar soon joined the army and the Guard, commanded by the grand duke, also arrived. Imperial headquarters was at Bartenstein, while the grand duke remained at Schipenbeil.[165]

---

[165] In late March, Alexander personally visited the army to encourage his troops for the oncoming campaign.

Parades and foppishness took over and, despite our hungry bellies, we had to turn to arranging ammunition.

Grand Duke Constantine visited us first as, after Suvorov's campaign in Italy, he had established friendly relations with Bagration. Observing our lack of provisions, he took care to improve our supplies. The first supply train, that he insisted on sending to the vanguard, was diverted en route to other troops. However, he assigned escorts to the subsequent trains, which reached us safely. Instead of a shortage, we soon found ourselves in abundance.

Among other officials introduced to him, the grand duke honoured me following Prince Bagration's commendation of my service. Until then, he had not known me because I had never served at the capital. We were soon ordered to prepare to meet the czar and the King of Prussia.

Having arranged our huts uniformly and made them look smart, we organized the rest of our camp. Picked men were chosen from various regiments, given the clothes of others and armed. The troops thus deprived of their clothing were hidden in the woods or sent to man an outpost on a distant hill. Here, I saw how the czar was shown his troops in the best light and assured that they lacked nothing. He introduced each commander to the King of Prussia, and, among others, he mentioned me and that he was satisfied with my service in the previous campaign. The czar's attention and benevolence fascinated everyone. Without any flattery, I must admit that he had the ability to encourage everyone. The Prussian king awarded the *Pour le Merite* to three staff officers,[166] and I was one of them. These were the first Prussian orders awarded and were not yet rendered worthless by their subsequent multiplicity.

Medals for Preussisch Eylau were soon issued. Instead of the order of St George (3rd class), to which the commander-in-chief had nominated me, I received the St Vladimir. Major General Count Kutaisov was portrayed as having assisted me in battle. Yet, it was only curiosity that had brought him to my company and since I was not subordinated to him, he did not interfere with my orders. However, he was awarded the St George (3rd class), even though

---

[166] Yermolov's note: Awards were given to the chef of the 5th Jäger Regiment (Colonel Gogel), myself and the commander of the Pskov Musketeers, Lieutenant Colonel Loshkarev.

he did not yet have the 4th class. They intended to describe him as my superior in the official report but Baron Steingel knew the facts and opposed this. Bagration explained this injustice to the commander-in-chief, who acknowledged that I was mistreated but did not do a thing. So, this was one of those many pleasant events that I experienced in my career.

It was beneficial to Napoleon to prolong the inactivity because he could send a large corps to reinforce the troops besieging Danzig. The corps of Davout, deployed at Allenstein, and of Ney, at Guttstadt, were small and parts of their cavalry and artillery had been detached for sustenance. So it was decided to attack Ney's corps on 1 [13] May. A day before, the Guard had arrived at Launau, the rest of the army had concentrated and everything was ready. The vanguard took up a position in the woods with the intention of occupying the Altkirck plain and cutting the French line of retreat towards Guttstadt.

The czar reviewed the vanguard and, in the company of the commander-in- chief, he visited those outposts deployed before Zechern and Peterswalde which screened the movement of the vanguard. I do not know why the offensive was called off. The czar returned to headquarters, the troops returned to their bivouacs and the vanguard returned to Launau.[167]

The enemy, meanwhile, continued besieging Danzig. Although Major General Count Kamenski was dispatched with a strong detachment to reinforce the garrison,[168] the enemy had superior forces and Count Kamenski was prevented from reaching the fortress and was repulsed with loss. Had it been undertaken earlier, this operation would have succeeded. Soon thereafter, the fortress had to surrender because of lack of ammunition, especially after an English ship carrying munitions was captured by the French.

---

[167] French scouts had detected the Russian movement and Ney was warned of the possible attack. The rumour also spread that Napoleon was marching to reinforce Ney. So, Bennigsen postponed his offensive but the troops were exasperated by these movements calling them 'the first of May ramble'.

[168] Yermolov's note: Danzig was defended by the Prussians, three garrison battalions and two Cossack regiments under Major General Prince Sherbatov. After the surrender, these troops were allowed to leave fortress on condition that they did not serve against the French. Sherbatov rejected this and rejoined the army.

It was unpleasant to hear about the capitulation of Danzig and there was no doubt Napoleon would recall most of the besieging force.

I do not know why we, after cancelling our offensive on 1 May, hesitated until the 24th when the enemy army had already been reinforced. The operation was so well planned that the entire corps of Ney should have been in our hands. The direction of the main parts of our army was as follows:

The vanguard moved to Altkirck to cut the French off in the woods extending from Peterswalde to Guttstadt while two Jäger regiments attacked them. The vanguard's action was to be cautious so as to allow other parts of the army to outflank the enemy.

On the right, Lieutenant General Baron von der Osten-Sacken was to outflank the enemy and prevent him from reaching the Passarge. On the left, Lieutenant General Prince Gorchakov was to cross the Alle and surround Guttstadt. Lieutenant General Dokhturov was to drive off an enemy outpost on our right and rejoin the main army. General Prince Golitsyn was to support Baron Sacken with his cavalry. The Guard was left in reserve. Ataman General Platov was to observe the movement of Davout's corps towards Allenstein.

The vanguard marched to Altkirck early on the morning of 24 May. To the left of the woods, we observed French sentries, calmly changing guard. Soon, a few artillery rounds signalled the start of the offensive and we observed the hasty movement of troops towards Altkirck. An intense cannonade ensued but we did not do anything much. Considering the amount of time which had elapsed, Bagration believed that Sacken should have outflanked the enemy by now but not a single shot was heard in that direction and the inaction of the French troops in front of us also raised doubts. Officers were dispatched to gather intelligence but no troops were observed except General Prince Golitsyn's cavalry moving in the distance.

Meanwhile, the French managed to concentrate at Altkirck and our vanguard was ordered to attack them. Bitter fighting followed. The enemy fought for a long time before retreating. The left wing of the vanguard, led by General Baggovut, came under ferocious fire. Baggovut moved through Amt-Guttstadt (a suburb of Guttstadt), leaving troops to contain 600 Frenchmen. We did not receive support from Gorchakov, as he encountered the enemy at the crossing of the Alle, took his time crossing it and then spent time seizing Guttstadt, thereby failing to arrive on time. It should be noted that this town had no fortifications, was defended by a mere 600 men and, had we marched on, it would have surrendered without having committed an entire corps to its capture. But, because of the hiatus in May headquarters had heard rumours that the French had fortified the town and they considered it important. So Gorchakov thought its capture would be considered a great exploit. Had Gorchakov left a small detachment there and moved forward, Ney would have suffered heavy casualties.

The vanguard pursued the enemy until nightfall and bivouacked near Quetz. We had captured many prisoners during the day; some of the French had been unable to reach a rally point at Altkirck and had found themselves cut off.

It was Sacken's fault that the plan did not work. He was late to his objective, excusing himself by claiming he had taken a long detour and needed further instructions. But rumour had it that, irritated by the commander-in-chief, Sacken had deliberately sabotaged the enterprise, preventing Bennigsen from succeeding. Many were furious that a favourable chance to annihilate an entire enemy corps was so wasted.[169]

The commander-in-chief saw how less than 600 French infantry had fearlessly opposed our cavalry. The infantry had deployed near the village. Our three cavalry regiments charged one after another but were repulsed, each time the French commander courageously appeared in front front of his troops to close ranks. Only after our two guns were deployed and opened canister fire did the French withdraw. Otherwise, we would have had to give up and look for other means to prevail. The French infantry escaped us.

General Dokhturov found the enemy weak but in strong positions and exchanged fire with them committing a battalion at a time. Two battalions of the Leib-Guard Jäger Regiment then made a swift bayonet attack and drove the enemy back at once.

---

[169] The main reasons for failure lay in the quality of the French troops as well as in the flawed campaign plan itself. But Sacken's delay was crucial too. In a letter to Alexander, Bennigsen accused Sacken of insubordination and held him responsible for the failure. Sacken was under court-martial for over three years. The court found him guilty of insubordination but did not impose a punishment due to Sacken's distinguished career.

By 25 May, our forces were facing an enemy fortified in strong positions so our artillery went into action. The vanguard's Jäger regiments under Major General Rayevskii were ordered to encircle the enemy's right. The French withdrew when our skirmishers approached their batteries and, having occupied some gardens near Quetz, they deployed some infantry supported by several artillery pieces. The vanguard hastily advanced along the main road. I opened canister fire and drove the enemy out of Quetz; however, when the Grodno Hussars attacked the French in the open, two enemy canister rounds routed it.[170] Although it was hot our Jäger regiments ran forwards. Despite their tenacious defence, the French could not hold their ground as their troops were in great confusion. The woods prevented us from coordinating our actions and helped the French rescue their artillery. Nevertheless, they sacrificed their rearguard, had many captured or killed and abandoned their wounded and transports.[171] Only two guns were captured; one by the Cossacks, another by the courageous Major Kulnev, who led two weak squadrons of the Grodno Hussars and caught up with an enemy artillery park on the Passarge, seizing a few artillery pieces. Informed by prisoners that the rest of the artillery was trying to escape nearby, he rushed to capture it but took the wrong road and encountered superior enemy cavalry which forced him to retreat. Returning, he came across the artillery park he took earlier. The enemy did not risk attacking him and Kulnev crossed the river. He captured many officers in this action.

The Cossacks, meanwhile, captured some French wagons, including Marshal Ney's personal carriage with his silver dining set and other belongings.[172] Earrings and bracelets were found and it would have been a mystery as to where the marshal had acquired

---

[170] Yermolov's note: This regiment was assembled from squadrons of different units which had never fought together. Its officers were excellent. Colonel Shepelev often hosted lavish breakfasts and lunches, bragging that he would make a gapping hole in the enemy at the very first engagement.
[171] Russian sources claim 1,500 French killed and wounded and two guns captured in two days of combat; Russian losses were unknown but may have been as many as 2,000 killed and wounded.
[172] Yermolov's note: It must be noted that Cossacks capture wagons not because they are always ahead of the troops, but because they stay with the wagons while everyone else pursues the enemy.

these trinkets if it was not for the coats of arms of various Polish families etched on the silver.

The vanguard bivouacked near Deppen on the Passarge. On the opposite bank, the enemy occupied Kallisten and the adjacent heights. Our outposts stretched along the bank towards Elditten, where the enemy had a detachment with a few guns. General Dokhturov, despite having his corps nearby, thought it unnecessary to capture it and so the French detachment remained alone on our bank, protecting the best crossing site. The army soon followed and bivouacked close by.

On 26 May [7 June], the enemy, taking advantage of the heights, harassed us with an artillery bombardment which lasted all day. We responded and a chain of Jägers was engaged in a fierce fire fight along the riverbank. We noticed that the enemy received reinforcements. The Cossack outposts kept us informed that the enemy had been observed near Elditten on the right flank. The day ended without incident.

At daybreak, movement was observed among the enemy deployed against our vanguard. Troops, artillery parks and transports were gradually concentrating. At 10:00 am outposts were reinforced and intense fighting began. Two enemy infantry columns and one of cavalry moved towards Kallisten. Having routed the 7th Jägers under the command of the timid Lieutenant Colonel Laptev,[173] one enemy column advanced quickly to the artillery battery where I chanced to be. I initially thought these were our troops; and I only perceived they were French after seeing their white shoulder belts (only our Jägers were deployed here). The enemy column was shaken by our canister. The Jägers, the 5th under Colonel Gogel and the 20th of Colonel Bistrom, engaged the French near the crossing, killed many of them and, pursuing the rest, they rushed into Kallisten and exterminated everyone.

Meanwhile, another enemy column, observing our reinforcements, turned back. Despite our fire, the French cavalry plunged into the river, but the 26th Jägers threw it into confusion with its battalion fire and then attacked with bayonets. The horses were stuck in the swampy river and the French suffered

---

[173] Yermolov's note: He should not be mistaken for a gallant Colonel Laptev, under whose command the 8th Jäger Regiment was renowned for fearlessness and discipline.

accordingly. We were not attacked for a few hours after this combat. Prince Bagration ordered the entire vanguard to be battle ready[174] and this precaution would prove very useful! At 6:00 pm the enemy opened artillery fire against Kallisten but we held on. The French advanced in large numbers against us in order to drive our Jägers back. They fought back tenaciously and the village changed hands several times before superior French forces finally captured it. We moved across the river and the combat ended with darkness. Just then, Major General Ilovaisky (IV) informed us that Soult's corps had crossed the river at Elditten and had advanced at least three verstas. This could have cut off our line of retreat. So at dawn, the vanguard retreated in two columns; the first of them was commanded by General Markov, who was accompanied by Bagration. General Baggovut led the second column along the main road and I was attached to it with most of our artillery. The enemy caught up with us half way to Guttstadt; cavalry and Cossacks engaged in action; several cavalry units were sent to our support. The army was, meanwhile, passing through Guttstadt.[175] Roads through forests are inconvenient and we moved slowly. Besides, the main army had started marching four hours later than it should have done; the headquarters was burdened by numerous creatures useless to the army, who, while we were fighting against the French, were calmly enjoying themselves. To protect such people an order was delivered to Prince Bagration instructing him to hold his ground as long as possible and a few cavalry regiments were sent as well.

Some of the French attacks went entirely to our advantage. One Italian dragoon regiment was pushed into the swamp, where it was forced to dismount. Surrounded, most of its soldiers were captured. But when the enemy infantry arrived in large numbers, we could barely hold our ground on the heights near Guttstadt. That

---

[174] Yermolov's note: On my request, several heavy (batareinikh) guns were sent to me because I often suffered from the enemy's larger calibre artillery. At Königsberg, I experienced firsthand what three-pound licornes could do against good artillery and I am sure the enemy was surprised that it did not rout us with their very first shot.
[175] Napoleon launched the offensive towards Elditen and Deppen. Murat's cavalry, supported by Ney, was ordered to cross the Passarge at Deppen. Lannes and the Imperial Guard followed them closely. On the right, Davout moved his corps across the river at Hasenburg.

day, I was under such ferocious fire that I destroyed one enemy battery using nothing but canister. The St Petersburg Dragoons protecting my company held their ground under fire with incredible restraint. We were last to retreat following the vanguard and burning a bridge over the Alle. The enemy had occupied the city. Its infantry filled the houses along the bank and I suffered from musket fire and retreated only after setting fire to the city in several places. This was my revenge on the rascals who lived there, those supporters of the French, who back in February, when the 5th Jägers were driven out, had expressed their joy with applause and jeering.

Having retreated to Heilsberg in the wake of our army, the vanguard stopped near the river.

On 29 May [10 June], the vanguard was dispatched to Launau, where another detachment was already deployed to delay any enemy move in this direction.[176] There was no doubt that the French would advance this way because this road was much better than the others passing through the forest; besides the other roads led to a plain too narrow to deploy an entire army.

The enemy, having beaten us to Launau, encountered the vanguard at Bewernick.[177] Meanwhile, our army took up positions in the trenches constructed at Heilsberg but it again acted so slowly that the vanguard had to delay the enemy forces for two additional hours, suffering heavy casualties in the process. The terrain sloped down from Bewernick to Heilsberg and the terrain was to the enemy's advantage. The vanguard deployed its line infantry on the left straddling the main road; the Jäger regiments were on the right, supported by cavalry that was sent from the main army. My company was attached to the cavalry.

We held our ground for a long time and our cavalry made several dazzling charges. However, the enemy soon came up in strength and attacked our trenches, having 150 guns against our 40 pieces. Its cavalry extended beyond our extreme right and we found

---

[176] A new vanguard under Mikhail Borozdin was at Launau, some 6 miles from Heilsberg, while Bagration with his detachment remained at Reichenberg.

[177] On 10 June, Murat's cavalry attacked Borozdin driving him to Bewernick. Bennigsen reinforced Borozdin and ordered Bagration from Reichenberg to Bewernick. He crossed the Alle at Amt-Heilsberg and joined Borozdin as he was retreating. Bagration rallied his forces in the valley between Bewernick and Langwiese.

ourselves in a very dangerous position. They broke our lines and some of my guns were captured from the rear. One of these cavalry attacks was so formidable that most of our cavalry was scattered behind Langwiese. However, General Rayevskii's Jägers limited the enemy's success and our cavalry, having rallied, returned to the battlefield, recapturing our guns. I escaped only because of my swift horse as part of the enemy attacked us from the rear and several French cuirassiers rushed toward me. Meanwhile, our infantry, having endured horrendous fire and suffered heavy casualties, began to withdraw. At this moment, duty officer Major General Foch arrived and demanded to know why Bagration was retreating without orders when the army was not yet deployed. Prince Peter was infuriated by Foch's question, he was known as a brave officer but was relatively junior. Prince Bagration took him into the very heat of the action to demonstrate why the troops were retreating. Five minutes later, Foch was seriously wounded and we were pursued back to our trenches. The vanguard lost at least half of its strength; no regiment returned with its commander unscathed, and very few staff officers survived.

Grand Duke Constantine witnessed the battle; the commander-in-chief having ordered him to move the vanguard's infantry and artillery across the Alle while its unscathed cavalry was to rejoin the army for further actions. Among those distinguished that day were Baggovut, Rayevskii (who commanded the Jägers) and Liven, head of the Liven Dragoons. The commander-in-chief thanked me for my service and the grand duke showed me his particular benevolence.[178]

Pursuing the vanguard, the enemy columns descended on our trenches. The French tried hardest from the direction from Langwiese; repulsed, they always resumed their attacks and fresh forces replaced their routed units. In the evening, a vicious attack was made and some of our batteries on the right flank were captured.[179] However, the French could not hold them because of the proximity of some fortifications, which brought fire to bear on

---

[178] Yermolov's note: He enjoyed my response to an adjutant he had sent to me with a message that the French column was too close to my battery: 'I will fire when I can distinguish blondes from brunettes.' He saw that column routed!

[179] Wilson recalled, 'About 11:00 pm, the [French] shouted arrêtez le combat along their line of tirailleurs … and the massacre, for no other term can be so properly applied, terminated.

them, especially a redoubt constructed on the height that dominated the vicinity. Without this fortification the French could not hope to succeed and so a strong column of French grenadiers advanced against it. A wide ravine protected them for some distance from our fire, but as they came out of it, they were caught in a crossfire from our batteries and canister rounds from the redoubt. Despite some confusion, this column still reached the ditch in front of the redoubt but our units, defending this fortification, made a bayonet attack and routed them. The entire valley was covered with bodies. It was difficult to repulse any attack by such a good army, but they simply could not withstand the crossfire. Other attacks faired no better and the enemy was pursued far beyond the fortifications. There were no trenches on our right flank and our cavalry was deployed to cover this direction. The French did not manage to bring sufficient cavalry to bear at this point and the commander-in-chief ordered a counterattack; the French could not resist our cavalry and were driven back to the forest, where the French infantry opened fire to cover their survivors and turned our cavalry back. Two Prussian cavalry units distinguished themselves in this action. In some places, the infantry clambered out of the fortifications and in one particular place entire lines fired by battalions. The darkness ended the battle and our joyous troops returned to their forts.

According to information we later received, the enemy lost some 12,000 men and our losses were considerably lower.[180] Napoleon was not present and his marshals fought the battle.

On 30 May [11 June], the enemy, occupying Bewernick and Langwiese, dispatched its main body towards Königsberg.[181] Our army stayed in trenches but during the night of 31st, it retreated to Bartenstein because the enemy movement threatened our lines of operation.[182] Napoleon, by forcing us to abandon our fortified

---

[180] Heilsberg is often overshadowed by other Napoleonic battles, although it was a bloody fight and both sides suffered enormous casualties. Soult lost 8,286 men while Lannes' attack cost his troops 2,284 dead and wounded. Russian losses were 2,000-3,000 killed and over 5,000 wounded, including eight generals. Bennigsen himself was so exhausted physically and mentally that he collapsed on the battlefield and regained consciousness some time later.

[181] During the night of 10 June, Napoleon arrived on the battlefield with the Imperial Guard and Ney's 6th Corps.

[182] The morning mist prevented Bennigsen from observing Napoleon's

positions, showed how imprudent his marshals had been when they decided to attack in view of our advantages and how useless was the battle itself.

The rearguard retreated at dawn. The enemy cavalry caught up with it around 10:00 am but only observed its movement from a distance. The rearguard spent the night near Bartenstein.

In the evening of 1 [13] June the rearguard passed Schippenbeil. The enemy cavalry was present in numbers, but the day ended with a futile exchange of fire. At Schippenbeil, Bagration received the order to quickly proceed to Friedland.

Many were surprised by the direction of our army, but we soon learned that squadrons of the Tatar Uhlans had captured some French cavalry[183] that imprudently entered Friedland and the prisoners revealed that the French army was advancing on Königsberg and only one corps was deployed nearby. It was therefore assumed that the commander-in-chief wanted to destroy this corps before it was reinforced and so he concentrated the entire army to ensure complete success.

The rearguard marched without rest during the night and reached Friedland at dawn; artillery fire could occasionally be heard. Prince Bagration dispatched General Rayevskii and his Jägers on ahead and ordered me to advance with the horse artillery. Having crossed the river at Friedland,[184] we were assigned a place on the left, where we found grenadiers of the Life Guard Izmailovsk Regiment already engaged in a skirmish. Our troops were gradually concentrating but there were still only a few of them. We

---

movements, but, around 10:00 am, he noted large masses of the French troops marching against his left and ordered retreat.

[183] Bennigsen dispatched Prince Golitsyn's detachment to beat the French to Friedland. As he approached Friedland, Golitsyn found the town already occupied by Lannes.

[184] Wilson described Friedland as 'a considerable town situated on the left bank of the Alle; a long wooden bridge connects the town with the right bank – west of the town is a capacious lake – the country for a mile in the direction of Heilsberg forms a semicircle of apparent plain, but is cut by a deep and narrow ravine full of water, and scarcely fordable, which runs from Domnau into the lakes. Near the town, on the left of the plain, the ground abruptly descends and woods border down the Alle – a deep wood fringed the plain from the Alle to the village of Heinricksdorf [sic], where there was a little interruption, but woods again closed round to the Alle, the banks of which were very steep, the fords, subsequently used, were yet unknown.'

replaced the Guards and their regiment moved back. The enemy, as we later learned, had 10,000 grenadiers under Marshal Oudinot, who masked his weakness by deploying his troops in the forest opposite our position. Soon most of our troops had come up while the enemy remained the same. Unfortunately, the commander-in-chief was not feeling well that day;[185] Quartermaster-General Baron Steingeil and new duty officer Lieutenant General Essen (I) were bruised during a reconnaissance of the position at Friedland and so we received no instructions for quite some time.

We should have attacked the French corps, which was dispersed and could not have properly defended itself or made an easy retreat. The French army was also extended on its march to Königsberg and could not have arrived in time to support this corps; even if it managed, the arriving troops would have appeared piecemeal and could not have resisted the combined forces of our entire army. Perhaps our commander-in-chief did not plan to intercept the French on their march but he should at least have taken the opportunity of destroying an isolated corps. Instead, we were occupied in a prolonged and useless exchange of fire and wasted so much time that some French cavalry arrived on our right and some infantry filled the forest in front of our rearguard. Our cavalry was routed and was only able to rally behind our infantry. However, taking advantage of the confusion engendered by pursuit, courageous General Count Lambert counterattacked with the Alexandria Hussars and, with the support of our other units, the enemy was driven back to the edge of the woods. The French remained there for the rest of the day, occasionally appearing at the edge of the forest. On the left, the rearguard, reinforced by many other units, captured the forest several times but was finally forced to relinquish it to superior enemy forces. The Life Guard Jäger Regiment fought with remarkable fearlessness. We made many successful attacks along our front, however our actions were uncoordinated and nothing decisive was achieved.[186]

---

[185] Bennigsen was exhausted by constant campaigning and late on 13 June, he left the army to spend the night in a house in Friedland. According to Alexander Mikhailovskii-Danilevskii, some Russian officers and participants later asserted, 'Had Bennigsen found proper lodgings to rest on the right bank… the battle of Friedland would have never taken place.'

[186] By now it was becoming clear that the Russian army had failed to annihilate Lannes' corps. Bennigsen could still have safely retreated across the Alle before

Around 6:00 pm Napoleon arrived and the entire French army too. With a forest concealing their movements, masses of French gathered against our left; a battery of 40 guns was deployed[187] on the edge of the forest and a fierce cannonade began.[188] Because of the range, the artillery fire was direct and our rearguard's cavalry greatly suffered from it.[189] The rearguard was soon retreating as well. The army soon began withdrawing to the bridges. The only way to reach the main bridge was through the city itself. Chaos reigned in the narrow streets and this was further increased by the enemy artillery. Based on the direction of the enemy columns, it was obvious that they intended to cut us off at the crossing; to delay them, the Life Guard Izmailovsk and Pavlovsk Grenadier regiments made an attack, but that same ghastly battery halted their gallant assault and the regiments turned back.

Its distinguishing gallantry was no longer with the cavalry of the Guard. I managed to cross the river via the nearest pontoon bridge with the rearguard's artillery but it was already under enemy fire and part of it was damaged. The bridge in the city (the main bridge) was prematurely set on fire for unknown reasons and without any orders. Only one bridge remained and a number of troops and artillery had not yet crossed. The enemy pressed them against the bank and every minute was extremely precious.[190] The artillery,

---

the arrival of Napoleon's army but the initiative swung away from the Russians with the arrival of Napoleon.

[187] According to Mikhailovskii-Danilevskii, 'The Russian gunners were surprised by the sudden appearance of the French 36-gun battery' and failed to react in time.

[188] General Alexandre Antoine Senarmont, chief of artillery of Victor's corps, recalled, 'The Russian batteries, deployed on the opposite side of the Alle, fired on our flanks; some of them were at very close range, including one battery, on the hill near the river turn, which decimated our ranks.'

[189] During the battle, General Senarmont organized two companies of 15 guns, with six pieces in reserve, and placed them on both flanks of General Dupont's division. As the French advanced, Senarmont outpaced the infantry and opened fire at Bagration's troops from close range. His guns initially fired at 600 paces, then moved as close as 300 paces. The Russians tried to capture the French battery but the French virtually wiped out entire regiments; the third battalion of the Life Guard Izmailovsk Regiment alone lost some 400 men out of 520.

[190] Lord Hutchinson later declared, 'The Russians would have rendered their success undoubted if courage alone could ensure victory, but whatever may be the end, the officers and men of the Russian army have done their duty in the noblest manner and are justly entitled to the praise and admiration of every

which we would have had to abandon, was saved when a ford was discovered nearby.[191] Thus, our total loss in guns, either damaged, abandoned or sunk during the chaotic retreat, amounted to 13 pieces. Lieutenant General Dokhturov's 7th Divison was among the last to cross the river, but it was now commanded by Colonel Benardos, chef of the Vladimir Infantry, an intrepid Greek.[192]

By nightfall two battery companies failed to cross the river and the road to the ford was already in enemy hands. Major General Count Lambert escorted them with the Alexandria Hussars, marching two miles along the enemy bank towards Allenburg and, having crossed the Alle at dawn, rejoined the army.

Thus, instead of defeating and annihilating a weak enemy corps, which could not have been reinforced in time, we lost a general battle. I cannot but repeat that had our commander-in-chief not been ill at the start, our situation would have been dramatically different. Lieutenant General Prince Gorchakov actually commanded the army during the battle. But he failed to rise to the occasion and the troops had no confidence in him.

On the morning of 3 [15] June, the rearguard arrived at Allenburg, finding there what remained of the retreating main army; everything was in complete disarray. The enemy was occupied constructing bridges and failed to take advantage of our disorder. Enemy cavalry detachments were observed on both sides of the river, but they had no communication with each other.

We reached Wehlau without difficulty. I do not know if the rumours that the commander-in-chief planned to give another battle here were true, but it was clear that the construction of redoubts was started; however, the approach of the enemy did not permit their completion.

As the rearguard retreated, our outposts discovered General Kamenski's detachment marching from Könisgberg pursued by large enemy forces.[193] There was a junction ahead and Count

---

person.'

[191] Yermolov's note: This ford was discovered by Artillery Colonel Begunov, who had lived at Friedland whist refitting his company, he often hunted in the vicinity and knew the local residents who told him about the ford.

[192] Yermolov's note: We should be relieved by the fact that all the divisional generals were alive. They probably wanted to be first to test the crossings.

[193] Soult occupied Königsberg on 16 June, capturing 3,600 sick and wounded Russians and 4,000 Prussians.

Kamenski would lead the enemy there, potentially cutting our line of retreat. Prince Bagration kindly listened to my observations and allowed me to propose the dispatch of our entire cavalry to the left, bringing it against the pursuing enemy, halting this threat and allowing our infantry to pass the crossroads and wait for Kamenski. Bagration ordered the plan carried out immediately and we just beat Kamenski there whilst our cavalry arrived with his last troops. Kamenski marched to join the army and the rearguard was left alone.

At the village of Taplaken, we awaited the enemy and a brutal combat with the enemy's vanguard was crowned with success.[194]

Some 12 verstas from Tilsit, we came across some cavalry who had been ordered to delay the enemy by the commander-in-chief while the army got across the Niemen. This wide river flows by Tilsit and there was only one bridge across it. It was impossible to establish a *tête du pont* there and everyone recognized the difficulty of the mission assigned to Bagration and what danger the rearguard was exposed to. The rearguard was deployed for battle and ordered to hold its ground by any all means possible until night. Bagration retained only his cavalry and Cossacks and, to everyone's delight, returned the rest of the cavalry so that it did not hinder his crossing. We prepared for this last battle on the land of our ally! Our outposts were driven back with gunfire and the enemy closed in. But it is possible that the resolution with which we faced the French filled them with respect and they shared our opinion that it would be impossible to defeat us without bringing large numbers against us as they remained inactive the entire day. They awaited their army while we eagerly looked forward to nightfall.

The rearguard, and our cavalry, reached Tilsit at dawn. The Cossacks and artillery had been first to cross the Niemen, followed by the line infantry. Only the Jägers remained in the town and prepared the bridge for destruction. Around 9:00 am large enemy forces approached and began reconnoitering. We abandoned the town and the Jägers had hardly crossed the bridge when Murat

---

[194] On 16 June, Bagration fought a series of rearguard actions against Murat's cavalry between Taplaken Biten and Polpiten. He received two Bashkir and one Kalmyk regiments, who were 'armed with bows and arrows, wearing caps with long ear-flaps and dressed in weird-looking caftans, riding on short, bulky mounts that lacked elegance.' They appealed to Bagration to allow them to attack the French, who, according to Davidov, 'greeted them with laughter'.

rushed it with his cavalry and the bridge was set on fire virtually under his horse.

The enemy occupied the town and deployed its artillery along the bank that was considerably higher than ours. During the rest of the day, the French army gathered and began to spread out. We did not try to guess what might happen next but simply awaited the future without anxiety.

Our army was weak and in disarray.[195] It had been weakened by the many stragglers who had fallen behind during the retreat. Gathering in bands, they wandered along roads, pillaged food and thousands of them crossed the Niemen at Urburg, Olit, Merech and some as far away as Grodno. As proof of the disorder I can cite the following. The Izumsk Hussars were forgotten in Prussia, where they had been quartered to rest their horses; hearing about Friedland from local residents, they marched to join us but ran into our and French marauders who told them that we were in retreat. So they marched to the Niemen and successfully crossed over. Similarly, Colonel Sisoev was forgotten with his Don Cossack regiment, and they were even deeper into Prussia. He encountered enemy forces, fought them, passed their quarters, captured prisoners and finally rejoined us. Part of our artillery did not receive orders in time and had itself to select the direction of its retreat, crossing the Niemen at Urburg, where it found a previously unknown ford.[196]

The army bivouacked some distance from the river; the wooded surroundings shielding its vulnerability. The vanguard was ordered to remain on the bank. Bagration was ordered to send his adjutant with a proposal for a truce. He was introduced to Murat and then to Berthier and told that Napoleon seeks peace, not an armistice! The following day, Berthier arrived at our headquarters with the details and a message was sent to the czar at Shavli. Two day later, the czar reached the army and Prince Lobanov-Rostovskii[197]

---

[195] Davidov described 'crowds of people [at headquarters]: Englishmen, Swedes, Prussian, French Royalists, Russian military and civilian officials who knew nothing of either military or civil service, men of intrigue without employment.'

[196] Yermolov's note: Naturally, one wonders who was issuing the orders? It was Colonel Aderkass. And of course who would have dared dispute them with a German? Since ancient times, we have been unable to find a Russian for the position of general quartermaster.

[197] Dmitry Lobanov-Rostovskii (1758-1838) conducted the peace negotiations at

was sent to Napoleon. An armistice was concluded and soon peace negotiations began.[198]

Meanwhile, a meeting between the czar and Napoleon was arranged in the middle of the Niemen. The Prussian king was left on the riverbank! Several days later, the czar visited Tilsit, where, in the middle of the French army, his escort comprised of one battalion of the Life Guard Preobrazhensk Regiment and two squadrons of the Life Guard Hussar Regiment. Peace was soon concluded; Napoleon had all to gain by it, but he showed respect to the czar. He also agreed to meet the Prussian king. Napoleon paraded his troops and, at the French camp, the czar was met with respect and honour on a par with Napoleon himself. The emperor's suite included all his marshals and numerous generals. Finally, the Prussian queen was invited to lunch. This beautiful woman, with eyes full of tears though trying to seem happy, appeared before the same conqueror against whom she had once incited her armies. Meanwhile, the armies began returning home and the day for departure was set. Napoleon's entire Guard was in new uniforms (thanks to Prussia) and in incredible order. With a battalion of Preobrazhensk Regiment at the head of the column, the Imperial Guard passed by both emperors, who said their goodbyes and left Tilsit.

The troops of the rearguard returned to those divisions from which they belonged; all of us, serving under Bagration, quit this beloved commander with an expression of devotion to him. Besides complete confidence in his abilities and experience, we felt the difference in his treatment of us as compared to that of other generals. There was no one better at ensuring that his subordinates knew who was in command. The soldiers simply adored him. Having said goodbye to my comrades, I travelled back to Russia.

Thus, I served throughout this war as an artillery commander in the vanguard. Due to my good fortune, I did not lose a single gun, whilst many others, facing less trying situations, lost many. Only one of my guns was abandoned – that in the Pskov Musketeer Regiment, but even then, an artillery officer could not have been reprimanded.[199]

Tilsit in 1807.
[198] The armistice was signed on 21 June 1807.
[199] Yermolov's note: During the battle of Heilsberg, the enemy captured many

I enjoyed the benevolence of Grand Duke Constantine Pavlovich, who often praised my service. I also enjoyed the confidence and friendship of Bagration. He often gave me orders that surpassed my rank and nominated me twice to the rank of major general, making every effort on his part for me to receive it; however, he was unsuccessful because, at that moment, promotion was mostly done based on seniority, not merit. In the meantime, I earned the respect of my comrades and the confidence of my subordinates. In short, new prospects opened up to me and I hoped to have less trouble than before. During the campaign, I received the following awards: a golden sword inscribed 'For Courage' for Golymin, the Order of St Vladimir (3rd class), the Order of St George (3rd class) for Guttstadt and the Passarge and the diamond insignia of the Order of St Anna (2nd class) for Heilsberg.

---

our guns because I ordered my officers if forced to abandon guns, to open fire at close range to avenge themselves. I explained to them that it would be less harmful to lose a gun rather than to remove them prematurely and expose our troops. Officers were told about incidents, which had taken place earlier in the rearguard, when the batteries remained in their positions at all costs and were not captured by the enemy despite their efforts. I explained that if any officer, concerned not to lose guns, left his position, then our troops would inevitably be destroyed. I issued certificates to my staff officers when they recaptured guns seized by the enemy and they later received the appropriate awards based on these documents. My superiors were informed about my instructions, which absolved the officers from any responsibility for the lost artillery pieces; the czar himself was told about it and later kindly asked me about them.

CHAPTER IV
PEACETIME, 1808-1811

I left Tilsit for Russia and passed through Vilna where I met General Bennigsen. He received me with his habitual kindness, a kindness he had shown me since my adolescence. Discussing the war, he told me that the summer campaign in Prussia had not been conducted as he would have liked. He had been promised reinforcements of some 30,000 men and with these he had planned to open the campaign in early spring while Napoleon's troops were still occupied with the siege of Danzig. However, reinforcements were first delayed and then promised for the first of May but in the end not a single soldier reached the army by the time peace was concluded. These reinforcements should have comprised two divisions of recruits who received weapons just as they were leaving for the front and therefore had no idea how to use them. As they marched through the provinces of Minsk and Vilna, at least half of the recruits were left behind in hospital.

General Bennigsen told me that after Preussisch Eylau he suggested to the Emperor [Alexander] that he shoul send an experienced and cunning envoy to Napoleon, who could have offered an exchange of prisoners and also looked for a way of inducing Napoleon to discuss peace and conclude a favorable peace treaty.[200]

At the town of Shklov, I joined a division (whose designation I cannot recall) deployed there. In late August, the Inspector of All Artillery Count Arakcheyev arrived to review the artillery; he reorganized it and, never liking me, he ordered me to remain in camp until 1 October while all remaining artillery brigades were ordered to return to their quarters on 1 September. In addition, he bluntly remarked that I should have come to see him at Vitebsk in order to explain some deficiencies. I replied that his dislike of me should not prevent the impartial consideration of my reports. I was

---

[200] Yermolov's note: He offered Major General Khitrovo (Nikolai Feodorivhc) for this mission, who stayed in Paris and enjoyed Napoleon's favor.

insulted by his rudeness and did not conceal my intention to quit military service. Hearing about my decision, Count Arakcheyev called for me, offered me leave to see my relatives and ordered me to visit him in St. Petersburg so that he could become better acquainted with me.

I was assigned to the 9th Division of Lieutenant General Suvorov, Count of Rimnic, Prince of Italy,[201] the son of the great Suvorov; my quarters were based in the town of Lubari in Volhynia.

1808

I soon received an Imperial decree and money to award those lower ranks who had distinguished themselves during campaign. It was the first time that such an award had been given out! At the same time, Count Arakcheyev told me that, to prove his respect for my superb service, he would recommended me for an award.

I reached St. Petersburg, when Count Arakcheyev had been appointed Minister of War. He received me with distinct benevolence and told me about my new award. The Emperor had awarded my and Prince Yashvil's horse artillery companies with special embroidered insignia on our uniforms. Arakcheyev personally introduced me to the Emperor and I could see that he recommended me.

Having spent three days in St. Petersburg, I wrote a letter to Count Arakcheyev telling him that during my exile under late Emperor Paul I, many officers had been promoted above me and that I was virtually the last colonel of artillery. I explained to him that even if I would not receive seniority in rank, I would still consider it beneficial that he, as the Minister of War, should be aware that I had been treated unfairly and not because of any incompetence. Without waiting for his reply, I left St. Petersburg

---

[201] Suvorov, Arkadii Aleksandrovich (1784 – 1811) enjoyed a brilliant career at the court due to his father's successes. Paul I made him adjutant general and Alexander I had him promoted to lieutenant general. In 1807, Suvorov commanded the 9th Division in Ukraine. He participated in the 1809 Campaign against Austria and fought Turks in the Danubian Principalities in 1810-1811. However, he drowned on 25 April 1811 in the Rimnic River while trying to save his coachman.

the same day. Staying with my relatives in Orel, I later received a message that, during general promotions in artillery, I had been promoted to major general and appointed inspector of some horse artillery companies, with a salary increase of 2,000 rubles.

1809

In this new position, I departed to review the horse artillery of the Army of Moldavia then commanded by the aged Field Marshal Prince Prozorovskii, whose headquarters was at Jassy. Military operations against the Turks were temporarily halted. I watched our troops moving into the camp at Kateni, which later became notorious for horrible diseases that took countless lives. No argument succeeded in persuading Prozorovskii to refrain from moving his troops into this lethal camp. Our troops made marches for some fifteen verstas but rarely accomplished them in less than ten hours because they were deployed in huge squares with heavy transports in the middle and moved very slowly, frequently without any roads. Field Marshal Prozorovskii constantly declared that he was exercising troops in maneuvers. Suffering under unbearable heat, the troops were completely exhausted. The field marshal soon passed on to eternal life but not after dispatching ahead of him an army as large as the one he left behind. Lieutenant General Miloradovich commanded in Wallachia and there was rarely a day without celebrations that Miloradovich loved to organize or forced others to arrange to entertain him. So I led a joyous life, attended celebrations, visited parties, listened to his stories about victories, including the one at Obilesti. "Hearing about an enemy movement," – he told me – "I advanced at once; rumour had it that the Turks were 16,000 men strong; in my report, I wrote about defeating 12,000 men, but in reality there were only 4,000 men." His ingenuity indeed did him great credit!

Leaving the army, I travelled through Bender and Odessa to the Crimea. I visited ancient ruins, saw the beautiful coast and spent some time at Karasu-Bazaar, where one of the artillery companies from my inspection was deployed. Returning through Kharkov, I visited most of the southern regions of Russia.

A division, to which I was assigned, was soon attached to General Prince Golitsyn's army as it moved against Austria. I was left commanding a reserve detachment of some 14,000 men in the Volhynia and Podolsk provinces.[202]

The Minister of War ordered the deployment of our troops along the borders of these two provinces because many local Polish nobles fled with large number of their people and horses into the Duchy of Warsaw, where a Polish army was organizing. Under this order, I reported directly to the Minister of War Count Arakcheyev and he confirmed my decisions. To subdue any unrest, I was given authority to arrest anyone, despite their rank, crossing the borders and to send them to Kiev for further exile to Orenburg and Siberia. I decided to severely punish those crossing borders with weapons and my superiors were satisfied with my decisiveness. I applied severe measures but no one was exiled.

At the end of the war against the Austrians, our army returned from Galicia and part of it deployed in the Volhynia provinces, forcing my detachment to move to the Kiev, Poltava and Chernigov provinces. My headquarters was transferred from Dubno to Kiev. With my departure from Volhynia, I had to abandon a most pleasant life. I would briefly say that I was passionately in love with W., a beautiful young woman who shared my feelings. For the first time in my life, I entertained the idea of marriage but both of us had economic shortcomings that turned out to be a major obstacle; besides, I had already passed that age when one believes that affection can be a substitute for food. In addition, military service was my primary passion and I knew for certain that I could only live a satisfactory life in military service. So, I had to overcome love itself! With great difficulty, but I still managed.

1810

My division, soon after returning from Galicia, was moved into Moldavia, but I was again left commanding reserves. I wrote to Count Arakcheyev requesting a different assignment, but he was soon replaced as the Minister of War by General Barclay de Tolly, who barely knew me. My activities in Kiev were limited to

---

[202] Yermolov's note: It was the first time that reserve was created by detaching two battalions from infantry regiments, one or two squadrons from cavalry units and entire companies from artillery.

overseeing my troops as they constructed a new fortress on the Zverina hill. To escape dreadful boredom, I reviewed regularly my troops at their quarters and occupied myself with organization of the Evpatoria and Simferopol Horse Tatar Regiments. So it was that, artillery general was inexplicably ordered to raise two units of irregular cavalry.

I spent approximately two years in Kiev but such miserable and ignominious service thoroughly depressed me. On the one hand, a sympathetic opinion of my superiors flattered me and General Prince Bagration, being appointed commander-in-chief of the Army of Moldavia, requested my appointment to command artillery in his army, but his request was denied. His successor General Count Kamenski, passing through Kiev, also offered me to serve with him. I considered it as a great honor and anticipated that as a brigade commander I would have two regiments; I would have taken this command enthusiastically since my current detachment of some 14,000 soldiers had been turned into navvies (lopatniki). Having joined the army, Count Kamenski wrote to the Emperor nominating me his duty general. This nomination far exceeded my expectations and I anxiously awaited permission to join the army. The Commander-in-chief enjoyed Emperor's especial confidence and all his nominations were usually confirmed. However, his recommendation on my behalf was rejected and he was told that I was still needed in my current position.

Later a recommendation was made to appoint me to replace the late Major General Count [Yegor] Zuccato[203] who commanded a special detachment and cooperated with the Serbs against the pasha of Viddin. But this proposal was also rejected on the grounds that I was too young. This probably meant seniority in rank since other younger officers were never disapproved of because of their youth. Lady Luck could not have given me opportunities more

---

[203] Zuccato, Yegor Gavrilovich (? – 1810) descended from an ancient Venetian family. He served in Württemberg army before entering Russian service in 1788 and distinguished himself during the Russo-Turkish War of 1787-1791 and the Italian and Swiss Campaigns of 1799. Promoted to major general in October 1799, he served in the War College until late 1808 and was appointed to the Army of Moldavia in 1809. In the summer of 1810, he led the Russian troops in Serbia and captured several Turkish fortresses along the Danube River. However, he died of illness in August 1810.

flattering to my pride, especially considering that I served without any patronage. But these refusals also saddened me because I had no battle experience at my current rank and I wanted to test myself first in the war against the Turks, where mistakes could easily be corrected and were less damaging. I needed experience and a chance to prove my abilities; serving as an artillery officer, I could only become famous for my gallantry, but, as a major general, I was not satisfied with this. Yet, I had to remain in Kiev and endure my prolonged appointment.

1811

Receiving a short leave, I travelled to St. Petersburg. I was introduced to the Emperor in his office, an honour bestowed only on a division commander. There were rumours about increasing disgruntlement with Napoleon and problems with him could be solved with nothing but weapons in hand. So many considered this as a reason for the Emperor's benevolent reception of officers. Deep down, I feared that if a new war began I might again be left in reserve. The Inspector of All Artillery Baron Müller-Zakomelsky wanted to transfer me to a Guard artillery brigade but I declined because I was worried I would be occupied with parade service and returned to Kiev. I soon received a letter from the Minister of War that the Emperor was inquiring whether I might agree to command an artillery brigade in the Guard. I replied that I hoped to attract the Emperor's attention through my service in the field army, could not support myself in St. Petersburg and did not want to ask for anything without having seen appropriate service. An Imperial order transferring me to the guard was a response to my letter! However, I could not depart for my new appointment in time because I had fractured my hand in two places and was unwell for quite some time. After reporting this to the Emperor, a courier was sent to inquire about my health and the local military governor was ordered to report about me every two weeks. I was surprised by such attention and decided to take care of my hand, which now belonged to the Guard. I used to care less about myself!

Two months before the new year, I arrived to St. Petersburg and assumed command of a brigade. I did not interfere with the administrative section of my unit to show that I did not seek any profit. The Emperor received me with his usual kindness and this was sufficient for me not to feel a stranger in the capital. The Grand Duke [Constantine] was benevolent to me following our last campaign. My fractured hand prevented me from participating in all training and maneuvers that consumed most of time of anyone serving in St. Petersburg, so I had enough free time. The Life Guard Lithuanian Regiment was soon organized and assigned with the Izmailovsk Regiment to a brigade that the Emperor appointed me to command, in addition to the artillery brigade I already had. My salary was increased by 6,000 rubles a year.

1812

Thus, my life of a poor army officer was suddenly transformed and I could serve as an example for anyone who shared my difficulties. In my youth, I began service under strong patronage but later lost it completely. During the reign of Emperor Paul I, I was imprisoned and sent into exile for life. All junior officers quickly became my superiors and, under the current Emperor, I had to resume my service without any support, endured numerous troubles from my superiors and achieved everything in turn through my best efforts; I often had equal claims with others to rewards but had unequal success in getting them. To illustrate my point, I will describe an example. Artillery Major Generals Prince Yashvili and Ignatiev also commanded reserve troops, however my detachment were on state border and I was entrusted with protecting it, so with my greater authority came greater responsibility. Yet, both of these officers were decorated with the Order of St. Anna first class, while I was not shown any gratitude for my service.

I explained my disappointment to the Minister of War Barclay de Tolly, who coldly responded with his German burgomaster's self-importance, "It is true that I failed to notice your service." I tried to see a noble man in him and sense some politeness in his rejection. Equally upsetting was the rejection of the Inspector of All Artillery's request to transfer me as an artillery commander to the Army of Moldavia commanded by General Kutuzov, who was well disposed towards me. Following this, I wrote to the Minister of War that I required treatment at a spa in the Caucasus and asked for a brigade command on the Caucasian front. He bluntly told me that I simply wanted to exploit the Emperor's benevolence to get a reward for myself and that I requested dismissal knowing full well that it would not be granted. Thus, to everyone's surprise, I incensed this icy German, who made himself colourfully clear I soon learned how difficult it was to change my appointment. With my consent, the Inspector of All Artillery requested my appointment to review and maintain the fortress of Riga and a bridgehead at Dunaburg.[204] However, the Emperor rejected it and informed me that, from now on, my appointments would depend only on him and that I did not need anyone's assistance to get them. When he later met me, he asked whether I was told about his order and added, "Why are you driven out of St. Petersburg? However, I already interfered and you will have enough business to attend." I did not dare to admit that it was me who wanted transfer to another branch of service and I was pleased that the Minister of War did not report about my earlier letter.

Meanwhile, it was already March and the Guard marched to Lithuania. His Majesty Grand Duke Constantine led a column of the Guard cavalry and I commanded a separate column of Guard infantry.

Quo fata trahunt retrahunque, sequamur

[We move where fate directs us].

Virgil

---

[204] Yermolov's note: Inspetor of All Artillery wanted to give me an opportunity to earn a reward that was earlier given to Major Generals Prince Yashvil and Ignatiev.

CHAPTER V
THE PATRIOTIC WAR
JUNE–AUGUST 1812

And so 1812 arrived, a year so memorable for every Russian, so ominous for our suffering and so illustrious for the brilliant glory of generations to come!

In early March, the Guard left St Petersburg and several days later I received orders to take command of the Guard infantry division.[205] This was an appointment that many people of higher status or rank would have envied[206] and, for a long time, I could not believe this miraculous turn of events. However, is there anything that happiness cannot accustom us to? So I gradually began to believe that I was worthy of this promotion, although I tolerated those that did not agree. The sudden rise of an obscure person always nurtures envy in others but our self-confidence overrides this and such was the case with me.

I accepted command of the division on whilst on manoeuvre at Vilna. Everyone found the Guard superbly organized and part of this praise, which in all fairness belonged to the troops, reflected on me although I had no right to it. After a brief stay in Vilna, the Guard returned to its quarters at Sventsyani.

Meanwhile, the French had concentrated large forces near our frontiers. Yet, rumour denied the possibility of war and no preparations were taken against an attack and nothing was done to prevent invasion. The czar's circle believed in the return of Count

---

[205] Yermolov's note: The division consisted of the following units: 1st Brigade (Major General Rosen): Preobrazhensk Regiment, Semeyonovsk Regiment. 2nd Brigade (Flügel adjutant Udom): Izmailovsk Regiment, Lithuanian Regiment. 3rd brigade (Colonel Bistrom): Jäger Regiment, Finland Regiment. The Marine ekipazh was also attached to this brigade.

[206] General Vorontsov wrote to Zakrevskii, 'Please tell me you are not ashamed for not giving us [the 2nd Western Army] even one good artillery general. This is not a joke, you have three such officers: Kutaisov, Iashvili and Yermolov, but no, you decided to turn Yermolov (who is the best artillery officer in Russia) into a Guard infantry commander. Meanwhile, we have all the ogres in that branch: Arakcheyev, Sivers and now, we hear, even Lowernstern, one worse than the other.'

Narbonne, Napoleon's adjutant, who had arrived here with instructions and very skillfully hinted at the possibility of further negotiations. Some people were convinced of this.

On the same day as a fete organized by the prominent noblemen and members of the imperial suite at an estate at Zakretye near Vilna, amid pomp and splendid festivity, a courier arrived from Kovno and was immediately taken to the czar. The state of the messenger and the reason for such haste was quickly deduced; soon news spread that the French had crossed the Niemen near Kovno and had occupied this town and that the Cossack outpost had retreated after a brief exchange of fire. Mutual fears concealed for so long now disappeared and, facing an enormous enemy onslaught invading our land, we had to surrender Vilna and then the whole of Lithuania without a fight!

Adjutant General Balashov was to deliver a letter from the czar to Napoleon at Vilna. The czar joined the Guard, which was ordered to camp near Sventsyani. The minister of war, Barclay de Tolly, was appointed commander of the 1st Western Army, the largest of our armies, with his headquarters at Vilna. The army corps were commanded by the following:

>   1st Infantry Corps (Lieutenant General Count Wittgenstein), at Keidany.
>   2nd Corps (Lieutenant General Baggovut) at Wilkomir.
>   3rd Corps (Lieutenant General N. A. Tuchkov (I)) at Troky.
>   4th Corps (Adjutant General Count Shuvalov) at Lida.
>   5th Corps (Grand Duke Constantine Pavlovich) at Vydza.
>   6th Corps (General of Infantry Dokhturov) at Slonim.
>
>   Cavalry Corps:
>   1st (Adjutant General Uvarov).
>   2nd (Adjutant General Baron Korf).
>   3rd (Major General Count (Peter Petrovich) von der Pahlen).

The Don Cossack forces were under the command of Ataman General of
>   Cavalry Platov at Grodno and around Belostock.

Prince Bagration commanded the 2nd Western Army with his headquarters at Pruzhany. General of Cavalry Tormasov led the 3rd Western Army,[207] with his headquarters at Dubna. The Army of

Moldavia under Admiral Chichagov was largely deployed in Wallachia, where it remained until the conclusion of a peace treaty with the Ottomans. The first two armies were deployed along our European frontiers and were to oppose the invading armies led by Napoleon; however, the ratio of forces was so uneven and our forces so widely spread that the only thing left for us was to beat a prompt retreat.

Napoleon's massive war preparations, some hastily made, were well known to us. His influence over the Confederation of the Rhine was enormous and after his brilliant successes in the last campaign against Austria, Napoleon could not expect that Emperor Francis I would dare to rise against him, and even Prussia, which had aspired to join us for so long, now had to side with Napoleon. The Russo-Prussian war against Napoleon in 1806–1807, which ended with the Peace of Tilsit, threatened to annihilate Prussia. Czar Alexander's active mediation saved her from destruction, however several major fortresses were taken and garrisoned by the French and the size of Prussian forces limited. Russia took every measure to prevent war in 1812 but was finally forced to take appropriate measures against it. Opinions on the nature of the coming war varied. Without daring to undertake an analysis of their merits, I shall only repeat what I happened to hear.

The minister of war preferred an offensive war. Some people[208] thought it useful to occupy the Duchy of Warsaw and, having entered Prussia, give the Prussian king a plausible reason to join us, every means to strengthen his army and to operate in accordance with circumstances. If superior enemy forces forced us onto the defensive, Prussia would be convenient because of its abundant supplies and because war would have been waged outside our borders, whereas the newly acquired Polish territories could not have been trusted.

We would have gained more had we occupied the Duchy of Warsaw the previous year and established a military alliance with the Prussian king. The Polish army, which was now organizing with

---

[207] It was officially designated as the 3rd Reserve Army of Observation. The designation '3rd Western Army' was adopted only on 30 September 1812 when it merged with the Army of the Danube.

[208] Senior officers, including Bagration, Wolzogen and Toll, suggested preemptive strikes against Napoleon's forces and the invasion of Poland and Prussia, where they hoped to incite nationalist uprisings against the French.

incredible energy, could not have numbered more than 50,000 men and would not have dared to oppose us under threat of being annihilated. The French troops in Germany under Davout were not yet strong enough and, to ensure Prussian cooperation, they were scattered and could not have concentrated in time. French garrisons were small in number and some fortresses were not garrisoned at all. A brutal war in Spain, so destructive to the French forces, required the continuous supply of large reinforcements and only allowed the French to turn to the creation of the enormous armies of France and the Confederation of the Rhine in 1811, a year before a war against us was declared. The states of the Confederation were forced to make excessive efforts and meet heavy expenses which could not have encouraged their voluntary participation in the war. Seeing the Duchy of Warsaw in our hands and Prussia rising, Austria would not have remained idle and a united Europe could have subdued the common enemy and returned peace to a Europe tired of war, liberating kings from captivity and using the fear that Napoleon instilled in everyone as a tool of revenge and terror against him. Thus, Napoleon would have tripped over the land where earlier his every step had led to victories. If Austria would not dare join us but continued stubbornly to maintain her neutrality, Napoleon then would have faced a united Russian and Prussian army and been forced to secure fortresses and territories to the rear of his troops. Therefore he might well have considered invading our territories perilous and his war arrangements unsatisfactory.

So, in 1812, it seemed everything was ready for us to wage an offensive war: armies were deployed on the borders, enormous magazines were established in the Belostock district and in the Grodno and Vilna provinces. However, at the same time negotiations were in progress to avoid war and some even expected another visit by Count Narbonne. Yet, accurate intelligence soon confirmed colossal forces being concentrated near our borders and the decision was made for our armies to retreat.

A former Prussian officer called General Pfuel, now a lieutenant general in our service, who gained that confidence that we so easily invest in foreigners, considering them always superior to us in expertise, offered, among other things, to establish a fortified camp near Drissa on the Dvina. Mr Pfuel's military talents were revealed by the location where this camp was established. He also resisted moving the 1st Army closer to the 2nd, arguing that the latter could threaten the enemy flank when the enemy attacked our 1st Army.

I not only refuse to believe but am ready to argue against any unsubstantiated claims that the minister of war supported the construction of the Drissa Camp and did not reject this proposed operation of the armies, separated by vast expanse, especially when the army designated for the flank attack had less than 50,000 men. Had Napoleon personally directed our plans, he could not have imagined anything more advantageous.

General of Cavalry Baron Bennigsen, who had commanded our armies in the last war with the French in Prussia, tried in vain to have the armies moved closer to each other so that we could either stay on the direct road to Smolensk or find another position where the enemy could not threaten us. However, despite his persistence, he succeeded only in moving the 2nd Army from the vicinity of Lutsk in the Volhynia to Prouzhany.

Our forces, deployed so close to the frontiers, now covered a vast expanse of territory and might have seemed ready to prevent his crossing of the Niemen.

It was difficult to suppose that such a deployment was made simply to facilitate our retreat when any separation actually complicated withdrawal and threatened troops with isolation and piecemeal destruction.

Having crossed the Niemen at Kovno, Napoleon perceived the intentions of our corps and decided to prevent them from uniting; he might have succeeded in this had he completed the crossing in time and not awaited more troops. Having many supporters among the Poles, he was undoubtedly well informed about the deployment of our troops[209] and might have already known about our intention to abandon Lithuania. Our 6th Corps, deployed in advance to maintain communications between the two armies, was able to rejoin the army not because of anything we did but simply because of the sluggishness of the enemy crossing. A hussar detachment from Grodno caught up with the 6th Corps en route because

---

[209] Yermolov's note: Among the documents later captured from the enemy, we found details of our troops in Lithuania, a list of our generals and a correct estimate of our forces that were supplied with bread collected instead of tax arrears. It could be seen that it was our intention not to leave supplies for the enemy in this region.

General Major Count Pahlen commanded it and forced it to cover almost 200 verstas [132 miles] in three days.

The Don Cossack troops under Ataman General Platov were deployed near Grodno and were instructed to cooperate with the 1st Army; yet, Platov could not join the army and, threatened by Davout's movement, he had to turn for support to Bagration's army. Among Ataman Platov's troops, there was Major General Dorokhov's detachment of one hussar and two Jäger regiments.

Thus, the 1st Army, although feebly pursued, defended itself and fell back towards Drissa which rumours claimed to be a first-rate fortification.[210] The rearguard had an intense engagement at Davgelishki. Thereafter, the enemy operated in small numbers, tending to observe our movements rather than pursue us. Due to Platov's absence, only three Don Cossack regiments were with the army and so the Guard Light Cavalry Division was employed in the rearguard.

The 1st Army finally entered the camp. The vanguard halted nearby. The 1st Corps crossed to the right bank of the Dvina and took up positions at Druya, while its vanguard was placed towards Opsa. The 6th Corps also crossed the river and halted near Drissa, with its vanguard deployed near Disna. Our movement was so rapid that it left the enemy far behind and we had to dispatch patrols to locate enemy forces. We soon learned that Napoleon was at Belmonte with a few troops while his main forces advanced towards the Disna on the left side of our camp.

Having observed the camp, the commander-in-chief found it had been built for larger forces than those now deployed there. General Bennigsen meticulously studied it and noted that many fortifications had unsatisfactory communications between each other which weakened their common defence whilst the enemy had favourable approaches to some of them. There were some places where the enemy could conceal its movements and concentrate forces. The fort's profiles were, in general, inadequate. Three bridgeheads were too narrow and their profiles so poorly designed

---

[210] Yermolov's note: This camp, which required extensive works, revealed the prudence of its designer. This type of fortification could not have originated in a sane mind. But Mr Pfuel could enjoy the consolation of the approval of a few of our generals and disregard the opinion of the French who described this camp as an example of ignorance in the art of fortification. I never heard anyone dispute this.

that every movement could be observed from the nearest hill. Even these flaws could not describe all of the errors of this camp, deficiencies that were obvious to anyone proficient in military matters. Russia had constructed other forts before the war. A bridgehead in Riga had been expanded and several fortifications added to it; the fortress was prepared for defence. The Dunaburg Fortress on the Dvina was begun a year ago, yet only a small bridgehead, gunpowder magazine and watchtower had been completed. The lines of the fortress itself were barely visible. As usual, our reports showed all costs and expenses in order; a foreigner, who planned and directed the works, was found to be a man of remarkable talent and, despite no other service, was promoted. During the war, this fortification withstood some enemy light troops for two or three days before the guns and ammunition were thrown in the river and the bridge destroyed.

Another fortification was built in front of Borisov on the right bank of the Berezina and it was designed to prevent the enemy from taking a bridge, though later our troops still had to seize it back from the enemy. The Bobruisk Fortress on the Berezina was built within a short period of time but in such a way that the enemy had no resources to besiege but could only blockade it.

A small fortress was built on the Zverinetsk hill near the Kiev Fortress and I took part in the construction together with a detachment of reserve troops; so I know all the hideous deficiencies it had. Some 400 sazhens away from the old citadel, this new fortification was of little support to, and had limited communications with, the old fortress. There was no benefit in the fact that the fortress could contain the enemy because having captured it, the enemy could inflict no damage on the old fortress.[211] It seems, the strength of these fortresses lay not in them as such, but rather in the hope that a siege would be conducted poorly. We owed the safety of Riga and Bobruisk to this factor and could therefore consider them impregnable.

While the 1st Army remained in the fortified camp, the enemy concentrated on our left towards the Disna. Davout hurried with a strong corps towards Minsk, but only his advance outposts

---

[211] Yermolov's note: It was Engineer Lieutenant General Opperman's idea to build this fort, and he was also responsible for the project and its execution. I cannot believe modern engineers have nothing else worthy of imitation.

approached the town itself. Bagration could have reached Minsk before Davout and if he had encountered troops there they would only have been Davout's advance outposts. An attack was necessary and Bagration should have launched one, despite casualties, in order to secure the road to Smolensk. However, Bagration's customary vigour eluded him for once. In addition, his movement was slowed by the terrible roads from Nesvizh and the flooded Niemen at Nikolaev. Receiving exaggerated reports on enemy strength, he turned to Nesvizh and marched to Bobruisk via Slutsk. He was pursued by the enemy forces under the King of Westphalia and Prince Poniatowski with the Polish cavalry. Thereafter, any hope of uniting our armies seemed in vain. The czar told me about the reports he received and did not conceal how disappointing it was for him to receive this news, but I was reassured seeing him remain resolute.[212]

It was finally decided that the 1st Army would abandon the fortified camp. On 1 [13] July, I was appointed chief of staff of the army. I tried my best to avoid this appointment, writing to the czar himself that I was unprepared for so demanding a position, had no experience and that circumstances surrounding our army required a more experienced and celebrated officer for this task. Of course, it would not have been difficult to find a more capable officer among the numerous generals in our army but either they were needed in their current positions or they simply refused to accept this position seeing how difficult the situation was.

I appealed to Count Arakcheyev to help me. Having confirmed how difficult this position was, he did not encourage me to accept it, but rather agreed with my decision to decline it, observing that this position was rendered harder because of the minister of war. It was known that Barclay de Tolly had proposed one of the senior lieutenant generals, Tuchkov (I) for this position due to his experience and long career.[213] The czar told me that Count

---

[212] Yermolov is overly critical of Bagration. On 29 June, he began to retreat on his own initiative after the main headquarters neglected his appeals for instructions. In his letters, Bagration emphasized the difficulties his army would face during the retreat. It had to march 250 miles to Minsk, while the French, who already occupied Vilna, were only in 160 miles from Minsk and could easily reach the city before the 2nd Western Army.

[213] Yermolov's note: He earned respect from many qualities but during his long service he never demonstrated any unusual military skills.

Arakcheyev informed him of my appeal and asked me, 'In your opinion, who among the other generals is more qualified?' I responded, 'The very first general you meet would be more capable than me.' As the conversation ended, it was the czar's firm desire that I accept this position. I told him, 'If I might be tolerated in this position, then it would only be due to the magnanimity and benevolence of Your Majesty.' Then I made my final plea: not to deprive me of the hope that I might resume command of the Guard division, where I was officially listed as on leave. I was promised this.[214]

Thus, I served under the commander-in-chief, who was also the minister of war, in the rank of chief of staff of the army and was able to learn much, not only connected to the army. Therefore everything I describe is based either directly on original sources or from other accurate information above suspicion. My predecessor Lieutenant General Marquis Paulucci remained in his post for six days before he was deprieved of it due to the displeasure of the commander-in-chief. My first assistant was Flügel Adjutant Colonel Kikin, who also acted as duty general. He had served during the introduction of the new system and the recent Establishment for the Administration of the Large Active Army. Unwilling to serve under my predecessor, he had feigned illness and Colonel Stavrakov, Commandant of the Main Headquarters, replaced him. The phrase 'this name full of destiny' fits Stavrakov exactly as fate pursued all those who had been commanders-in-chief with him. Only Suvorov had selected him whilst the rest could not get rid of him. Stavrakov served under Suvorov in Italy, under Buxhöwden and Bennigsen in Prussia, then transferred to Finland serving under each commander-in-chief there until finally General Barclay de Tolly could not escape him either! So why, after all of this, did they still keep him in his post of duty general? I made a plea to replace him, but the commander-in-chief found him very capable. Despite my attempts to bring Colonel Kikin round, he refused to free me from Stavrakov!

The Quartermaster General was Colonel Toll, an officer of excellent skill who would contribute greatly in the future; however,

---

[214] Nikolay Rayevskii noted in a letter, 'Alexey Petrovich Yermolov is appointed chef d'etat major of the main army and everyone is happy about it…' Rayevskii to Samoilov, 17 July 1812, Arkhiv Rayevskiikh (St Petersburg, 1908), I, pp. 153-154.

his excessive egotism needed to be contained and his superiors must never be weak personalities or he would wield too much power. With talent, quick judgment, hard working and enterprising, he was also opinionated, sometimes refusing to accept sound advice or common sense and declining to believe that others might have equal or even superior skill.

On 2 [14] July, the army crossed the Dvina and took up positions at Drissa. It was clearly disadvantageous for us to have a river like the Dvina in our rear since the army still found itself in some confusion. Half of the bridges were kept intact for the rearguard of Adjutant General Baron Korf.

The 1st Corps was deployed to the right of the former camp, with a detachment near Druya and outposts near Dunaburg. The 6th Corps approached the Disna to reinforce Count Pahlen's vanguard on the left bank of the Dvina, where our outposts detected enemy movement.

The czar instructed Flügel Adjutant Count Potozky to destroy the crossings over the Disna if necessary. Burning with desire to carry out this order, Potozky also set fire to a large supply magazine, though the French were no closer than 70 verstas, and he then returned so hastily that he did not notice that local inhabitants had plundered supplies. Probably Potozky later presented this incident in a better light, although I do not know if he left a description of it in his memoirs. Thus, there was no bridge over the Disna but Count Pahlen's vanguard, reinforced with an infantry division of the 4th Corps, was still on the far side of the river and had to remain there to cover the army's march to Polotsk.

On 4 [16] July, the army advanced and reached Polotsk three days later. Major General Baron Korf's vanguard remained at its earlier location and, having observed no enemy forces, it crossed to the right bank of the Dvina.

Count Wittgenstein's 4th Corps of 24,000 men was deployed near Druya with orders to retreat to Pskov and cover St Petersburg if facing superior enemy forces. If the enemy had not thought about marching there, concern in the capital was sufficient cause to spread fear. Such antics can be justly described as courtly. The enemy appeared with a few light troops, occupied Druya with one of their detachments and approached Dunaburg with substantial forces. Count Wittgenstein informed the commander-in-chief that he intended to reinforce a detachment deployed against Druya and to defend Dunaburg. Major General d'Auvray, chief of staff of the 1st Corps, informed me that 10 infantry battalions with artillery and cavalry, which was already deficient, were allocated to reinforce that detachment. The commander-in-chief allowed me to express my opinion and supported my objection to such a division of forces. It was strange that, despite being aware of enemy movements on the left, some still proposed defending Dunaburg, although it was not prepared for defence and it was impossible to manoeuvre an army before it.

Meanwhile, General Yorck's Prussian corps had entered Courland, occupied Mittau and his light troops had appeared near the suburbs of Riga. His forces were combined with troops from other nations for a total of some 40,000 men under Marshal Macdonald.

The 3rd Western Army under General Tormasov was near Brest Litovsk facing a Saxon corps under the French General Reynier, who had invaded our territory with the support of Austrian troops under General Prince Schwarzenberg.

Lieutenant General Ertel's detachment of some 14,000 men was idle at Mozyr, with a small unit located at Pinsk. Having served in the police and earned the rank of lieutenant general in this branch, Ertel was now perfecting his policing skills by oppressing the inhabitants around Mozyr.

The Army of Moldavia under Admiral Chichagov began to leave the territory of Wallachia following the peace treaty with the Ottoman Porte, but it faced a lengthy march which prevented it from supporting the other armies. Its advance units had hardly reached the Dniestr yet.

The czar left Polotsk for Moscow, accompanied by Count Arakcheyev, Minister of Police General Balashov and State Secretary Shishkov as well as Adjutant General Prince Trubetskoy and Flügel Adjutant Chernishev. The other officials in the czar's retinue remained with the army. General Pfuel also stayed with the army, with a bitter feeling in his heart that the czar no longer needed him and despair in his soul that the camp at Drissa had been found wanting. Neither his slavishly adoring Prussian Flügel Adjutant Colonel Wolzogen nor Adjutant General Count Ozharovskii, whom Pfuel had tutored in the art of war, spoke now of his glory. His wise proposals on continuing the retreat as far as the Volga were finally silenced; no one now listened to his benevolent concern for Russia. Oh, fate would judge your ingratitude, Russians, you who would not see the banks of the Volga![215]

The czar's departure had an unpleasant effect on the troops. Appearing every day with a serene and calm look, no one thought about danger and everyone was encouraged by his presence. But others, deep in Russia, also needed such encouragement. It was necessary to uplift despondent souls and prepare them to endure the coming woes. Moscow, where 200 years of tranquility and prosperity, and an entire century of grandeur and glory concealed the deep wounds of the past, now needed to be consoled. Oh Moscow! Is there any other place where devotion is more clearly expressed to the czar? Departure was necessary! The disheartened army was promised a speedy return and everything soon returned to order or, at least, disarray did not increase.

Marching from Polotsk, we learned that the enemy had appeared in numbers on the Disna and had proceeded upstream along the left bank of the Dvina. Count Pahlen's rearguard crossed to the right bank and defended the crossing until the evening. The 6th Corps, supported by a division of the 4th Corps, bivouacked for the night between the rearguard and the army.

The army continued towards Vitebsk. The 6th Corps was one march behind. Count Pahlen, having dispatched quantities of supplies to the army, now left the banks of the Dvina. The enemy crossed the river at Disna and began the pursuit the following day. Count Pahlen was reinforced by Baron Korf's cavalry corps and a few Jägers. Numerous enemy troops were seen along the left bank near Polotsk, but the rearguard arrived in time.

At Polotsk, I threatened to put Commissioner (7th Class) Yuzvitsky into shackles for planning to take an army treasure chest to the enemy-occupied riverbank to pay for supplies he had allegedly bought from local Jews but that no one even thought of transporting to our lines although the army was already suffering from lack of provisions. General Intendant Kankrin had taken prudent measures and had gathered large amounts of bread, but he

---

[215] Yermolov's note: Retreat was not planned but rather, after learning about the remarkable strength of Napoleon's troops, it was decided that retreat was necessary for the time being.

later had to abandon most of it because the army retreated and it was impossible to transport these provisions.[216]

An intelligent man, Kankrin lacked the gift of enterprise that people in the supply branch find essential in order to conceal state expenditure. I would not attempt to presume whether he might turn a blind eye to such activity or whether he could be used as an example to others.

At Polotsk, the quarrel between Grand Duke Constantine Pavlovich and the commander-in-chief got deeper. The latter arrested Colonel Arsenyev, commander of the Guard cavalry, who had marched too slowly. This was enough to revive and worsen the long-standing spat between the two. The Grand Duke was exasperated and the reserved Barclay de Tolly did not try to cool his anger.

After the czar's departure, I chanced to have lunch with his remaining entourage at Polotsk and I immediately noticed the change in tone and attitude! The czar had taken his greatness with him and left everyone alone. Those condemned to be courtiers should earn respect through their own abilities or, if basking in someone's brilliance, at least learn to reflect it! Can it be true that throughout history courtiers have been so similar? General Pfuel lunched with us. His Gothic egotism and disdain to everyone was now transformed into the politeness of a courtier. He bowed without even waiting for others to bow. Slavish respect towards him now disappeared and the first signs of insanity became visible. Sir James Wylie [the czar's personal physician] confessed that his trusted remedies had failed to repair his mind.

The army reached the crossing site at Budilov. During the crossing, a small detachment was left at Beshenkovichy to cover 6th Corps and Count Pahlen's rearguard remained too to protect the bread that was being brought over from the other bank. The enemy was still far off because of the difficult and steep road on the left bank; besides, the river had a wide turn on the enemy side, which shortened the distance we had to cover and the flat terrain facilitated our movement.

---

[216] Yermolov's note: For four days, some 3,000 rank-and-file, accompanied by a colonel and officers, were allocated to bake bread. Strict discipline was maintained.

Meanwhile, Davout's corps passed Borisov and occupied Moghilev, seizing Orsha with a small detachment. Prince Bagration's army proceeded from Nesvizh to Bobruisk and had a few rearguard actions. On 27 and 28 July [9–10 July] at Mir and later at Romanovo, Ataman General Platov had a chance to show the Polish cavalry that we still had the upper hand over the Poles and the Cossacks had the pleasure of reviving that sensation in their hearts.

Since the partition of Poland in 1794 its name had disappeared from the face of the earth and Poles existed no more. In 1807 Tilsit gave birth to the Duchy of Warsaw and the hope of expanding it should the neighbouring powers [France and Russia] fail to agree. Napoleon took advantage of the fear that he instilled in the hearts of many of his royal contemporaries: each of them had suffered enormous losses, his continuous triumphs fed on that same fear and led to the hope of restoring Poland. Many seized this idea and measures were taken to give it a veneer of reality! In 1809 Warsaw was our ally against Austria but we had to relinquish part of Galicia for their benefit and contrary to our interests. In the current war, Poland was now against us in a common alliance with Europe and in cooperation with Austria. We had increased her forces and had armed her against ourselves. For her benefit, we were now stabbing each other's hearts with swords and, in our blindness, providence was complaining that the wounds were not deep enough!

Passing through Bobruisk, Bagration left his wounded, and those exhausted by the rapid marching, in the fortress; he reinforced the army with six infantry battalions from the local garrison and appointed Major General Ignatiev, commander of the regional artillery, as military governor of the fortress. Enemy troops soon appeared in the vicinity but General Ignatiev, keeping the local population in order without overdoing it, managed to supply the fortress and due to his efficient management, the army received substantial resources. The fortress was not besieged since the enemy did not have the means to do this and could only blockade it. So should General Ignatiev have been more forceful when protected by stonewalls than he had been at Austerlitz where he did not consider it necessary? Well, fate postponed the test until another time.

Prince Bagration's army now proceeded from Bobruisk to Bikhov. The King of Westphalia pursued with his corps and the

Polish troops but, either exhausted by prolonged marching or unable to keep the pace and falling behind, they lost the Russian army which continued its movement undisturbed.

At Dashkovka, Lieutenant General Rayevskii's corps encountered part of Davout's troops from Moghilev. The enemy forces were weak at first but were reinforced later; Rayevskii's troops, however, were insufficient but he retained fearlessness and firmness and, leading his column, attacked the enemy. The fiercest action took place on the left, where the enemy failed to halt the 26th Infantry Division, which Major General Paskevich led fearlessly and with incredible vigour through thick forest to threaten the enemy flank. But he had to concede to superior forces. General Rayevskii's actions concealed the movement of the [2nd Western] Army and gave Bagration the opportunity, which he failed to utilize, of making a forced march to gain some distance and avoid further pursuit. Instead, the army bivouacked in the same position as General Rayevskii had occupied after the battle. Davout considered Rayevskii's corps as Bagration's vanguard and withdrew to Moghilev, where he began preparing for an attack. Ataman Platov, who appeared near the very trenches of Moghilev, kept him busy for quite some time. Prince Bagration had dispatched him to join the 1st Army and ordered him to take this direction. Thus, the junction of our armies was a result of Davout's grave mistake; otherwise, this could not have been possible before Moscow and hope, which endures in desperate times, had already been disappearing![217]

---

[217] Once again, Yermolov fails to give Bagration and his troops due credit. The 2nd Western Army had been marching constantly since 29 June and had suffered considerable losses. He had decided to attack Davout with only the 7th Infantry Corps of Rayevskii to fight a delaying action to keep the French on the right bank of the Dnieper while he crossed the river with the army to the south of Moghilev. However, the battle proved bloodier than expected. The Russians suffered 2,548 killed and wounded and claimed the French losses were 4,134 dead and wounded, although Davout himself admitted to only 900 casualties. Davout remained in position waiting for a renewal of the offensive. By this time, Bagration completed the construction of a bridge at Novy Bikhov and moved his army across the Dnieper. Marching to Smolensk, Bagration wrote, 'To the great shame of the King of Westphalia, Marshal Davoust [sic] and Poniatowski, and despite their tricks and attempts to bar my way, I arrived at Smolensk marching right under their noses and beating them in the process.'

Had any of our generals committed such a mistake, public opinion would have castigated him. Davout, who served for over 10 years under the great commander, participated in illustrious battles, adorned his sovereign's crown with numerous laurels of victory and earned many titles for himself, had committed a mistake that many of us would have avoided. Bagration had no other choice but to fight his way to the 1st Army. Davout's aim was to prevent this and he should have fought resolutely, knowing that superior forces were pursuing Bagration. Of course, Davout expected nothing from the King of Westphalia, but he could not have guessed that the latter would not even march and would lose sight of the enemy.[218]

So, students of military art take note and generals be surprised that experience alone is no substitute for skill, cannot be subordinated to the rules of war and is always subject to chance. Of course, similarity in circumstances provide some advantages in dealing with such challenges or, it might be said, in repeating the same methods should similar incidents recur; however, insignificant variations do significantly alter circumstances! Generals are all too aware of this! In his marshals, Napoleon found the best executives of his will. In his presence, they commit no mistakes or Napoleon immediately corrects them. So, his own orders exposed Davout.[219]

At Budilov, I proposed crossing to the left bank of the Dvina; I based my plan on the calculation that the enemy was advancing over difficult and unfavourable terrain along the river and only his cavalry was observed at Polotsk. His main forces and artillery were far behind and at least three marches away from us. Having crossed the river, we should have marched to Orsha, forced Davout to scatter while his attention was concentrated on the 2nd Army and assisted Bagration in joining the 1st Army. In addition, we could have destroyed the enemy at Orsha, crossed to the left bank of the Dnieper and protected Smolensk. Meanwhile, the supply trains and heavy transports could have been sent to Smolensk via Vitebsk to avoid slowing us down. All this could have been accomplished without danger because the enemy was distant. Convinced that I

---

[218] In his letter to Yermolov on 7 July, Bagration criticized French actions and concluded, 'Hardly escaped from hell. Those fools (duraki) let me escape.'

[219] Yermolov is overly critical of Davout. His effective forces amounted to only 22,000 infantry and some 6,000 cavalry. In the circumstances, he had achieved his goal of preventing Bagration's breakthrough at Moghilev, but he had no means to prevent the Russian escape across the river.

did not have the commander-in-chief's full confidence, I nevertheless sent two cavalry corps forward and two pontoon companies began to construct a bridge at Budilov.

The arrangements for the crossing were underway and success was imminent for us. However, less than an hour after my orders, the commander- in-chief changed his mind. I guessed who might have influenced him and my suspicion fell on Wolzogen. This sombre German pedant enjoyed Barclay's full confidence. I realized that we were losing valuable time and that this often cost us dear. Although I had no right to the commander-in-chief's trust because of my age, so incompatible with my experience, I still persuaded some corps commanders to share their observations with him, but he remained determined and the army continued to Vitebsk. A strong detachment was left at Budilov, with instructions to reinforce the rearguard. Adjutant General Count Orlov- Denisov was dispatched across the Dvina with the Leib-Cossack Regiment to observe enemy movements. He was ordered to provide intelligence directly to Vitebsk and retreat to the opposite bank of the river.

The army arrived at Vitebsk. 6th Corps was still around Stary. The rearguard was conveniently protected by the river and lakes. The detachment from Beshenkovichy was recalled. Enemy movement was insignificant. The French cavalry appeared near the rearguard on the left bank of the Dvina, but its infantry was still rare.

The army calmly spent two days ay Vitebsk, assuming that Count Orlov- Denisov would warn it in advance of the enemy approach; however, the outposts were probably not well deployed or patrols were conducted incompetently because an enemy detachment was observed only three verstas from our camp. The commander-in-chief had to dispatch several cavalry regiments with one infantry corps to meet the enemy. I offered him Lieutenant General Count Osterman-Tolstoy, who had distinguished himself through his gallantry and steadfastness in battle during the last campaign. We need generals who can wait for the enemy and not be afraid of them. Osterman was exactly such a general and he marched on with the 4th Corps. The 6th Corps was ordered to form in front of the town. The bridge over the Dvina was still intact and another pontoon bridge was constructed. The rearguard was moved closer to avoid isolation.

Count Osterman encountered a few enemy detachments some 12 verstas away and pursued them to Ostrovno. Here he faced superior enemy forces and a fierce engagement began. The enemy attacked vigorously; our troops, having grumbled about continual retreat, seized the opportunity of engaging the French and the distance from reinforcements seemed to double their courage. The forested and rolling terrain prevented the enemy from utilizing his advantage; cavalry acted in isolation which helped our weaker cavalry. Facing fresh enemy forces, Count Osterman had to yield ground for some distance and darkness ended the battle.[220] Due to their commander's carelessness, two squadrons of the Leib Hussar Regiment managed to lose six horse artillery guns.[221] Both sides suffered considerable casualties.[222] Count Osterman was reinforced by Lieutenant General Konovnitsyn's 3rd Infantry Division.[223] Early on the following morning, Konovnitsyn deployed and, with his characteristic fearlessness, he resisted for a long time, refusing to yield an inch to the enemy. Assisting him, Osterman kept his troops in reserve; a cuirassier division soon arrived but could not be employed because of the terrain. Artillery continued to do us great service. To get precise information, the commander-in-chief ordered me to go to the battlefield. Lieutenant General Tuchkov (I) soon arrived with a grenadier division and we held on! For two days the enemy brought all of his weight against us in a series of impetuous attacks. Neither the courage of our troops nor the fearlessness of General Konovnitsyn could hold them back. Our tirailleurs were routed and retreated in groups.[224] Stung that

---

[220] The battle of Ostrovno took place on 25-27 July 1812.
[221] Yermolov's note: Pursuing some enemy advance posts, the squadrons entered the forest, but were suddenly counterattacked and their guns, still unlimbered, were captured.
[222] The Russians lost some 4,000 men.
[223] Yermolov's note: Under Catherine II he had commanded an infantry regiment; in the last war against the Poles [in 1794] he distinguished himself as a courageous and enterprising officer. His division was known for its exemplary discipline.
[224] The French doctor, Raymond Faure, recalled, 'The ground was ploughed up and strewn with men lying in every position and mutilated in various ways. Some, all blackened, had been scorched by the explosion of a caisson; others, who appeared to be dead, were still breathing; as one came up to them one could hear their moans; some had their heads on the body of one of their comrades who had died a few hours before; they were in a sort of apathy, a kind of sleep of pain,

Tuchkov had been given command, Konovnitsyn did not try to reestablish order while Tuchkov did not understand what was happening or show the necessary energy. I told them it was necessary to withdraw from this mess and rally the troops. They sent back the cuirassiers and other superfluous units, making sure the retreat did not turn into a rout. It is indisputable that, having successfully started a battle, it is pleasant to finish it off; but it is unforgivable to allow envy and ego to allow disorder just so it shows the other commander in a bad light. Just now this was all too apparent!

Having dispatched Konovnitsyn's division to Count Osterman, the commander-in-chief ordered the 6th Corps and Pahlen's rearguard to rejoin the army; communication with the right bank of the Dvina had been interrupted, the bridge destroyed and pontoons dismantled.

Over the following days, the commander-in-chief reconnoitred some positions selected by Colonel Toll. I accompanied him and was surprised that he did not spot the numerous flaws. The place was covered by such thick scrub that the quartermasters could not see each other and had to communicate through signals. Behind lay a deep ravine and there was no time to correct its slopes. Our goal was to protect the town of Vitebsk. I voiced my opposition to this position and explained my views. It would be dangerous to fight a battle here because there was no way to reinforce the army. There was still hope that we could join the 2nd Army – the main purpose of our retreat. If we experienced a setback, the troops would either have to pass through the town or cross the ravine. If it was still decided to give battle, then it would be better to deploy the army on the opposite side of the town, controlling the shortest route to Smolensk. By surrendering Vitebsk we would only be adding one loss to all the lost provinces we had alredy sacrificed. The commander-in-chief agreed but continued to prepare for battle and ordered a position behind the town on the road to Smolensk to be selected.

The battle at Ostrovno began in the evening, and I delivered my report to the commander-in-chief that night and there learned

---

from which they did not appear to wish to awake, paying no attention to the people walking around them. They asked nothing of us, probably they knew that there was nothing to hope for.'

about the new position. I examined it the following day, when the troops were already deployed. I found that it was covered with woods, that it might be difficult to maintain communication between the troops, that it was too wide and so required a much greater force than the one available. On the right, two corps – those of Osterman and Baggovut – were isolated by a deep ravine, which artillery would have difficulty in crossing even without an enemy presence. On the left, batteries could be deployed on heights that could rake our lines; it was impossible to adjust our deployment without complicating a retreat. Should the enemy attack our right, we would have to reinforce it but it was impossible to do so quickly or with artillery.

A special vanguard was organized under General Count Pahlen, who engaged the enemy, relieving the troops of General Tuchkov (I), Count Osterman and Ivarov. He contained the enemy attack for some time before finally retreating across the Luches, skilfully taking advantage of its steep banks to protect the fords. The French army, having occupied the nearby heights, made it possible for each French soldier to see what a small force can achieve with exemplary order. They saw Count Pahlen fighting and he made it clear that if the Russian army had more men like Pahlen then the French would need extraordinary efforts and all possible courage to win! Oh, you who did not witness this event, Pahlen's admirable comrades in arms – Rayevskii, equal to him in steadfastness and discretion, Count Lambert, equal in gallantry and enterprise, and you, Müller-Zakomelsky, who combine their best traits and virtues and can be chastised for modesty alone.

The enemy managed to get some of his troops across and it was apparent that he intended to drive the vanguard right through the town. Thus, the moment was approaching when Count Pahlen's efforts might have proved futile. If it could defeat our vanguard, the enemy would be able to reconnoitre our position. The commander-in-chief dispatched several infantry battalions as reinforcements and ordered Major General Shevich, with some of the 1st Cavalry Corps, to support the left of the vanguard and observe the area between it and the army.

After scrutinizing the flawed deployment of our army, I dared to urge the commander-in-chief to abandon the position immediately. Of course, this was a bold suggestion coming from a young man but it was a calculated risk: it was better to commence a retreat with some misgiving and complete it unhindered than to accept battle without having any hope of success and potentially suffer a complete defeat. In my opinion, battle should only be accepted when our army could overwhelm the triumphant enemy after it had been reduced by constant losses. Here we were in a completely different situation. Our nearest reinforcement in Kaluga was small, weak and their commander, General of Infantry Miloradovich, called them soldiers only because they wore uniforms. Had we waited for the attack here, the enemy would not have assaulted us from the front, but rather would have pinned us down with part of his forces, then crossed the Luches upstream with most of his troops and turned against our left, our weakest point as mentioned above. It seemed impossible that the enemy would fail in such an endeavour, but even if they had, the French could have retreated unimpeded towards the road to Borisov, and reinforced by Davout's corps, launched another offensive.

So I took the plunge and became certain that an extreme situation is the best stimulus for action and this itself sweeps away the complexity of the issue. However, it is important that the same conviction and spirit guide those who execute orders. There should be no time for deliberations at the moment when action alone is necessary. A minute often decides the outcome!

The commander-in-chief hesitated in accepting my proposal. As the minister of war, he was well aware of the difficulties which beset us and these required serious consideration! Quartermaster General Toll, against the opinion of many, argued that the position had many advantages and that we should accept battle. General Tuchkov (I) saw the necessity for retreat but was timid in expressing his views; decisiveness was not one of his traits and he suggested we retreat during the night.[225] Adjutant General Baron Korf shared my opinion but did not run the risk of arguing for it. He did not seek glory in danger. Like me and many others, his soul was subject to fear. Trepidation is pardonable when danger threatens common security! I was both afraid of the commander-in-chief's stubbornness and of his consent. Finally, he issued the order

---

[225] Yermolov's note: I told him, you must be sure Napoleon will let you survive until evening. However we had to gain time to avoid an enemy that could have taken advantage of our delay.

to retreat. The die was cast and destiny snatched the laurels of victory from the enemy!

It was about 1:00 pm, the vanguard was engaged in ferocious fighting, two armies were in close proximity and prisoners informed us of Napoleon's presence.

Oh, audacity, a deity before whose altar man must kneel so many times in life! At times, you are the companion of prudence, who often leaves us timid, and you lead the brave to greatness; today a worthy sacrifice was made for you!

Our entire camp was in movement. The army marched in three columns: the left column, with the 5th and 6th corps and most of the reserve artillery, moved down the shortest road to Smolensk. Its rearguard comprised of regiments from the 1st Cavalry Corps under Major General Shevich. Count Osterman with the 2nd and 4th corps proceeded along the main road to Porechey; he was to reinforce the rearguard should the enemy launch a vigorous pursuit. The central column included the 3rd Corps and the main headquarters; Baron Korf's 2nd Cavalry Corps formed its rearguard. In half an hour, the forest concealed an entire army from the enemy's sight. Everyone moved by forced marches. Lieutenant General Lavrov, commanding the Guard infantry, had to awaken his dormant energy to show the agility the occasion required. Demands were placed on all and on every effort! I cannot conceal some sense of pride that the commander-in-chief, an experienced and extremely cautious general, found my suggestion for retreat correct and accepted it.

I could not take my eyes from the vanguard and superb Count Pahlen. The departing army, having entrusted its security to him, could no longer protect him from superior enemy forces but nothing could have shaken his courage. I will quote Horatio, 'if the universe crumbles, it will bury him, fearless, beneath its ruins.' The rearguard action continued relentlessly until 5:00 pm when we retreated to the far side of the town, leaving the enemy surprised by our orderly withdrawal. The French occupied the town cautiously on the following morning.

The same day as we abandoned Vitebsk, Bagration's adjutant Prince Menshikov arrived with news of the battle at the village of Dashkovka and that the army was now marching uninterrupted to join us. Dispatching Ataman Platov and his [Cossack] host, Prince

Bagration instructed him to accelerate his movement and, taking account of time and distance, he was to join us soon.

One march from Vitebsk, the rearguard fought an intense cavalry battle. Personally directing the cavalry, Pahlen won and thereafter the enemy limited his actions to observing the movements of our columns.

An officer and NCO of the Bug Cossack Regiment, whom I dispatched with a letter to Ataman Platov, soon returned with a response. Coming back, they often passed close by the enemy and the commander-in-chief awarded them with promotions.

Having missed Bagration, Davout might strike for Smolensk with those troops at Orsha and Dubrovna, prevent the organization of the militia, destroy the supply magazines and sack the town. The loss of the magazines would have been significant for us since our supply system was inefficient. Seeing the risk, the commander-in-chief ordered the 5th and 6th corps to hurry and instructed Ataman Platov to cover their movement.

After leaving Vitebsk, the commander-in-chief instructed Grand Duke Constantine to travel to Moscow. I am not sure, but I doubt that he was responsible for this decision. The grand duke was upset believing that anybody could carry out this mission. I noticed that many regretted his departure and, to his credit, many of them were subordinates. Commanding a Guard division, I was also subordinate to him and cannot recall any trouble from him.

The army soon quit Porechye; the 5th and 6th corps meanwhile arriving at Smolensk. When the czar had passed through the city he had instructed Adjutant General Baron Winzegorode to organize a local militia. Major General Olenin, newly returned to service, commanded a detachment that included some of these poorly-armed men, a few reserve squadrons, the troops of Adjutant General Baron Müller-Zakomelsky and the reserve artillery. Reinforced by one regiment from Ataman Platov's troops, this detachment was deployed near Lyadi before Krasnyi.

Meanwhile, the enemy dashed into Velizh, cut down some recruits from a battalion assembled in the main square, and having routed the rest, captured a bridge across the Dvina. This happened because a staff officer, bringing up eight battalions of recruits from Nevel, was told the French were close, set outposts in the town, strictly maintained discipline and kept the entire battalion under arms all night, although the cartridges were all in wagons and had

143

not been issued to the men! Other battalions on the right bank veered off the road and escaped a beating. The enemy destroyed one artillery park of 166 horses that had been left behind because they were exhausted. Colonel Tishin, sent from Porechye to collect this park, barely escaped alive.

At Porechye, General Laba reported to the minister of war that a commissioner, in a praiseworthy gesture carried out to prevent the enemy capturing a large supply depot, had burned it to the ground. There were several thousand quarters of oats and 64 thousand puds of hay in it. The minister was not thrilled by such efficiency and I asked for his permission to inquire exactly when the depot had been established. The order establishing it had been signed two weeks ago. Was it possible to gather so many supplies in such a short time, especially when the army was using nearly all the transport? I dared to tell the minister that for such an act of robbery the commissioner should have been burned with the magazine as well.[226]

Porechye was the first Russian town on our retreat and the sentiments of the locals towards us were very different. We had previously passed through Lithuania where the nobility, keeping the hopes of restoring Poland alive, agitated the feeble minds of peasants against us. In Byelorussia too the oppressive authority of landlords forced the peasants to desire change. However, here, around Smolensk, people were ready to see us as their saviours. It was impossible to express more hatred towards the enemy, or a more fervent desire to assist us without sparing property or life!

The peasants came to me with a question: could they take up arms against the enemy themselves and not be held responsible for it by the state? The commander-in-chief issued an appeal to the residents around Smolensk, calling on them to oppose the enemy who dared to desecrate holy shrines, pillage houses and dishonour families.

We left Porechye at night to avoid the heat. To understand the soldiers' mood and morale, I often walked among them unrecognized asking questions: the soldiers complained about the retreat and expected to find a solution for everything in battle; they

---

[226] Yermolov's note: Laba listened to this discussion without a hint of embarrassment; of course, this was not the first time he had been in such an incident. The manipulation of supply regulations often exhausted justice and rescued criminals. A commissioner never sinned alone.

were dissatisfied with the commander-in-chief, who, in their eyes, was guilty because he was not Russian. If success is not decisive enough, or less than expected, the very first quality that a Russian soldier ascribes to a foreigner commander is treason, and the latter cannot escape their condemnation. There is only one remedy for this – victory! A few of them bask in the trust and love of soldiers. Yet, circumstances were not favourable for the commander-in-chief and this meant victories, or even small successes, were rare. A few residents remained in Porechye and, scattering between abandoned houses, the troops turned to pillage and robbery. I personally drove them out of some houses and, I must admit, on one occasion even from the church.[227] I did not encounter any of their officers who should have noticed their absence. So, the reason for a decline of effectives should be attributed to this negligence of duty and not only regimental commanders should be reprimanded for this.

During our march from Porechye, Grand Duke Constantine suddenly returned from Moscow. We also received a message from Bagration that he was approaching Smolensk and, if necessary, would enter the town one day after us. The commander-in-chief's intention was not clear when he told me, 'There are insufficient supplies for two armies, while there are plenty of provisions collected at Toropets and on the Volga and those provided by Tver. Therefore, I think that the 1st Army should take the direction of Belyi upstream on the Dvina.' It was easy to counter this suggestion but lacking prudence, it was difficult for me to do this with discretion. I passionately told him, 'The czar expects success and a revival of our chances from the junction of the armies. The troops also eagerly await this union. What was the purpose of all the hardships and dangers that the 2nd Army overcame if you would again place it in the position from which it escaped? Your movement to the Dvina will benefit the enemy: the French would destroy the weak 2nd Army, isolate you from the south and the support of other armies! You cannot dare do this; you must join Bagration, adopt a joint plan and thus carry out the will and desire of the czar! Reassured, Russia will have no right to reprimand you!'

---

[227] Yermolov complained about this to Barclay de Tolly, who had several soldiers hanged for looting churches on 22 July [3 August]. However, Grand Duke Constantine later chided Yermolov 'I will never forgive you that you had 15 men hanged on the birthday of my mother.'

The commander-in-chief listened to me patiently. It seemed to me I had seen through his scheme. Joining Prince Bagration could not have been pleasant for him; although as the minister of war, he held the higher position, Bagration was senior in rank and could refuse to obey.[228]

Power is an invaluable gift! Why does it not brighten the lives of those leading an honourable life? Why does it bless those who gain by ignoring the law?

After our discussion, I do not think that the commander-in-chief changed his attitude towards me, or perhaps it was difficult to notice, or it was simply impossible to be less cold or distant.

The army continued towards Smolensk. The commander-in-chief left the army a march from the city and travelled ahead to get there first. The following day the army arrived and began preparing bread and biscuits. Supply magazines were almost empty and supplies could not be brought in in bulk from the provinces.

Thus, we were at Smolensk, where I had spent my childhood with my relatives, where I had served in my adolescence and where I had many pleasant and hospitable friends among the nobles. Now, I was old, my passionate youth gone and, at least according to others, an honourable man in a prominent position. Such twists and turns of fate were amazing for me too!

The day after our arrival at Smolensk, the 2nd Army was 12 verstas from the city. Bagration arrived to see the commander-in-chief accompanied by several generals, a large retinue and a magnificent escort. They met each other politely with a show of amity, but with aloofness and distance in their hearts. They had contrasting characters and the contrast was apparent. They had both served at the same time, for a long time in the lower ranks, and had together achieved the rank of staff officer.

Prolonged service in junior positions had kept Barclay in obscurity, made him accustomed to slow promotion, frustrated his hopes and ambition. Having no remarkable talent which might set him apart, he valued his skills modestly and so did not enjoy that

---

[228] Yermolov's note: It was impossible to know Bagration better than I did and to know how infinite his devotion to the czar was, for whom he considered even his life a small sacrifice. Yet, despite all this, nothing would have forced him to subordinate himself to Barclay de Tolly, who had served under him in 1806-1807. Yet, to him the patriotic war was not waged for ambition and he was ready for everything.

trust which opens doors otherwise closed. He made his mark as a major general following service as commander of a Jäger regiment which had prepared him well for war. He urged many officers in the regiment not to limit their study of tactics and had improved their knowledge.

Providence made Bagration famous. The war in Italy in 1799 brought quick promotion; Suvorov, that genius, showered him with fame and brought him honours that attracted attention to him. Encouragement inspired self- confidence and trust in his own skills.

Being quickly promoted to the rank of general, then unexpectedly appointed minister of war and soon after commander-in-chief of the 1st Western Army, Barclay de Tolly aroused envy in many around him, gaining many enemies. Awkward at court, he did not earn the good will of the people close to the sovereign. His reserved attitude did not secure the amity of his colleagues or the loyalty of subordinates. Having begun reforms in the administration, he exposed flaws and provoked the resentment of his powerful predecessor [Akarcheyev], who took advantage of every chance to expose Barclay's every mistake. He had a handful of competent men around him but rarely thought of sharing his work with them, wanting to accomplish everything through personal hard work. So matters proceeded very slowly, then were gradually muddled, leading to an unavoidable mess.

On the other hand, Bagration was also appointed to high positions (except for minister of war) but his success was based on the opinion and hope of many. Certainly he generated envy, but he did not gain enemies. Shrewd and cunning, he made powerful connections at court. He was responsible and pleasant, stayed friends with his equals and retained old acquaintances. Surrounded by fame, he shared his accomplishments with others and cited any assistance he received. He generously rewarded subordinates, who were delighted to serve and always idolized him. Bagration, like nobody else, tried not to abuse authority; no other subordinates obeyed orders with more delight. His manners were enchanting! It was, however, easy to manipulate him in matters in which he knew little. But he had an independent character. Ignorance or faults were only apparent to those close to him.

Prior to his rise, Barclay enjoyed a small, one may even say humble, fortune and had to limit his desires. Such limitations did not subdue his aspirations or extinguish the talents of the mind; but poverty finds a way of showing them in a dignified way. Poverty isolates people from society, restricts them to a small group of acquaintances, prevents those contacts which require mutual favours or sacrifice. His family life could not keep him satisfied: his wife was not young, without that charm which can enchant a man and captivate him. His children were still infants, and a military man did not have to run a house! He spent his leisure time in practical studies and enriched himself with knowledge. By nature, he was reserved, in wealth, unpretentious and in habit, he endured shortcomings without a murmur. With his intelligent, positive and dedicated mind, he applied himself to any task entrusted to him; yet, he was not resolute, being shy of responsibility. He was indifferent to danger, untouched by fear. Of a compassionate but patronising spirit; attentive to the work of others, especially to those close to him. He remembered disapointments: I do not know if he remembered acts of kindness. Sensitive to any public expression of respect, yet mistrustful of the sentiments behind it. Cautious in his relations with subordinates he did not allow any freedom he considered disrespectful to rank. Timid before the monarch, devoid of eloquence. Fearful of losing the patronage he had only recently earned beyond his expectations. In short, Barclay had weaknesses which we all have, but he also had the skills that quite a few of our most celebrated generals have had. He made use of his talents with diligence and devotion to the sovereign.

Bagration was thrown into the society of young men, a whirlwind of confusion, with equally limited fortune. Of lively character by nature and passionate, he made acquaintances and kept in touch with them. Similar personalities masked the inequality in wealth. The extravagence of his friends satisfied him and he gained the habit of not limiting himself by moderation. These connections facilitated his career, but the war, although it separated him from his friends, brought him under the flags of Suvorov in Italy. This war required courageous and decisive men; its hardships filled men with good will. Suvorov turned his attention to him, weighed his soul, distinguished him and raised him up! No other contemporary, except for Miloradovich, was near Bagration. Suvorov led them in a common purpose and prevented any clash between them. Bagration returned from Italy in the glow of fame, a sparkle of honours. It would have been indecent not to renew his previous connections, not to acknowledge previous assistance: a fortune of his own was now required. The sovereign chose a most beautiful wife for him, with enormous wealth, but could not instill love in her heart or endow her with fidelity! There was no domestic bliss, nor family harmony! Solitude was not Bagration's trait; it was late to seek a solution from within, absence became a necessity; it was further worsened by constant service. Never having had a tutor and no wealth to speak of, Bagration was without education. Well endowed by nature, he remained untutored and entered military service. He drew his knowledge from experience, his conclusions from events and was never guided by rules or science. Sometimes he was at fault, however, his opinion was quite often sound. Fearless in battle, impassive to danger, he was often less enterprising at first, but always decisive later. He was untiring in work, caring about the condition of his subordinates and yet demanding every effort from them in time of need. He always selected them on the basis of merit and awarded them accordingly. However, he sometimes promoted those with strong connections or patronage at court. He showed refinement before the sovereign and flattering manners to his entourage. He was humble by nature, undemanding and generous to excess. He was slow to anger and always open for reconciliation. He renounced malice and was of a kindly disposition. In short, Bagration's positive traits can be found in ordinary men, but using them for the common good, and enjoying doing so, belonged to him alone! Had Bagration been as educated as Barclay, the latter would not have been able to hold a candle to him.

So, the 2nd Army finally arrived at Smolensk and the junction of two armies was accomplished. Our gratitude to you, oh eminent Davout, who benefited Russia so much![229]

Delight was all the two armies had in common. The 1st Army, exhausted by continuous withdrawal, grumbled and showed signs of disorder and lack of discipline. Confidence in the commander-in-chief was undermined at the top, while the lower ranks hesitated in trusting him. The 2nd Army arrived in a completely different state. The sound of incessant music and joyful songs animated the souls of the soldiers. These troops showed pride in the dangers they had overcome and readiness to face new perils. Here the commander-

---

[229] Yermolov refers to Davout's failure to prevent Bagration from joining the 1st Army.

in-chief was a friend to his subordinates, while the latter were his trustful comrades!

Judging by such spirit, it might seem as if the 2nd Army had not retreated from the Niemen to the Dnieper but had performed a triumphal march! What other troops can match you, incomparable Russian warriors? Your loyalty cannot be acquired with gold, or with a blind eye to disorder or toleration of insubordination. You are not afraid of obedience and the sovereign's will transforms you into heroes! When will a man like Suvorov stand before you and astonish the universe?

While we gathered at Smolensk, the Don Cossacks under Platov, reinforced by one hussar and two Jäger regiments, were some 15 verstas on the road to Rudnya. Count Pahlen's vanguard was nearby. Colonel Creitz and a dragoon regiment were covering Katan. At Kholmy on the road to Porechye, Major General Ilovayski (VI) with his Cossack regiments and the Elisavetgrad Hussars protected the right flank through constant patrolling. Adjutant General Winzegorode, with the Kazan Dragoons and three Cossack units, watched the enemy around Velizh. A detachment under Major General Olenin was posted at Krasnyi, with its outposts at Lyadi. The 1st Army remained idle.

Due to my rank I had frequent contact with the Civil Governor Baron Asch in Smolensk. There never was a more useless man for the army; he was so negligent that he was still dispatching bread supplies to Vitebsk, although we were heading to Porechye. The least threat to his district should have made him more curious. Neither did the army benefit from the local marshal of nobility, Leslie, and many remained surprised that the distinguished and titled Smolensk nobility had elected him.

At Smolensk, we came across the *zemstvo*[230] militia: crowds of men had collected regardless of age, poorly clothed and virtually unarmed. It was commanded by Lieutenant General Lebedev, an old and completely incompetent man, who had cheated death and achieved his rank only by longetivity. On the commander-in-chief's instructions, damaged weapons were taken from the cavalry and given to the militia.[231] Some commanders felt bad about releasing

---

[230] Each province or *gubernia*, comprised of several districts or *zemstvos* which provided opolchenye [militia].

[231] Yermolov's note: The General Inspector of Cavalry, Grand Duke Constantine

such weapons, and many thought it a strange order; yet, none dared to admit that these weapons were useless! A company to repair roads and bridges was organized from some cavalry militia, whilst the infantry was tasked with field works. At Smolensk, we received news of Count Wittgenstein's and General of Cavalry Tormasov's victories and the latter also sent some captured flags.

Passing Polotsk, Napoleon had left Marshal Oudinot's corps there, which was more numerous than Count Wittgenstein's forces opposite Drissa. At the same time, Marshal Macdonald's corps entered Courland and its advance posts were seen near Creitzburg. Circumstances became serious: Wittgenstein could neither remain at Drissa nor retreat or remain inactive since the enemy had placed him between two fires. Count Wittgenstein decided to act and marched towards Klyastitsy on the road from Polotsk to Sebezh. Then he shielded himself with a small detachment against Macdonald and moved with his main forces against Oudinot.

The gap between the enemy corps and their difficulty in coordinating their actions gave Count Wittgenstein the advantage. Whilst Oudinot was marching from Polotsk, Macdonald had not yet crossed the Dvina. A burden was thus removed from Wittgenstein's shoulders. Believing that our move to Klyastitsy was a retreat, Oudinot imprudently pursued us with part of his troops. When he encountered our concentrated forces, he could not resist and fled. His troops had scattered on the march, arrived piecemeal at the battle and were destroyed in detail. Having lost those advantages he had at first enjoyed, Oudinot suffered heavy losses and returned to Polotsk. Wittgenstein pursued him and, having halted his vanguard a march from Polotsk, he returned to his earlier position with the rest of his troops. Oudinot remained idle for a long time. Macdonald did not undertake any operations, either because he did not trust his Prussian and Confederation of the Rhine troops against our corps from Finland or because he was preparing for the siege of Riga, which was his main objective. So Wittgenstein claimed a victory and boasted of a clever plan of action. However, some asserted that his chief of staff, Major General d'Auvray, should have been credited for the plan. It was an assertion provoked by envy but, well, I have no precise information on the matter.

Pavlovich, opposed this order, but it was still carried out.

General Tormasov had attacked a Saxon corps under General Reynier which had crossed our borders at Brest-Litovsk. He prevented its juncture with the Austrians under Schwarzenberg[232] and defeated enemy forces despite their fierce resistance. The enemy suffered heavy casualties and retreated in confusion. One general, 2,000 men, eight guns and four flags fell to us.

During our four-day stay at Smolensk, arrangements were made to gather bread. The commander-in-chief invited the grand duke and major generals and suggested a discussion on the current state of the army. Common opinion called for an offensive. Grand Duke Constantine Pavlovich's considerations, modestly delivered but well thought out, were taken into account with due respect. The commander-in-chief was reluctant to give his consent to an attack, waiting for more precise intelligence on the enemy from the advance posts. It was known that the French had occupied Porechye with a small cavalry force. More were at Velizh and Surazh. The rest of their cavalry was facing Platov and the King of Naples, Murat, who commanded it, was close nearby. Napoleon's headquarters was at Vitebsk, with his Guard and the strong reserve artillery. Davout's corps was slowly gathering at Orsha, with a strong detachment at Lyadi. Everything seemed favourable for an attack. The enemy were scattered over a vast area, encouraged by our inactivity, and resting; all of this favoured our success. The enemy might not learn of our movement and would need at least three days to concentrate his forces, not to mention his more distant troops. Finally an order to attack was issued and it was impossible to describe the joy of our troops! Smolensk watched in bewilderment as the militias prepared themselves. The Dnieper flowed on, proud of our troops streaming forwards.

The 1st Army advanced in two columns towards Rudnya via Prikaz Vydra. On its left, the 2nd Army moved along the Dnieper. A detachment of several Jäger regiments under Major General Rosen was in Katan and the nearby woods. Similarly, another detachment under Major General Prince Shakovskii had been sent to Kasplya. Major General Neverovskii's infantry division, reinforced by the Kharkov Dragoons, was sent to Krasnyi to support Major General Olenin's detachment. The division had been

---

[232] Yermolov's note: Even had they united, Tormasov would still have been stronger. Success was guaranteed, although probably with higher casualties.

recently organized from recruits and two of its regiments were replaced with older, more experienced units. Bakers from regiments in both armies were left at Smolensk. One regiment was kept behind to keep order; the wounded and sick were evacuated to Vyazma.

The armies halted a short march from Rudnya. The commander-in-chief hesitated, while Bagration insisted on advancing. Instead of the rapid movement that would have secured success, the armies were given a useless rest and so the enemy gained an additional day to concentrate his forces! The French might already have been aware of our advance.

Platov, reinforced by Pahlen's vanguard, encountered a strong cavalry detachment at Leshnya, routed it and pursued it to Rudnya, which the enemy promptly abandoned. One wounded colonel, several officers and 500 lower ranks were captured.[233] The colonel told us that they had no knowledge of our advance. Among the papers captured in General Sebastiani's quarters were orders to the outposts and instructions to generals on their units on how they were to support and maintain communications. Circumstances still favoured us and had our commander-in-chief showed more resolution we would have succeeded. Of course, the defeat at Leshnya stung the French, but they would now suffer from further attacks and had no time to avoid them. But the commander-in-chief not only evaded executing the adopted plan but completely changed it.

The 1st Army withdrew to the village of Moshinki some 18 verstas down the road from Smolensk to Porechye. Prince Shakovskii's detachment remained at Kasplya. Count Pahlen's vanguard was sent to Lushe to reinforce Shakovskii and maintain communications with the army. Five Jäger regiments were taken from him and garrisoned Lavrova. Platov's troops occupied Inkovo with their left and, covering Kasplya, extended further towards Vorony.

The 2nd Army moved to replace the 1st Army; its vanguard was before Gavrikov, outposts were spread to the left of Inkovo, through Leshnya to Katan and the Dnieper. Baron Rosen's

---

[233] Yermolov's note: Grand Duke Constantine Pavlovich met this courageous colonel with particular respect and helped him. Learning that the czar's brother had spoken to him, he was very surprised.

detachment was disbanded and replaced with a stronger force from the vanguard. A day later, the 2nd Army was forced to return to Smolensk because of the lack of water, the local water was poor and harmful to the troops. Its vanguard under Vasilchikov remained in place and was reinforced by Lieutenant General Prince Gorchakov's corps.

The 1st Army remained inactive for four days at Moshinki. Advance posts found nothing of importance. Patrols from Winzegorode's detachment were dispatched to Velizh and reported that the 4th Corps of the Viceroy of Italy had left the area and it was devoid of French troops as far as Surazh. A small detachment of Platov's troops rushed into Porechye, but was immediately driven back. The local residents soon reported that the French had abandoned the city.

It is possible to understand why the commander-in-chief expected the enemy from the direction of Porechye. Davout's corps, reinforced by the Westphalians and Prince Poniatowski's Polish cavalry, moved towards their main body and strengthened it so it could overwhelm us and directly dispatch a substantial part of its troops to Smolensk. Even assuming Napoleon would make a serious mistake (which seems foolhardily to expect), he could concentrate at Vitebsk and have the same number of troops before which we had previously retreated. Assuming that he returned to the regions he had passed during his advance, we still would have been unable to shift the war to Lithuania where the French were prepared to destroy the province and its resources.

It was more likely that the Viceroy's corps, recently at Velizh but now gone, and other troops, previously at Surazh, would retreat and lure us to Vitebsk. Napoleon would lead his Guard and the troops at Rudnya and Liubavichi in crossing to the left bank of the Dnieper, where Lyadi was already occupied by Davout's troops, and would approach the walls of Smolensk long before Barclay could arrive. The

2nd Army, unable to protect the city alone, would have been forced to retreat towards Dorogobuzh. The returning 1st Army would be forced back and unable to link with Bagration. Our movement on Rudnya was unknown to the enemy, as became obvious from the statements of prisoners. An attack against scattered troops and their destruction would have been easily completed, and the army could then return to Smolensk, as was initially planned. I believe that an experienced and reasonably cautious commander-in-chief would have done this and certainly would not have been carried away by success.

I will never forget your strange intentions, Barclay of de Tolly and I still hear reproaches for calling off the attack on Rudnya. Why did I have to endure the reprimands from you, Bagration, my patron? Was it not me, who, having had the idea, insisted on its execution; was it not me who tried to urge its accomplishment as quickly as possible? I did everything to maintain good will between both commanders, fearing even the slightest tension between you. I might add that I frequently concealed the coldness and insolence in Barclay's correspondence in such terms as to make them appear more amiable. As for you, Bagration, I conveyed your occassional coarse and acerbic opinion in a more respectful tone. You often told me that you found better qualities in Barclay than you expected.[234] Barclay often told me that he did not think it possible to serve with you without problems. Because of your confidence, I could have maintained good will between you, but, Bagration, it was your assistant Count St Priest, who generated hostility between you two. He envied the fact that I was more trusted and better employed than he. My position at headquarters with the minister of war gave me precedence over him and made my accomplishments more visible. He did not place the common good first. He desired more than he was entitled to and more than he should get. You, Bagration, my patron, respected this spoiled young man's connections at court and so you were not prudent by trusting him.

After wasting so much time, the 1st Army quit Moshinki taking the same road back to Rudnya. It is unknown what the intention was, whether we would engage in battle or await the enemy here so that Prince Bagration could hurry to join us.

The 1st Army soon arrived at Gavriki, where Vasilchikov's vanguard was deployed; the troops of the 2nd Army were already on the march from Smolensk and were to cover our right. The corps of Lieutenant General Rayevskii had moved less than 15 verstas from Smolensk because it had departed three hours late. The 2nd Grenadier Division was ahead of it, but the division had halted.[235] This delay later proved to be of great advantage for us,

---

[234] Yermolov's note: When inquiring about Barclay, Bagration always asked me, 'How is your Davout?'

since General Rayevskii was destined for an entirely different mission.

On the day our army arrived at Gavriki, Platov made a forced march from Kholmy to Inkovo; without stopping, he overtook Vasilchikov's vanguard, reconnoitred Rudnya, which, according to local residents, had been abandoned by the enemy one-and-a-half days ago, and then crossed to the left bank of the Dnieper at Rossasna. Our vanguard knew nothing about this foray.[236] One of the parties, dispatched by Platov, encountered enemy troops moving towards Rossasna, while others followed enemy tracks towards the right bank of the Berezina creek but no longer found them there. Halting in Rudnya, Ataman reported everything to Barclay and awaited further orders.

Just then, Bagration received a report from Neverovskii that, on 3 [15] August, superior enemy forces had attacked him near Krasnyi. He fought back but was driven out and vigorously pursued, suffering heavy casualties, including several guns, and retreating to Smolensk. The courier took twenty-four hours to deliver the message, and therefore it was possible to assume that the enemy was already near Smolensk. The distant sound of gunfire could be heard; outposts along the Dnieper also reported hearing a strong cannonade.

Lieutenant General Rayevskii was ordered to reinforce Neverovskii. The 2nd Army headed for Smolensk, followed by the 1st Army. Platov, recalling his outposts, deployed his troops near Prikaz Vydra. Shakhovskii's detachment returned to the army; some of the Jägers and cavalry retreated along the road by the Dnieper and watched the fords. I ordered Rotmistr Chechensky, famous for his gallantry, to select volunteers from the escort of the Bug Cossack Regiment and to watch enemy forces on the march down the left bank of the Dnieper. Returning from Gavriki, I persuaded Flügel Adjutant Colonel Kikin to act as duty general.

---

[235] Yermolov's note: Lieutenant General Charles von Mecklenburg commanded this division. Having spent the previous night with friends, he was drunk, awoke late the next day and only then was he able to order his troops to march.

[236] Yermolov's note: Vasilchikov, the vanguard's commander, was one of the best officers in the army, having recently distinguished himself by his courage, he was still inexperienced since he was engaging the enemy for the first time as major general. He had commanded the distinguished Akhtrysk Hussars and was promoted because of powerful connections at court.

Goodbye, Stavrakov, you lamentable duty general, incomparable commandant of the headquarters. Now you will not be able to test my activity, and, thanks to Colonel Kikin, I will now have a few minutes of repose! Oh laziness, always valued by me! Take this soul, so eagerly returning to you; I swear eternal loyalty.

Lieutenant General Rayevskii arrived at Smolensk and deployed his men in the suburbs. He ordered Neverovskii, who was some seven verstas from the city, to join him. If the 2nd Grenadier Division had not prevented Rayevskii from leaving Smolensk on time, his corps would have had to have made a long march before turning back and might have arrived at Smolensk too late or found it occupied by the French.

The town of Krasnyi had been protected by Olenin's vanguard supported by Flügel Adjutant Colonel Voyeikov's Jäger brigade from the 27th Infantry Division. The French were already in the streets but were driven back. Our regiments, which had never seen the enemy before, knew no danger and fought doggedly; but, yielding to renewed attacks, they fell back to the detachment on the main road two verstas behind the town. The French pursued with cavalry and some artillery. Their infantry appeared on the approaches to Smolensk. Neverovskii was a brave officer and unafraid of danger, however, he had rarely, and then in a subordinate position, seen action and here he was suddenly placed in a difficult position which required experience and skill. Anyone familiar with French cavalry will understand how to hold it back with 6,000 infantry whilst retreating across broken terrain, along a road planted on each side with trees and covered by a battery. Neverovskii's Kharkov Dragoons suffered heavy casualties. Due to his poor use of infantry and his decision to send back the artillery, the enemy cavalry was able to launch successful attacks. Taking advantage of its superiority, the French charged his rear and captured most of his artillery as it fell back. Had Neverovskii been able to form a square, which so many had excelled at in the wars with the Turks, events would not have forced him to seek flight, and you, Apushkin, would have saved your battery.[237] Despite this,

---

[237] Yermolov is too critical of Neverovskii. He made a fighting retreat to Smolensk with his two dense columns via Merlino and Korythnya. At about 8:00 pm Neverovskii reached Korythnya, where he rallied his cavalry and rearguard and continued his retreat to Smolensk the next day. Contemporaries and modern

the enemy could not but respect Neverovskii's fearlessness and, fortunately, the French infantry only appeared after Neverovskii joined Rayevskii.

On 4th [16 August] Rayevskii and the 27th Division fought for Smolensk for the entire day, preventing the enemy from capturing the suburbs. Only a few generals would have risked doing what seemed uncomplicated to Rayevskii. It might seem easier to abandon Smolensk and defend the crossings over the Dnieper since the army might not arrive in time. To defend the citadel, it was necessary to deploy artillery on the walls and risk losing it should we retreat since the exit road lead through narrow gates. The enemy forces were massing, but they had no knowledge of the city and its vicinities and thus wasted their efforts, striking down the road from Krasnyi and attacking the Malakhov Gates. Had the French turned left near the river, followed the walls and deployed a strong battery against the bridge, Rayevskii would have been placed in an untenable position and his troops would have suffered appalling losses from the enemy artillery. The 2nd Army arrived late in the evening, followed by the 1st Army around midnight; both armies bivouacked on the right bank of the Dnieper. Rayevskii had prevented capture of any suburbs and held his ground everywhere. The following day, he was replaced by Dokhturov, who with his corps and the 27th Infantry Division, again held the suburbs, preventing the enemy from reaching the city walls. Rayevskii joined the army on 5 [17] August. Around 10:00 am our troops entered the fortress and deployed near the walls protected by some batteries. Artillery, in large numbers, was deployed in earthworks before the walls. Earlier, Lieutenant General Konovnitsyn had come up with his 3rd Division to reinforce the defenders by taking up a position in the city. The buildings closest to the walls, extending down to the Dnieper, were still in our hands and our *tirailleurs* were outside the walls. Taking advantage of weight of numbers, the enemy surrounded the city and attacked the suburbs; fierce musket and artillery fire resonated and various parts of the city caught fire. On Konovnitsyn's orders, the 3rd Division drove the enemy back; Major General Olenin's detachment assisted and Colonel Potemkin's Jäger brigade distinguished itself. Finding more favourable terrain to the left, the enemy diverted his attacks in this

---

historians agree that Neverovskii did form squares.

direction and reached the Nikolsk Gates. A breakthrough could have decided the fate of the city, but the courage of Major General Neverovskii and the presence of the commander of the artillery of the

1st Army, Major General Count Kutaisov, who directed the fire of our batteries, triumphed over the enemy. Lieutenant Colonel Nilus' batteries, deployed on the right bank, also inflicted casualties on the enemy. Repeated attacks against the same places and the increasing presence of artillery revealed the enemy's intentions and led to the decision to dispatch the 4th Division of Prince Eugene of Württemberg to reinforce our left. His regiments flew in the wake of their young commander, so distinguished for his gallantry and admired by his troops!

The commander-in-chief ordered me to report on our positions in the city. The battle raged with intensity; we had already suffered considerable casualties; the French losses were much higher since massive fortress walls protected us from their artillery. An hour before nightfall, the French was very close to the walls; some suburbs on the left side were already in their hands. The only remaining bridge over the Dnieper now came under artillery fire; the city was engulfed in flames, while not a single skirmisher survived beyond the walls. Napoleon did not spare his Polish troops and they slavishly obeyed his will suffering the most in this battle. Initially, strong enemy forces had moved upstream along the road to Yelna on the left bank of the Dnieper. The 2nd Army watched their movements and, on the 5th, it moved down the Moscow road towards the crossing over the Dnieper some 40 verstas from Smolensk. Its vanguard under Lieutenant General Prince Gorchakov was left six verstas from the city; most of the Cossacks were deployed on the left bank of the Dnieper, watching the enemy. Communications with the 1st Army were maintained through cavalry outposts. The enemy, having marched for 12 verstas towards Yelna, then returned to Smolensk and so the 2nd Army bivouacked nearby.

Prince Bagration persuaded the commander-in-chief to continue our defence of the city for another day, then cross the Dnieper and attack the enemy, while he struck from the other direction. When the commander-in-chief inquired further, Colonel Toll responded that we should issue from the city in two columns. I was surprised by such an answer from a man of his standing. I noted that there were few gates in the city and large bodies of troops could not possibly pass through them quickly, nor deploy in the confined space between the enemy batteries and the walls. How would our artillery cope and how could such numbers of troops pass through the narrow streets of the city and amid destroyed buildings and ruins without confusion? I offered to discuss the possibility of retreat when all these inconveniences would become even more menacing. The minister rejected my comments. We agreed that if we had to attack, then it would be better to cross the Dnieper to the right of the city, having constructed bridges under the protection of our batteries by the fortress. The suburb here was still in our hands; only a single enemy battery was deployed here and extensive gardens improved our chances. In case of retreat, we could occupy the churches and monasteries in the suburb and repulse the enemy attacks on the bridges. The 2nd Army should neither have crossed the Dnieper upstream nor attacked the enemy right flank, as Bagration proposed. The French could easily have prevented this crossing or, having repulsed the attack, they could sever communications with the 1st Army and impair our ability to act together. The French could then contain our troops in the fortress and act according to the situation. Yet, even my own considerations did not prevent me from taking an unreasonable decision. I still supported the idea of continuing the defence of the city for another day. Major General Count Kutaisov informed Barclay of the corps commanders' requests. A defence would be necessary even if the commander-in-chief still planned to attack. Otherwise, it was completely useless to defend Smolensk since the city was in ruins. The army could not leave a strong garrison here, and even a small one could not find the means to survive amid such destruction. So, Barclay decided to abandon Smolensk! There were a few difficulties in concentrating troops and artillery that were spread over the entire expanse of the city. The battle continued late in the evening; our troops withdrew unhindered from the city during the night and the last units to retreat destroyed the bridge at dawn. The enemy soon entered the city in their wake.

Several Jäger regiments were deployed in the suburb on the right bank of the Dnieper, defending the crossing. The fire soon spread from the bridge to the nearby buildings. Taking advantage of the confusion, the French forded the river near the bridge under cover of their artillery, occupied the suburb and immediately appeared on the hill where our battery did not expect them and was unprepared. However, Lieutenant General Konovnitsyn ordered the nearest infantry battalions to charge with their bayonets and the enemy was routed. Having rallied, the Jägers pursued the fleeing French, some of whom drowned in the river. As the houses burned to the ground, they provided no protection to our Jägers, who found themselves under canister fire and our casualties mounted. The enemy cavalry reconnoitred in various places, but did not attempt anything of importance.

I ordered the icon of the Most Holy Mother of Smolensk to be evacuated to protect it from desecration. A special mess had an inspirational effect on the troops.

On 6 [18] August, the 1st Army was ordered to retreat. That same day, the 2nd Army fell back to Pneva Sloboda, where it was to cross the Dnieper and await the 1st Army. Prince Gorchakov's rearguard was left six verstas from the city with orders to remain in position until replaced by the troops of the 1st Army. Major General Tuchkov [Paul Alekseyevich] was dispatched with a detachment to replace him. A difficult road delayed this detachment and when it finally reached the main road at the 12th verst from Smolensk, Tuchkov did not find Gorchakov as he had marched to join the 2nd Army without informing us and had removed outposts which maintained communications with the 1st Army. Prince Bagration had ordered him to march at dawn to avoid exhausting troops during the night, but only after he had been replaced.[238] Gorchakov was not bothered by the enemy and in the orders of the day, the direction taken by the 1st Army should have been clear to him and he should have seen that had the enemy captured the crossroads towards which the 1st Army was marching, then Barclay's army had no way to escape since the enemy was also pursuing it from behind. Circumstances should have warned Gorchakov to remain in position, even if it went against Bagration's orders. Having reached the main road, Tuchkov wanted to move to Smolensk to protect this important crossroads, but he encountered

---

[238] Yermolov's note: Prince Gorchakov will accomplish any mission requiring courage and resolution with great success and is not afraid of danger; however, an equal measure of talent for command is also required alongside these praiseworthy traits.

and engaged the enemy only one verst away. So he awaited the main forces in this position.[239]

Convinced that Prince Gorchakov was waiting for Tuchkov's detachment, which now covered his movements, the commander-in-chief ordered part of his troops to march at 8:00 pm; the rest, which could be seen by the enemy, were instructed to move under cover of night. Adjutant General Baron Korf was to remove all outposts during the night and take the rearguard out of the city.

Thus, we abandoned Smolensk after bringing adversity upon it and turning it into the abode of horror and death. It was as though the city reproached us with the fire which consumed it but yet, to hide our shame, it also spread smoke and gloom to cover our retreat.

The destruction of Smolensk introduced me to a completely new feeling which a war outside your native land cannot inspire. I had never witnessed the destruction of my homeland or seen my cities burning. For the first time in my life, my ears heard the lament of my compatriots and eyes were opened to the horror of their terrible condition. I do consider mercy a gift from God, but now I could never allow it into my heart before revenge was satisfied.

And so 7 [19] August had begun, so memorable for its events. Believing that the troops which had left in the evening had covered some distance, we were surprised to encounter Lieutenant General Baggovut's entire corps. Dreadful local roads and an unusually dark night had complicated the movement of our artillery and the troops had hardly progressed. It was a few hours before dawn and soon it would be impossible to retreat without the enemy noticing. The French would certainly pursue so our position was becoming perilous.[240] I had been ordered to go and hurry the troops by all means possible. Having travelled three verstas and urging the artillery on, I found two squadrons of the Sumsk Hussars amid an infantry column and an officer told me that he had been attacked by the French and lost a few wounded some 300 paces from this place;

---

[239] Yermolov's note: Major General Tuchkov faced unforeseen circumstances and danger, but he showed firmness of character. The enemy had large forces nearby, while he was far from the army and could not expect reinforcements any time soon. Nevertheless, he decided to defend his position and thus kept the army free from trouble.

[240] Yermolov's note: The perils of our situation were obvious as Barclay gave me his instructions in French so that only a few could understand them.

he also informed me that Jägers from Prince Gorchakov's vanguard had abandoned this place without waiting for Tuchkov's arrival and the enemy had soon appeared in force. We had to press on as fast as possible so I reported my findings to the commander-in-chief and then continued onwards.

Dawn was breaking when the troops, having marched for some ten verstas, had to halt because Uvarov had ordered the 1st Cavalry Corps to gather forage and load hay on their horses. I sent him a very respectful note and, based on my rank, invited him to proceed, without infantry, to the crossroads. Soon, we heard the sound of artillery fire and I ordered the infantry to march as fast as possible. Yet, we could not find Tuchkov, the commander of the entire column, as he was calmly resting in a nearby village; I explained the situation to Konovnitsyn and, knowing about his determination and love of order, I was convinced that he would accomplish the task in the best possible way. If the artillery fire came from the rearguard, then we would suffer a few casualties and that was it; however, if it was Major General Tuchkov's detachment engaged in action, then the French might overwhelm it and capture the crossroads; as a result, we would be attacked on the march and forced to abandon our artillery by heading to the crossing over the Dnieper at Pneva Sloboda. Having explained my concerns to the commander-in-chief, I also dispatched my adjutant to him. To hurry the troops, I ordered the soldiers to sit on the cannon and move them at the trot. Barclay soon informed me that the French were pursuing the rearguard, had occupied the heights along the road and had isolated our troops so that part of our cavalry had to gallop through their musket fire to escape. So Barclay had to send Baggovut's corps against them, driving the enemy from its positions and opening a way through for the rearguard.

Meanwhile, Uvarov's cavalry corps had reached the main road followed by the 1st Grenadier and 3rd Infantry divisions. At the crossroads, were the Elisavetgrad Hussars from Major General Tuchkov's detachment which was assumed to have been six verstas further forwards where Gorchakov's vanguard should have been deployed. The commander of the hussars told me that Tuchkov's detachment was only one verst away and confirmed that Gorchakov had not waited for them and had marched off to the 2nd Army leaving only three Don Cossack regiments under Major General Karpov. I ordered the Cossacks to remain in position and they continued exchanging fire with the enemy. Taking advantage of the enemy's inactivity, Major General Tuchkov gained some distance. Following my request for reinforcements, Lieutenant General Tuchkov (I) ordered Colonel Zheltukhin to support Tuchkov with Arakcheyev's infantry, the Leib-Grenadier regiments and half a company of battery artillery. The rest of the troops bivouacked six verstas behind them.

By now, it was around 10:00 am and everything was calm towards Smolensk; however it was doubtful that this calm would continue for the rest of the day since the French could clearly gauge our intentions and they would gain enormously by frustrating us. Lieutenant General Count Osterman's corps was still on the march and his artillery was stretched out along the road; the rearguard was far behind and Baggovut's corps was with it, protecting us from the French. So, we had to hang on until these forces rejoined. Our right flank extended to a hill, the defence of which was crucial since it covered the road junction, and made it easier to reinforce various units in our battle formation. Our centre was marshy and covered with thick undergrowth. A strip of thick forest covered our left flank, with an open field, good for cavalry, on its edge running down to a narrow stream. It was necessary for us to occupy this field and position artillery in this direction to frustrate enemy batteries which might fire on the roads leading to our position. Major General Tuchkov reported that enemy forces were increasing and delivered two captured Württemberg hussars, who told us that the enemy cavalry was only waiting for infantry before attacking. Karpov soon informed us that his outposts had spotted the French army crossing over pontoons to the right bank of the Dnieper. I reported this intelligence to the commander-in-chief and received the order to give battle while he would arrive after taking care of the rearguard.

All the details of this battle are described in the report cited below. When I later presented it to Barclay, I was ordered to send it on to Field Marshal Prince Kutuzov.[241] Despite the grave danger, our troops completed this important battle with honour. Recalling this action provokes a pleasant feeling of satisfaction within me

---

[241] Yermolov's note: Preparing to leave the army, Barclay could not devote his time to it and ordered me to report directly to Kutuzov, which I did.

because I had been shown such a high level of confidence and I was credited for much of this success.

Report on the Battle of 7[19] August at Zabolotie or Valutino

After the three-day defence of Smolensk, the army was ordered to retreat. The 2nd Army protected the crossing over the Dnieper, menaced by large enemy forces; its vanguard was some 6 verstas [4 miles] from Smolensk on the Moscow road. The 1st Army proceeded in two columns: the first column under General of Infantry Dokhturov, comprising the 5th and 6th corps, and General of Cavalry Platov's rearguard, marched on safe roads free from the enemy. The 2nd, 3rd and

4th corps and Adjutant General Baron Korf's rearguard had to make a flanking march to reach the main Moscow road and they moved along difficult roads, which delayed their movement. During this march, the vanguard of the 2nd Army withdrew prematurely and Major General Tuchkov (III)'s detachment of the 20th and 21st Jäger, the Revel Infantry and the Elisavetgrad Hussar regiments encountered the enemy on the eleventh verst [7 miles] from the city.

Superior enemy forces attacked Baron Korf's rearguard near Smolensk. Your Excellency [Barclay] witnessed this resolute action and had to commit the 2nd Corps of Baggovut, allowing the other corps to continue their march. Your Excellency ordered me to accelerate their movement. Circumstances required us to occupy the crossroads and we had to do everything possible for this. The crossroads was close to Smolensk and Major General Tuchkov (III)'s detachment was too weak to withstand superior enemy forces. On Your Excellency's behalf, I ordered the 1st Cavalry Corps of Adjutant General Uvarov to hurry towards the junction, which it did without delay. The 3rd Corps of Lieutenant General Tuchkov was eager to engage the enemy and followed behind the cavalry. I ordered Major General Passek to move his artillery at a trot. The 4th Corps of Lieutenant General Count Osterman-Tolstoy arrived shortly afterwards. I found Major General Tuchkov (III)'s detachment two verstas from the crossroads and ordered part of its infantry to move forward, reinforced by Colonel Zheltukhin's brigade of the Leib-Grenadiers and Count Arakcheyev's regiments and six battery guns. Our outposts were already engaged, but the enemy was not numerous. The 3rd and 4th corps withdrew six verstas to designated positions.

By 2:00 pm our outposts were reporting that fighting had intensified and two deserters told us that an enemy force of 12 infantry and cavalry regiments was preparing to attack as soon as they received reinforcements from the left bank of the Dnieper. The commander of the Don Cossack outposts, Major General Karpov, soon reported that the enemy was crossing the river in large numbers. I informed Lieutenant General Tuchkov about this and ordered the 3rd Corps to hasten to the battlefield. Our outposts withdrew before superior enemy forces but 4th Corps was also expected to arrive by 5:00 pm. I reported to Your Excellency and you instructed me to deploy the troops for battle whilst waiting for you and the rearguard. The battle soon began in earnest. The enemy directed its attacks down the main road, but advantageous terrain and the fact that the enemy artillery had not arrived yet allowed us to retain our position. The enemy increased its tirailleurs against Major General Tuchkov (III)'s left, but, on Tuchkov's orders, the 20th Jägers under Major General Prince Shakhovskii contained the enemy and gained time for the Chernigov, Murmsk and Selenginsk regiments of the 3rd Division to arrive and take up their positions.

The enemy's artillery soon arrived and artillery fire on both sides greatly increased. Just then Your Excellency arrived. The enemy cavalry also appeared and halted on their right flank like a dark cloud. We needed to shift our cavalry, except for the 1st Corps, to our left. The enemy had superior forces and the advantage of better terrain. Our cavalry and artillery had a marshy stream behind them, which was difficult to cross. However, Major General Prince Gurieli's brigade quickly drove the enemy infantry from the forest and inhibited their progress. In addition, the Pernov Regiment under Major General Choglokov, supported our cavalry by falling on the enemy. Twenty-four guns then made our cavalry invincible. Even so, it seemed as though a single cavalry attack would annihilate our left wing, but, because of the gallantry of our troops, each French attack was driven back with heavy casualties much to the shame of the French. I ordered Adjutant General Count Orlov-Denisov to take over the command the cavalry and Cossacks. Both sides attacked for a prolonged period of time.

Meanwhile, the 17th Division of Lieutenant General Olsufiev arrived and the exhausted regiments of Adjutant General Baron Korf's rearguard went to reinforce our right, which was some distance from the enemy's attacks. The enemy batteries were increased in the centre, but the Chernigov, Murmsk and Selenginsk regiments of the 3rd Division fearlessly held their ground and repulsed the enemy who fled in disorder to the main road and disorganized the French troops deployed there. At this moment, Flügel Adjutant Colonel Kikin, serving as duty general, my adjutant Lieutenant Grabbe of the Life Guard Horse Artillery and General Milioradovich's adjutant, Staff Rotmistr Dejunker, who was attached to me, rallied our troops, led a bayonet attack and *quickly cleared the road, restoring communications between our various units. Failing in its designs, the enemy directed its last attack against our right. Our battery of four guns was destroyed and, not trusting the exhausted regiments of the*

17th Division to restore order, I personally led the Leib-Grenadiers against an enemy battery, as Your Excellency witnessed yourself. Acting with competence and courage, Colonel Zheltukhin overthrew everything in his path. I had already reached the battery, when devastating canister fire routed my gallant regiment. However, the enemy attacks ceased. My regiment returned to its position and a fierce exchange of musket fire began. The Ekaterinoslav Grenadiers arrived to reinforce my troops and the regiments of the 17th Division were now mostly deployed as tirailleurs. Major General Tuchkov (III) overwhelmed a strong enemy column but, carried away by this success, he was captured. Despite intense enemy fire, Lieutenant General Konovnitsyn drove the enemy back on the right and retained the field. He then established his outposts, withdrew the artillery and troops in complete order and we retreated to Dorogobouzh, joining the 2nd Army.

I have the honour to present to Your Excellency a list of the troops who distinguished themselves and seek to prove Your Excellency's confidence in me with this truthful report.

There were moments in this battle when it was impossible to foresee a successful outcome. I wrote a message to the grand duke saying it was essential to hurry to cross the Dnieper so that our fighting troops faced no impediment as the enemy were sure to pursue us energetically.

The rearguard commander, Baron Korf, was a long way from the main road, and he noticed that the enemy was trying to pin him down with skirmishing, hoping that our troops would be driven from the crossroads and that the rearguard would thus be isolated. The enemy's scheme was frustrated and the rearguard successfully joined the army.

On 8 [20] August, Adjutant General Count Stroganov took over a rearguard composed of the 1st Cavalry Corps and the Pavlov, St Petersburg and Tavrida Grenadier regiments with sufficient artillery. Considering the forces involved in the battle and its short duration, the enemy were not thought to be in strength but some captured French officers claimed otherwise. So, the enemy limited its actions to simply observing our position. I remained with the rearguard for most of the day, concerned about its weak composition and doubtful of its commander's abilities. Barclay ordered reinforcements to be close at hand.

I left the retreating rearguard and, having returned to the army late in the day, I was surprised to see it still crossing the Dnieper. This was because General Dokhturov had arrived late and crowded the crossing. One may consider it a stroke of luck that the French had not followed us because we would not have been able to oppose them here and would have suffered considerable casualties.

On the 9 [21] August, the entire 1st Army concentrated, marching in to Usvyatie. The day before, the 2nd Army had bivouacked near Dorogobouzh. Several Jäger regiments and cavalry were assigned to the rearguard now under Major General Baron Rosen, who was subordinated to Platov, and ordered to remain at the crossing to allow the stragglers to rejoin. Strong outposts were to move up the Dnieper and make sure that the enemy did not trouble the transports dispatched via Dukhovshina to Dorogobouzh. All the other transports and wounded were moved from Dukhovshina to Vyazma and were already safe.

On 10 [22] August, the armies had a rest. The rearguard was far behind. The commander-in-chief, the grand duke and Prince Bagration, accompanied by the corps commander and many other generals, went to examine a defensive position selected by Colonel Toll. The commander-in-chief noted that there was a hill to the right which could be used to threaten our lines, which we should note. His proposal of protecting this hill with a redoubt was countered by turning his attention to a small lake between the hill and our centre which might prevent the redoubt from being reinforced or supported by our batteries. If we constructed a large fortification, its garrison would simply witness the battle from afar. If driven back, these troops would be isolated. Colonel Toll told Barclay that it would be impossible to find a better position and that he did not understand what was required of him, implying that he knew the art of war quite well. Barclay listened to this tirade with incredible patience, but Bagration reminded Toll that responding to the commander-in-chief, especially in the presence of the czar's brother, with such impudence was intolerable and that Barclay, instead of being lenient, should have him reduced in ranks and given soldiers' belts to carry. He, as a mere pup and should remember that others were as familiar with military affairs as he was.[242] The left flank of this position was also defective and so the troops bivouacked near Dorogobouzh. Colonel Toll was ordered to deploy them near the town the next day. The infantry of the rearguard had meantime occupied Usvyatie. Its outposts were nearby, already pressed by the enemy. Adjutant General Vasilchikov's detachment, deployed to the left of the earlier position, engaged the enemy, and Lieutenant General Rayevskii's corps was committed to support him. The action, however, degenerated into a skirmish and the enemy made no further attempts. Ataman Platov's rearguard remained at Usvyatie and Vasilchikov remained on the left.

Ataman Platov told me that during the interrogation of a captured Polish NCO, serving as aide-de-camp to a colonel, he confessed that he had seen one of our officers with large silver epaulettes visiting the Polish camp at Smolensk, describing our forces to the colonel and making critical statements about our general. So General Platov and I began talking about the untrustworthy mob that jammed the headquarters and Flügel Adjutant Colonel Wolzogen's name came up in conversation. This officer enjoyed the commander-in-chief's particular attachment. Being in a boisterous mood, Platov said, 'This is what we should do, brother. You suggest sending him on reconnaissance and pass him to me, leave it to me to separate these Germans [Wolzogen and Barclay]. I will assign him special guides, who will show him the French so that he never sees them again.'[243] Platov then named a few others who he believed also deserved such treatment. He told me, 'It would be very nice indeed if Bagration sent Mr Jamber, who serves under St Priest and always interferes in command decisions.' I laughed but told him there are people who might be offended by such jokes and that these philanthropists often assume the disguise of lovers of humanity and compassion in order to portray themselves as defenders of human rights.

Both armies were located near Dorogobouzh. Lieutenant General Baggovut's corps replaced a detachment of the 2nd Army on the right bank of the Dnieper, while Colonel Creitz's dragoon regiment and Cossacks took over from Major General Count

---

[242] According to Captain Puschin, 'everybody was silent. Barclay de Tolly remained taciturn… while Toll began to cry and tears ran down on his face.'
[243] Platov usually referred to Wolzogen as wohl-gezogen, a play on words meaning well-bread.

Sievers' cavalry. The armies occupied a bottleneck and faced away from the enemy. The commander-in-chief made a note of Toll's severe mistake. There was no room to deploy the troops. Toll was reprimanded and others were ordered to correct his mistakes. However, there were no unfortunate consequences and we decided not to await the enemy.[244] Colonel Toll, with precise knowledge of his art, would not have committed this mistake if he had not been distraught by Bagration's harsh remarks on his inappropriate response to the commander-in-chief. Toll's excessive pride was further injured by the presence of so many witnesses.

The 1st Army remained in position until evening; the 2nd Army marched at once and fanned out along the left bank of the Osma to cover the road leading to Yelna and prevent the enemy from using it. Bagration rashly ordered his rearguard to follow the army. Its commander, Adjutant General Vasilchikov, withdrew leaving a small cavalry detachment under Major General Panchulidzev (of the Chernigov Dragoons) to maintain communications with the main rearguard of Ataman Platov and to conceal our retreat. However, Panchulidzev withdrew without informing Platov. The enemy immediately seized a position on our rearguard's flank and cavalry observed our movements. The enemy soon confused their roads, inadvertently got ahead of Panchulidzev and found itself between him and our army. The encounter was sudden so Panchulidzev and the French cavalry let each other pass without firing a single shot.

During our stay at Dorogobouzh, the French outfoxed our rearguard and, having advanced on the Old Smolensk road, they took up positions three verstas from the town on our left. Trusting its security to the rearguard, the army was ignorant of the proximity of the enemy, but the French made no attempts against our combined forces. This incident may be used as a lesson that if there are several rearguards located close to each other, they should be placed under one commander to maintain contact and coordinate actions. There are only incidents when units are placed under local commanders and there is no central command. Learning from its own experience, the high command modified its instructions.

---

[244] Yermolov later recalled, 'Bagration insisted on punishing Toll who had deployed the army with its rear facing the French. Bagration requested a reduction in ranks for this unjustifiable blunder.'

During our retreat from Dorogobouzh, Platov's rearguard had an intense encounter with the enemy. Our infantry, composed of Jägers, earned the right of respect from the French and taught them another lesson in prudence. After numerous vain attempts and heavy casualties, the enemy stopped attacking. The rearguard remained in position and retreated only once the army had covered some distance. Finally, the rearguard marched for two verstas through Dorogobouzh, whilst the army reached Semlevo. It was decided to give the exhausted soldiers two days of rest so they could repair their footwear. In addition, we wanted to allow the local inhabitants, evacuating the nearby towns and villages and delaying the army with their wagons, to get as far ahead as possible. On the first rest day, Platov sent a message asking that a camp for the rearguard be prepared as the enemy were attacking him vigorously. He would arrive at Semlev at midnight. The retreat was so hasty because the rearguard's infantry were not committed and a single body of 200 Cossacks had to contain the enemy alone. The environs were covered with woods and a few tirailleurs were enough to disperse the Cossacks and clear the enemy's way.

The 1st Army was ordered to quit Semlevo and follow the 2nd Army moving on the left. It had been noted that Platov was being careless and Bagration told me that during the retreat from Lithuania he learned Platov wanted to become a count and so urged Platov to be more enterprising and active.[245] It seemed to me that the cause of Platov's inactivity lay in his ignorance in commanding regular troops. To be a forceful and courageous commander of Cossacks does not mean you can be a good general as it calls for different skills. Platov, being the clever and shrewd man that he was, could easily comprehend that the war of 1812 was different in its character from the other wars in which he had demonstrated his worth.

We received news from General of Infantry Miloradovich that he was hurrying to join us with 16,000 troops, mostly infantry that he had organized in Kaluga. Ordered to abandon their knapsacks and using wagons, the infantry covered no less than 40 verstas [26

---

[245] Yermolov's note: Bagration turned Platov's attention to one of the Don Cossack host generals (Denisov), who had the title of count. I did the same. After that, Platov was constantly asking me about who received what awards and he was unable to conceal his impatient expectation.

miles] per day. We greatly needed these troops as the cavalry especially had suffered losses in the constant rearguard fighting.

Platov was ordered to delay the enemy for as long as possible and not to keep his infantry idle. Lieutenant General Baggovut, marching with his corps to the right of the army, was instructed to watch the large enemy forces following him; his rearguard was to maintain communications with Platov's outposts and with Major General Krasnov's Don Cossacks, which were also being pursued by enemy forces from Dukhovshina. These regiments were to leave strong outposts at Pokrov, a crossroads leading from Dorogobouzh to Sichevka and from Vyazma to Belyi.

A detachment of two dragoon regiments, two grenadier battalions and four horse artillery guns was placed under Major General Shevich, and he was ordered to pass through Vyazma, proceed down the road to Dukhovshina and reinforce Major General Krasnov in order to allow the wagons and heavy transports of the 1st Army to move through Vyazma, where even a small enemy detachment could wreak havoc.

Adjutant General Baron Winzegorode's detachment, comprised of light troops, was ordered to operate on the enemy's flank and harass its rear. Based between Dukhovshina and Belyi, he was to retreat to Sichevka if the enemy forces increased and maintain contact through Major General Krasnov. Lieutenant General of Engineers Trousson and both quartermaster generals were sent to Vyazma to find and fortify a position for the army. In general, everything pointed to something significant. The chief of the artillery was ordered to have the reserve parks close at hand.

In my report to the commander-in-chief, I also had attached Colonel Toll's report asking to be relieved of his duties as quartermaster general because he felt he was not competent enough. I explained that he was one of my subordinates and I knew his hard work, dedication and endeavour and that he demonstrated experience and prudence in battle. So, no he continued to serve in this capacity. However, the commander-in-chief's leniency did not last long since Toll was soon ordered to leave the army and travel to Moscow, where he remained without position.

I made arrangements to have the wounded evacuated from Vyzma. On the insistence of the Head of the Medical Inspectorate [Sir James] Wylie, I also arranged the evacuation of the wounded from the 2nd Army to prevent any confusion on the road. The sight of thousands of wounded would have further dismayed a Moscow already petrified.

Platov sent us a captured French colonel who had been dispatched by the Viceroy of Italy to the King of Naples to drive our rearguard from Semlevo. Our infantry resolutely defended it and the French suffered heavy casualties which forced them to leave the village in our hands. Some credit for this belongs to Major General Baron Rosen, who received support from Ataman Platov. Lieutenant General of Engineers Trousson did not find a favourable positions which might protect Vyazma. The enemy was more numerous, could turn our flank and threaten our line of retreat to Gzhatsk. The commander-in-chief spent a day in Vyazma and then moved to Fedorovskoe some 10 verstas [7 miles] from the town.

Most of the wounded were evacuated, but some 1,600 men still remained. Thanks to Duty General Kikin's efforts with help from Commandant of the Headquarters, Stavrakov, none of these were left behind. We even managed to rescue 100,000 arshins [71,000 metres][246] of canvas which one merchant offered to donate to the hospital and 70 puds [1,141 kg][247] of various medicines from the local apothecary. The enemy was approaching and the merchant needed the sound of the French guns to inspire such generosity towards the defenders of the motherland. The commander-in-chief stayed in the beautiful house of a wealthy merchant who had a collection of wine in his cellar worth more than 20,000 rubles. It was impossible to get even a single bottle from him for any price. The merchant even refused to disclose where the wine was to be buried. However, astute French soldiers later found his treasure to the chagrin of this thrifty merchant and the local landowners.

The position at Fedorovskoe had a few advantages and some fortifications had already been constructed here. The lack of drinking water was its major deficiency. A lake on the left wing of the army was marshy and hardly accessible. Colonel Manfredi, of the army communications service, built a dam but it was no use. So the army continued its retreat.

---

[246] Arshin was an old Russian measurement of length equal to 28 inches or 71 cm.

[247] Pud was an old Russian measurement of weight equal to 16 kg or 36 pounds.

Another favourable position was found near Czarevo-Znaimische and the commander-in-chief decided to give battle here. Engineer works began immediately and the army deployed. Open ground prevented the enemy from concealing its movements. We controlled the nearby heights which helped our artillery and made it difficult for the enemy to approach. The terrain was also favourable for an organized retreat.

After so many preparations for battle, the army refused to believe that a decisive one would ever be fought, although it eagerly awaited combat. However, our halt and the accelerated work on fortifications indicated that the commander-in-chief's intention was firm and everyone was hopeful that this would finally end the retreat.

We received news about General of Infantry Prince Kutuzov's appointment as supreme commander of the armies and his impending arrival from St Petersburg. Prince Kutuzov himself arrived at Czarevo-Znaimische immediately after this news [on 29 August] and assumed the command of the 1st and 2nd Western Armies. Though the unified command could not put an end to the disagreement between the army commanders, it was now restricted. His arrival revived hope in the hearts of every subordinate for an end to retreat and for better discipline and success. It is unfair to blame Barclay de Tolly for the retreat. At Smolensk, it was perfectly clear that the French superiority and precise intelligence they received made it a necessity.

On his way to the army, Prince Kutuzov had ordered the Moscow militia to join us. Barclay, rightly discontent with Platov's disorganized command of the rearguard, had dismissed him and allowed him to leave the army for Moscow, where Platov remained until Prince Kutuzov ordered him to return and resume command of the Don Cossacks. The rearguard was placed under Lieutenant General Konovnitsyn, who retreated from Vyazma contesting every inch of ground. Prince Kutuzov's first order was to retreat to Gzhatsk. He justified it with the need to strengthen the armies with the approaching reinforcements.

The rearguard had several fierce engagements which resulted in heavy casualties on both sides, but Lieutenant General Konovnitsyn gained more breathing space for the army than Ataman Platov had. At Gzhatsk, 16,000 men under General Miloradovich arrived and were assigned to the regiments.

CHAPTER VI
THE PATRIOTIC WAR
SEPTEMBER – NOVEMBER 1812

Prince Kutuzov intended to give battle near to the Kolotsk monastery.[248]

Fortifications were constructed there but the position was soon abandoned as it had just as many flaws as advantages. The right was anchored on some heights which dominated the surrounding area but a failure to hold them would have complicated our retreat since a narrow valley lay behind them. Our rearguard was left there and another position was selected some 12 verstas further back near Borodino on the Moscow River.

The importance of this place makes a description essential. The Kolocha flowed within its steep banks, impassable in some places, covering our right wing. This flank was covered by forests and extensive earthworks were made; fortifications protecting the flank and rear of the flank were also constructed in a vast field adjacent to the woods. This field, convenient for cavalry, exposed any enemy movement. Not far from Borodino, along the main road, on the heights near the settlement of Gorki, a battery was positioned; the bottom of the hill was protected by entrenchments and infantry. The village of Borodino, occupied by our advance troops, was

---

[248] Yermolov's note: It is doubtful that Barclay de Tolly was unaware of Prince Kutuzov's appointment. The speed of the works on the occupied positions certainly revealed his intention to give battle before Kutuzov's arrival. In 1805, Kutuzov, with his small army dispatched to support Austria, accomplished the celebrated retreat from Bavaria amidst superior enemy forces trying to surround him. He commanded at Austerlitz – a defeat never to be erased from the memory of a Russian – and although he disagreed with the decision to attack, he still suffered disgrace at the will of a sovereign present with the army. Kutuzov then served as the military governor in Lithuania. He later commanded the Russian army against the Ottomans, whom he decisively defeated and forced to the peace table. Recalled back to the capital, Kutuzov was instructed to raise the St Petersburg militia (not a flattering appointment). His appointment as the commander of our armies facing a superior and dangerous enemy invading Russia, was the result of a common desire which the sovereign had the magnanimity not to oppose.

connected to our position by the bridge over the Kolocha. At the centre of our position, in front of our lines, stood some more heights, which dominated the surrounding area in all directions, and was occupied by a strong battery from the 1st Army. This was the extreme left flank of the 1st Army. There was an open field limited by a deep, wide valley, which stretched out for the range of canister before the battery. On the far side of that valley, a thick forest extended into the valley. A strongly constructed redoubt defended some low heights on the left of the battery.[249]

The extreme left wing of the 2nd Army was adjacent to an extensive and thick forest, separated from the redoubt by a narrow valley, the only place on this wing convenient for cavalry action. A deep hollow, which hindered communications, stretched behind the troops. The old postal road to Mozhaisk wound through the forest for a mile from the left wing, snaking around our positions. After checking the deployment of the troops, Prince Kutuzov ordered the left to move back so that the deep hollow lay before it; he also ordered the flank to be strengthened with several fleches. Following this adjustment, the redoubt at Shevardino was out of our artillery range and so was rendered completely useless. It should have been abandoned. The straight line formed by the army was now bent at its very centre.

On 24 August, the French struck the rearguard which fought for a long time against superior enemy forces but had to return to our position a little earlier than expected. On the left, a part of the rearguard, comprising of some troops from the 2nd Army, withdrew so quickly and unexpectedly that the pursuing enemy appeared on the heights before Kutuzov's orders to change position had come into effect. Thus, we redeployed in front of the enemy, and, notwithstanding the speed in which we did so, the enemy was presented with a chance to attack. An otherwise useless redoubt now had to be defended in order to give the troops time to adjust to their positions, since the enemy could try to impede and even to throw our entire army into confusion. The redoubt at Shevardino should then have been abandoned immediately after the troops took up their new positions. However, Major General Neverovskii, the commander of the 27th Division, did not dare move without

---

[249] Yermolov's note: Near the village of Shevardino.

orders, while the commander on the ground, Prince Gorchakov, failed to perceive the benefits of abandoning the redoubt.

So, the enemy attacks on the redoubt and forest continued while we fought back. Soon, this small action escalated into a running battle that forced us to commit a large part of the 2nd Army. The fighting continued until late in the night. The French were determined to capture this redoubt and we lost and recovered it with our bayonets on several occasions. Enemy guns were captured more than once but a galling fire from the French batteries forced us to relinquish them. The attack of the cuirassiers of the 2nd Division on the enemy batteries met with complete success and several guns were captured; however, finding itself between the forest and the heights occupied by the enemy in force, the troops suffered considerable casualties. Our infantry, desperately defending the redoubt, was finally forced to abandon it with a few guns and the combat closed.

On 25 August, the armies spent the day idly observing each other. The redoubt by Shevardino had fallen so our left flank lay exposed with all its flaws and its incomplete fortifications visible[250] and there could be no doubt that it would be the point selected for the enemy's attack. General Bennigsen had already remarked that substantial enemy forces were massing in this direction, although, because of their superiority, the French did seem to be everywhere. Serving as the chief of staff on the armies under Prince Kutuzov's command, Bennigsen offered to take action to reduce the length of our lines; he suggested leaving several Jäger regiments in the forest and the *abatis* on the right and moving two infantry corps, pointlessly deployed nearby, towards the centre in order to support the 2nd Army. His proposal was not accepted.

The enemy deployed the Italian army in some defensive positions on its left; trenches and batteries were constructed facing the open ground convenient for massive cavalry attacks.

Early in the morning, Prince Kutuzov inspected the army. However, his large carriage could not pass everywhere. So, a few generals and a small suite accompanied him; I rode near the carriage

---

[250] Yermolov's note: The engineers did not have enough tools and so all fortifications were constructed using the meager resources of the commanders on the ground. The minister of war demanded more tools from Moscow but they were delivered only on the day of the battle.

wheel ready to receive his orders. General Bennigsen[251] stopped him near the hill, which dominated the surrounding area, where the extreme right flank of the 2nd Army were to occupy a fortification of 12 battery and six light guns that had just been recently started. An infantry division from General Rayevskii's corps[252] defended it. General Bennigsen called this hill the key to our position, explaining the importance of committing all available resources to its protection since its loss would lead to disastrous consequences for us. Prince Kutuzov limited his reaction to not changing the deployment of the 1st Army and ordering its left flank to curve far back to avoid any sudden attacks from enemy hidden in the forest and prevent any possibility of being outflanked. At the same time, the retraction of the line, which now formed an angle, gave the enemy the advantage of making longitudinal ricochet shots. Giving no other orders, Prince Kutuzov returned to his quarters.

26 August. This much-desired day had finally arrived! The sun, hidden in the mist, maintained the deception of calm until 6:00 am. Its first rays then illuminated the place where the Russians were ready to accept this unequal battle with complete devotion.

Here, oh majestic Moscow, your die will be cast. A few more hours, and if the firm resolve of the Russians fails to avert the dangers threatening you, ruins will mark the place where you once haughtily rose up and prospered.

Dispositions of the 1st and 2nd Armies

Three Jäger regiments, were positioned in the forest, abatis and fortifications on the extreme right. They were to take no direct part in the battle but lost several men because of stray shots fired from distant batteries. The following infantry corps were deployed between these Jägers and the centre: Lieutenant General Baggovut's 2nd Corps, Lieutenant General Count Osterman-Tolstoy's 4th Corps and General of Infantry Dokhturov's 6th Corps, which marked the end of the 1st Army's line. Next were the troops of the

---

[251] Yermolov's note: He was the commander-in-chief against Napoleon in 1806 and 1807 before the conclusion of the peace at Tilsit. Among our contemporary commanders, he was indisputably the most experienced and had a sound theoretical grasp of the military arts.

[252] Yermolov's note: Therefore this fortification was called the Rayevskii battery or sometimes the Rayevskii lunette.

2nd Army: the 7th Corps of Lieutenant General Rayevskii, the 8th Corps of Lieutenant General Borozdin and, on the extreme left, the 2nd Combined Grenadier Division of Major General Count Vorontsov and the 27th Infantry Division of Major General Neverovskii, both under overall command of Lieutenant General Prince Gorchakov (II).

The following troops were placed in the joint reserve: the entire cavalry, except for some parts assigned to the infantry corps and the Guard cavalry; the

3rd Infantry Corps of Lieutenant General Tuchkov (I); the 2nd Grenadier Division of Prince Karl Mecklenburg; the infantry (under Lieutenant General Lavrov) of the 5th Guard Corps of Grand Duke Constantine Pavlovich;[253] the Guard Reserve Cavalry Corps of Lieutenant General Uvarov and the Don Cossacks under Ataman Platov, were posted on the right of the 1st Army. The Moscow militia, some 25,000 men armed with pikes, had arrived two days ago, and was assigned to various corps to attend to the wounded to avoid diverting troops from the front.[254]

Around 6:00 am, a movement was observed, in the enemy forces opposite our right and soon an attack was launched against Borodino. A battalion of Guard Jägers, with outposts in front of the village, was routed and, in less than half an hour, the entire regiment was driven back in confusion towards the bridge over the Kolocha. Clouds of enemy tirailleurs then fanned out along the left bank of the river. The 1st Jäger Regiment, deployed by the bridge, swiftly counterattacked, repulsed the enemy and rescued the Guard Jägers, who were immediately sent back to their division.[255] Isolated from the rest of our forces, the

---

[253] Yermolov's note: The minister of war had sent the grand duke to the czar bearing dispatches. Considering their relationship, there was no doubt that the minister did not want him in the army.

[254] Yermolov's note: To organize the evacuation of the wounded, entire postal stations with carriages, coaches and horses were removed from those provinces occupied by the enemy. No less than 600 troikas [a carriage drawn by three horses] were gathered at headquarters.

[255] Yermolov's note: There was such carelessness in the outposts of this battalion that many soldiers were asleep, having taken off their uniforms. Some other battalions were equally negligent, but only a few were as disorganized. This courageous unit had never been reproached until now.

1st Jäger Regiment was now in a dangerous situation and its commander …[256] was ordered to abandon Borodino, withdraw across the river burning the bridge behind him. A light artillery company, deployed nearby, drove the enemy tirailleurs back and the action in this direction was thus limited to an exchange of fire. It was evident that nothing of import could be expected here.

Suddenly musket and artillery fire opened up on our left. Masses of enemy troops attacked, and despite our resistance, they maintained their advance, moving forwards steadily, and capturing our earthworks in front of Semeyonovskoe. However, the French could not hold them for long and they had to retreat with staggering losses. Infuriated by this failure, the enemy rallied, were reinforced and soon resumed their assaults. As they attacked, the French were mown down by the devastating fire of our batteries and infantry, yet they marched forwards bravely.[257]

The divisions of Count Vorontsov and Neverovskii met them with the bayonets and the Russian soldier's favourite weapon helped us hold out. Batteries constantly changed hands: our losses exceeded all expectations; Count Vorontsov was wounded, Colonel Kantakuzin, the commander of the Combined Grenadier Brigade, was killed while driving the enemy out of one of the captured earthworks; Lieutenant General Prince Gorchakov (II), in command on the extreme left of the army, was also wounded.[258]

Prince Bagration inspired our troops by his very presence but he was suddenly hit[259] and, to avoid any harmful effect on the morale of our troops, who idolized him, he concealed the agonizing pain. However, weakened by loss of blood, he collapsed and fell from his from horse in front of everyone. The rumour of his death instantly passed down the ranks and it became impossible to maintain order among the troops. No one worried about imminent

---

[256] Yermolov's note: Colonel Karpenko was in command but his intellectual abilities were limited to the single order, 'Forward!'

[257] The 57th Line particularly distinguished itself. Living up to its nickname Le Terrible, it advanced steadily with muskets levelled, holding its fire, while the Russians mowed them down. Impressed by the courage of these soldiers, Prince Bagration clapped his hands several times and cried 'Bravo, bravo!'.

[258] Andreev of the 27th Infantry Division recalled, 'Our division was virtually annihilated…. When the remaining troops were rallied, only 700 men gathered… Just 40 men survived from my entire regiment….'.

[259] Bagration was injured by a shell splinter that smashed his shinbone.

danger, no one was concerned about personal safety: one feeling seized everyone – desperation![260] Around noon, the 2nd Army was in such confusion that parts of it had to be moved to the rear to rally.

Colonel Prince Kudashev reached Prince Kutuzov with a report, which described in detail the state of the 2nd Army. Kutuzov ordered Osterman's corps to hasten to join Baggovut's corps sent forwards only a short time before. In addition, units of the Guard Infantry Division were dispatched. General of Infantry Dokhturov was given the command of the 2nd Army and all the troops fighting on the left. I was ordered to proceed to the 2nd Army and provide its artillery with ammunition, which was running low. I was also entrusted to report back to Kutuzov any suggested actions I might consider useful in the circumstances.

I was aware that the chief of staff of the 2nd Army, Count St Priest, had been wounded and knowing only some of the officers who had replaced injured commanders, I expected to encounter difficulties. In order to avoid being ineffective, I therefore requested that Count Kutaisov, the commander of the artillery of the 1st Army, assign three horse artillery companies under Colonel Nikitin, known for his exceptional gallantry, to me. The companies quickly arrived from the reserve and Nikitin was soon at my side awaiting orders.

Meanwhile, General Tuchkov, seeing complete disorder in the 2nd Army, which had lost its commander-in-chief and many subordinate commanders, realized that the remnants[261] would not be able to maintain an effective resistance and ordered his 3rd Corps to immediately join the combat; he placed the 1st Grenadier Division alongside the 2nd Army's left on the old postal road to Mozhaisk, where the Polish troops under Prince Poniatowski had already appeared around Utitsa. A cannonade began against our weak battery deployed on the barrow but the enemy's advance was soon halted. It would have been very dangerous for us to allow the French to establish a presence in this location. General Tuchkov (I)

---

[260] Barclay later noted, that after Bagration's injury, 'The 2nd Army was in a state of utter confusion.'

[261] Yermolov's note: If the 2nd and 4th Corps had been deployed closer to the 2nd Army, as Bennigsen suggested, then the troops of the 2nd Army would not have been alone against repeated enemy attacks. Yet, Kutuzov's dispositions were not farsighted, as would become apparent.

personally led the courageous grenadiers of the 1st Division forward under canister, held the place and awaited reinforcements; however, a mortal wound prevented him from attempting any other feats. Near Utitsa, the 3rd Infantry Division routed enemy tirailleurs and battled against those enemy forces supporting them. The gallantry of General Konovnitsyn shone in all its splendour. The 3rd Infantry Corps was placed under his command. General Baggovut with his 2nd Corps moved on to the old Mozhaisk road.

When I was dispatched to the 2nd Army, Count Kutaisov was eager to join me. I genially pleaded with him to return to his command and reminded him of Kutuzov's earlier reproach that he was never around when he was needed.[262]

However, Kutaisov did not accept my advice and stayed with me. Approaching the 2nd Army, I noticed its right wing on the heights, where General Rayevskii's corps was located. It was shrouded in thick smoke and the troops protecting the heights were in disorder. Many of us knew and, it indeed seemed obvious, that the loss of this vital point, as Bennigsen described it, would result in the most disastrous consequences for us. Therefore, I immediately rushed to this place. A minute lost could have been fatal so I ordered the 3rd Battalion of Major Demidov from the Ufa Infantry of 7th Corps to follow me in open order, hoping to halt the fleeing troops.

Our feeble fortification and handful of troops had long withstood the concentrated fire of superior enemy forces but there was not a single caisson for any of its 18 guns and their weak fire facilitated the French advance. Due to the limited space inside the fortification, only a small number of infantry could be deployed there at any one time and any troops outside the redoubt were mown down by canister and scattered. There were insufficient means to defend this point despite all the efforts of the fearless Major General Paskevich, who commanded that division. General Rayevskii also reconnoitred the position but he was not present during the attack.

Approaching a small valley that separated us from the enemy-occupied heights, I found the 11th, 19th and 40th Jägers acting as

---

[262] Yermolov's note: Count Kutaisov observed the actions of our batteries, directing them and appearing at those places where a commander's presence was most necessary.

reserves. Despite the steep slope, I ordered them and the 3rd Battalion of the Ufa Regiment to attack with the bayonet, the Russian soldier's favourite weapon. The combat was fierce and terrible but continued for no more than half an hour: we faced tenacious resistance, but seized the heights, recaptured the guns and not a single musket shot could be heard.

The gallant General of Brigade Bonammy, who was so badly injured that one may say he was brought down on the points of our bayonets, was spared;[263] but no other prisoners were taken, and only a few from the French brigade escaped.[264] The French general was very grateful for the respect shown to him. Casualties on our side were heavy and disproportionate to the number of battalions involved.[265] The three horse artillery companies of Colonel Nikitin, which had been assigned to me, greatly contributed to our success. Deployed on the left side of the elevation, they exposed themselves to the fire of enemy batteries of a much higher calibre.

Count Kutaisov separated when the attack began and I never saw him again. I also could not find General Paskevich, whose division was scattered but was now rallying in groups in order to pursue the fleeing enemy. It was said, that Kutaisov and Paskevich had been seen together amidst the throng. Having occupied the hill, I ordered the call to rally to be beaten and the wounded Colonel Savoini[266] appeared with a small number of officers and lower ranks. I feared that, if we were counterattacked, the enemy would

---

[263] Yermolov's note: I sent him to my family estate in Orel and asked my father to take particular care of him.

[264] Yermolov's note: I had seen on many occasions how troops follow those commanders who lead them from the front: my troops followed me in this fashion, seeing that I was giving orders even to their regimental commanders. Furthermore, I carried some medals of the Military Order of St George and threw handfuls forward so that our soldiers went after them. These soldiers showed examples of incredible bravery. There was no time for thinking and we could not retreat. My encounter with the Jägers was completely unexpected. The venture was no more than reckless audacity and many envied my luck.

[265] Yermolov's note: Regiments were composed of two battalions, the second line battalion was assigned to the reserve army and organized from recruits from the provinces.

[266] Born to a noble family from Florence, Savoini entered Russian service in 1784. In 1812, he was serving as commander of the Ladoga Infantry Regiment and was wounded in the left leg and hand at Borodino, earning promotion to major general.

bring strong forces against our depleted bands and deprive us of our recent success; so I dispatched my adjutants with a few other officers to recall our troops and to clear the valley before us.[267] Following this fierce combat, my battalions were reduced in strength and there was not a single caisson inside the earthworks, and the enemy were about to attack again. Still, wherever there was danger, one could find Barclay de Tolly. Scrutinizing the action, he had seen my predicament, and, without waiting for my appeal for reinforcements, he dispatched a battery company and two infantry regiments so that I had all I needed and was prepared to face the enemy. At the same time, Barclay had managed to contain the attacks against our right by the Army of Italy.

Having firmly established myself, I replaced our exhausted troops with fresh ones and moved them into reserve; Nikitin's three horse artillery companies had suffered disproportionately heavy losses and were moved back to their earlier position. On our left, the 2nd Grenadier Division of Prince Karl von Mecklenburg arrived from the reserve and would greatly assist us in this battle, although the prince himself was soon wounded.

Surrounded by danger, General Dokhturov encouraged his troops and they witnessed his fearlessness and determination;[268] but yet he could not replace the characteristic swift efficiency of Bagration or gain the complete trust of the troops who had idolized the prince. Because of the terrain, the cuirassier regiments fought in isolation and, in general, our cavalry enjoyed certain local advantages, but could not exploit them because of the hordes of enemy who came forwards again and again. Pursuing our depleted cavalry, the French appeared in front of our Guard regiments. The Life Guard Izmailovsk and Lithuanian regiments, formed in square, held their ground, but their volley could not halt the enemy cavalrymen, many of whom found death on our bayonets, before heavy losses finally obliged the enemy to retreat. As for the other Guard regiments – the Life Guard Preobrazhenskii suffered from

---

[267] Yermolov's note: Some of the minister of war's adjutants as well as officers serving under him and officials from the headquarters honoured me by accompanying me.

[268] Yermolov's note: He had neither harvested the laurels of his glory under the banners of Suvorov, nor on the fields of Italy, or amid the narrow paths and precipices of the Alps.

artillery fire, the Semyonovsk Regiment suffered fewer casualties, whilst the Finland Regiment was deployed as skirmishers.

To assist the 2nd Army, Prince Kutuzov had ordered Adjutant General Uvarov and the Guard Reserve Cavalry Corps and Ataman Platov with all his Cossacks and their artillery to attack the left flank of the enemy. Their sudden appearance caused great commotion in the enemy camp: infantry was hastily mustered, artillery redirected and reinforcements diverted from various positions. The enemy pressure was relaxed along the entire line and many believed that it was a moment of respite.

The commander of the Guard Light Cavalry Division, Orlov-Denisov, had hesitated during the attack, halting his regiments but exposing our weak artillery. He then, although under strong fire, moved across the Voina stream. Meantime, the Army of Italy was already ready, some of its units arranged in squares with the viceroy himself in the centre of one. Ataman Platov had the same objective but was more efficient. Yet, our troops did not succeed in this venture, inflicting minor losses and suffering casualties in turn. General Uvarov was ordered to return and Ataman Platov followed him.[269]

After a lull, the battle flared up with renewed intensity; the thunder of more than 1,000 artillery pieces produced a continuous roar; musket fire could not be heard anymore; wherever possible, cavalry replaced infantry. On the old Mozhaisk road, the 2nd Corps of the intrepid Baggovut held firm against superior enemy forces but our weak battery near Utitsa was already in enemy hands; the unusual density of the forest was all that saved Baggovut. It was obvious that he could not maintain his position for much longer, unless given some extraordinary assistance. Our forces were insufficient for this task, and Prince Kutuzov, watching from the battery near Gorki, could not see where danger threatened most, hoped for a favourable outcome. Meanwhile, the minister of war, personally observing everything, directed the action and nothing escaped his attention.

---

[269] Yermolov's note: The trains of Napoleon's headquarters and prominent personalities, ministerial chancelleries, correspondence and materials of various corps commanders, mobile hospitals, artillery parks, bakeries and enormous supply trains were in the rear of the French army. By threatening them, Platov forced the French to commit cavalry forces to protect these assets.

By 3:00 pm, whilst on the height I had retaken and provided with all the means for defence, I was suddenly informed about the death of Count Kutaisov. His horse had returned to the camp with its saddle covered with blood and brains.[270] Soon afterwards, I was wounded and had to leave the battlefield.[271] But first, I asked for Major General Likhachev, who commanded a division of the nearby 6th Corps,[272] to replace me.

From now on I ceased to be an actual eyewitness, so I will continue to describe the events of that day using information provided by the participants whom I dispatched to report on the rest of the battle.

On our left, the infantry under Miloradovich, Konovnitsyn and Count Osterman – generals of battle-hardened valour – had to relinquish the earthworks to the enemy despite every effort. Their resistance had aided the defence of the redoubt. Despite its reduced strength, Lieutenant General Rayevskii's 7th Corps continued to hold its ground and maintained communications between the two armies with exemplary steadfastness. Around 4:00 pm, infantry attacks ceased almost everywhere or, at least, no decisive actions were undertaken. In their place cavalry combat began. The terrain allowed large masses of cavalry to operate. Local advantages could only be overturned by the numerical superiority of the French and their ability to replace exhausted troops with fresh ones. The French could not match the rapidity of the attacks of our light

---

[270] Yermolov's note: His life ended still as a blossoming youth, having enjoyed a brilliant career and occupied an important position. His loss was mourned not only by his friends: gifted with valuable abilities, he would have rendered great service to his Fatherland. I had introduced him to the danger of war in 1806. I will forever regret that he did not heed my advice to return to his post, and if not for his burning desire to be with me, he might not have become another victim of this battle. The following day, an officer, who had caught him falling dead from his horse, delivered his orders and sabre to me and I sent these to his brother.

[271] Yermolov's note: A canister shot, which killed a non-commissioned officer in front of me, penetrating right through his ribs, pierced the collar of my overcoat and tore a lapel of my jacket. A silk scarf softened its impact. I fell down unconscious; my neck turned blue, a large bruise quickly appeared and all my neck muscles were damaged. I was brought down from the heights and regained consciousness there.

[272] Yermolov's note: He had commanded Jägers on the Caucasian Line under the renowned Prince Tsitsianov. He was an equally courageous and enterprising officer.

cavalry. The Chevalier Guard and Life Guard Horse regiments, as well as other cuirassier regiments, acted with particular valour.

At 5:00 pm, after a fierce combat against enemy cavalry, the Rayevskii redoubt was isolated from our troops, surrounded by large enemy forces and, only being defended by Major General Likhachev and his weak division, it could no longer hold out and fell into enemy hands. Likhachev was captured and several guns were lost. Fearing our attempts to recover this lunette, the French decided not to occupy the heights with their artillery, which could have inflicted heavy casualties on us, and that is why our troops remained in their positions. Baggovut's 2nd Corps was committed to the far left to prevent the enemy from outflanking us along the old postal road. The forests greatly assisted us in this and made it difficult for the French to deploy large forces against us. By the end of the day, however, the 2nd Corps had lost much ground and might easily have been isolated from the rest of the army, something which might not have been immediately apparent in the gloom.

Thus ended Borodino. Prince Kutuzov ordered an announcement to be made to the army that he would resume battle tomorrow.[273] It was impossible to express more gratitude for the heroism of troops than through such confidence in their courage and determination. Everyone, accepted this announcement with great enthusiasm.

However, after obtaining a detailed report that the 2nd Corps had been driven back and our left exposed, Prince Kutuzov withdrew his decision and ordered new orders to be drafted for retreat. The reserve artillery, wounded and heavy transports were immediately moved in order to avoid some of the expected difficulties because the roads from the position occupied by our army merged into one near Mozhaisk. In addition the shortness of the night and an inconvenient slope near the town ruled out speed. Retreat was carried out in relatively good order.

On the day of battle, Russia's warriors crowned themselves with immortal fame! The superiority of the enemy army

---

[273] Yermolov's note: My adjutant Lieutenant Grabbe was sent with this announcement. In some regiments, he was asked to dismount, officers embraced and kissed him for delivering such good news, while the lower ranks were also delighted.

compelled us to be on the defensive, something we were unused to. The loss of such officers, so many comrades, and everything else seemed to weigh against us but there certainly had never been an occasion when more indifference was shown to danger, more persistence, more steadfastness or a more resolute contempt for death. Success was uncertain for a long time, and although it often seemed to be in the enemy's grasp, it never weakened the spirit of our troops but rather inspired them to superhuman acts. Everyone was tested; and the day demonstrated how high man's virtues can be raised. Love for the fatherland and devotion to the sovereign had never had more commendable sacrifices; an infinite obedience, strictness in the observance of order and a feeling of pride to be defending the fatherland have no other or more glorious examples.

The French had won a victory which did not meet their expectations, and exhausted by our stout resistance, they needed rest. Only after several hours had elapsed did they begin to pursue our rearguard, commanded by Platov and composed of regular troops, artillery and all the Don Cossacks.[274]

In Mozhaisk, we came upon the wounded from the previous day and large transports of the 2nd Army as well as numerous large wagons of the Moscow militia. Hitherto unknown disorder began to reveal itself in the army. Our troops moved raggedy along the same road, transports crowding in on all sides.

The czar had been presented with a report announcing complete victory. Prince Kutuzov even stressed the possibility of saving Moscow; he was shrewdly massaging public opinion; he said that the loss of Smolensk was the precursor to the fall of Moscow without casting doubt on the actions of Barclay, whom even enemies respect for his experience, caring and efficiency.

Not long after Prince Kutuzov's arrival, I became aware of the tension he was provoking with Barclay who was exasperated by the disorder in the army, something which was now becoming widespread. Initially, the prince's orders were sent to the chiefs of staff, that is to me and Adjutant General Count St Priest, via Colonel Kaisarov, who was serving as duty officer to Kutuzov, as

---

[274] Yermolov's note: A French prisoner, captured in one of the skirmishes, told us that the redoubt, which General Likhachev defended, was abandoned that night because of concerns that the Russians might try to recapture it. The Cossacks reached the redoubt during the night and reported to Platov.

well as through many other officers, including even Captain Skobelev. They frequently contradicted each other, which caused misunderstandings, confusion and unpleasant recriminations. Sometimes, the orders were delivered directly to the corps and local commanders, who carried them out and reported back on when troops left camp and returned. Quartermaster General of the 2nd Army Toll[275] and Guard Colonel Prince Kudashev were also authorized to issue orders.[276]

Following Borodino, the 2nd Army existed in name only; its troops merged with the 1st Army and the headquarters of both armies were combined. I remained in my previous position as the chief of staff of the 1st Army.

On 27 August [8 September], the army bivouacked near Mozhaisk for the night. Platov's rearguard initially occupied the town, but was later driven out by the enemy, though the French did not pursue further. On the 28th, the army continued its retreat, the enemy pursuing us with more vigour and the rearguard was involved in heated engagements.

Kutuzov said it was his intention to give battle before Moscow in order to save the capital. Commanders on the ground already knew about this. General Baron Bennigsen was instructed to select a position and the quartermaster officers accompanied him. Anyone, who had precise information on the enemy forces and our losses, naturally found this incredible. Yet many expected it, even I believed it may have been possible. Kutuzov made brazen promises: 'It is better to die within the walls of Moscow than to let it fall into enemy hands.' General of Infantry Count Rostopchin, who governed Moscow, was not deceived by such statements; although he made public his correspondence with Kutuzov and pretended to be calm and secure, in reality he was the last to believe such promises. He endeavoured to leave Moscow in such a state that the enemy could neither find nor extract anything useful in the city.[277]

---

[275] Yermolov's note: Toll was an officer of outstanding abilities and enjoyed the particular confidence of Kutuzov, who, demonstrating his usual sagacity, often recalled that while being the director of the cadet corps, he recognized the unusual military talents in young Toll. Yet, after he got to know him better, Kutuzov could not perceive any such thing.

[276] Yermolov's note: Prince Kudashev was Kutuzov's son-in-law and suffered due to this close relationship because his achievements were mostly ascribed to this bond rather than to his abilities.

I allow myself to make some private observations. I thought that our army could have taken the road from Mozhaisk to Kaluga and abandoned Moscow. The French would not have dared to occupy it with a weak detachment and also could not have dispatched large forces there in the presence of our army, which they had to pursue. Certainly, they would not have brought their entire army after us, leaving Moscow in their rear and having their communications threatened.

If the enemy, observing our movement on Moscow, had done this, we would have faced a different set of problems. The French could have procured substantial supplies from Kaluga. Our communications with Admiral Chichagov and the troops under Tormasov would have been significantly delayed. The richest provinces that had supplied our armies with all our necessities would have been isolated from us. The enemy would have preserved his lines of communication intact, shifting them from Smolensk through Yelnya towards Kaluga across regions that had not been devastated by war. Moscow could have been rescued in this manner, but our army would have been forced to give battle before receiving fresh reinforcements or the recovered wounded. A battle would have been necessary to beat the relatively less disorganized enemy army.

Having occupied Moscow, Napoleon probably thought he would strike terror in the heart of Russia and put a quick end to this difficult and brutal war. Yet, he failed to perceive the courageous nature of Alexander or understand the character of the Russian people, who are firm in danger and patient in the face of adversity. So it was that the Lord, avenging Napoleon's insatiable desire for power, had chosen Moscow to be a tomb for him and his glories.

Meanwhile, our army, pursued by the enemy and having its rearguard constantly engaged, could not find any suitable position

---

[277] Police reports contain Rostopchin's instructions of 14 September to Pristav (constable) Voronenko to destroy as many buildings as possible by fire. For this purpose many convicted criminals were set free. The constable soon reported that '[he] had set fire to several places by 10:00 pm'. The same day Kutuzov ordered the destruction of magazines with supplies and ammunition. Rostopchin ordered all the water pumps taken out of the city and later acknowledged that 2,100 firefighters with 96 pumps had been evacuated. Rostopchin and Kutuzov paid so much attention to this that they left considerable supplies of armaments in Moscow: 156 guns, 74,974 muskets, 39,846 sabres and 27,119 cannonballs.

in the places it passed through and, without halting anywhere, it approached the suburbs of Moscow.

One position which had been suggested as a possible site for battle stretched from the village of Fili, across the Karpovka, towards the Vorobyev heights. Colonel Toll selected this position and he considered it rather advantageous. It was hard to believe that Kutuzov could not see its obvious deficiencies, but, to assure everyone of his firm intention to give battle, he pretended to agree with Toll's opinion, arguing that although our forces were disproportionately small additional artillery could be deployed to compensate for this.

Early on the morning of 1 [13] September, Kutuzov arrived at Fili and immediately ordered the construction of a large redoubt on a nearby hill, known as the Poklonnaia Gora, and another battery near the main road, designating them as the boundary for our right flank. Jägers were deployed in a small forest on the right whilst other troops were moved to their assigned places. Surrounded by generals, Kutuzov suddenly asked me what I thought of the position. I respectfully answered that it was difficult to judge at one glance a place where 60,000 men or more were to be deployed, but its apparent deficiencies caused me to think that it was impossible to defend. Kutuzov took my hand, checked my pulse and asked,

'Are you well?' Such a question was certainly justified in response to an objection expressed in so lively a manner. I said that he would not fight here or he would be defeated. None of the other generals expressed their opinion, although some already understood that Kutuzov had no need of their ideas and simply wanted to show his resolve in defending Moscow, when in reality he never contemplated doing so. Having listened to my observations, Kutuzov, with a sympathetic expression, ordered me to scout the position and report back to him. Colonel Toll and Colonel Crossard of the General Staff accompanied me.

After a thorough examination, I reported the following observations to the prince: the terrain from the right flank to the centre had a favourable slope that could be protected with intense fire. It was intersected by the Karpovka, flowing within steep banks towards the Vorobyev heights; these had difficult slopes which required time to correct. Bridges constructed over the river were exposed to enemy guns whilst more remote crossing sites slowed down our communications.

The left of the army, occupying the Vorobyev heights, needed strong fortifications, and had to be protected by the larger part of the army, since the enemy could deploy 30,000 men on the plain before us. In our rear, we had the Moscow River and the only way to retreat was via a flank movement towards the Karpovka creek. Having listened to my report, Kutuzov ordered a second reconnaissance. Returning again, I told him that, if we deployed the army on the Vorobyev heights and secured the Kaluga road, it could be possible to defend the Serpukhov road and retreat along this route into the Zamoskvorechye region. In conclusion, I said that this position was extremely disadvantageous for us, retreat could prove to be extremely dangerous and it would be difficult for our rearguard to hold its ground long enough to allow the army to retreat safely. Having listened to my observations, Prince Kutuzov said nothing while our troops continued deploying according to his earlier order. General Dokhturov's corps was directed to the Vorobyev heights and the construction of earthworks had already begun.

I found Rostopchin in Kutuzov's quarters and, as I later learned, the two had argued for quite some time. Seeing me, Rostopchin took me aside and asked:[278] 'I do not understand why are you trying so hard to protect Moscow, when the enemy would gain nothing valuable from it. All the wealth and property of the State Treasury has already been evacuated; church treasures, the gold and silver from most of the churches have been removed, with just a few exceptions. Important state archives have also been removed. Owners of private houses have already hidden their best property. Some 50,000 of the poorest people will remain in Moscow since they have no other shelter.' His last words were particularly remarkable: 'If you abandon Moscow without a battle, you will soon see it burning in flames behind you!'

Count Rostopchin left without getting any definite response from Kutuzov. Although Rostopchin's proposal found a response in Kutuzov's heart, Kutuzov had recently sworn on his gray hair

---

[278] Yermolov's note: Of course, it was my distinguished rank that turned his attention to me. Before, this haughty grandee had never even noticed me. I politely responded: 'Your Excellency, I am only executing the will of my commander, who does not allow freedom of thought.' He did not hide from me his suspicion that Kutuzov was reluctant to give battle.

that the French would find no other way into Moscow than over his dead body. It seems that he could only abandon Moscow if the idea was found to have originated not with him but from somebody else. On 29 August [10 September], Kutuzov had signed an order to the governor of Kaluga to redirect the supply trains from Kaluga to the Ryazan road.

Prince Kutuzov told me about his conversation with Count Rostopchin, and, with all the simplicity and innocence of his soul, he assured me that, before then, he had been unaware that the enemy would gain nothing by capturing Moscow and that there was now no reason to defend it and incur heavy casualties. He then asked me what I thought. Wishing to avoid having my pulse checked a second time, I remained silent; but when he ordered me to speak up, I told him that it would be appropriate to have our rearguard show some resistance in order to honour our ancient capital.

It was late afternoon by now and yet there were still no special orders for the army. The minister of war summoned me and, with marvellous sagacity and insight, he explained the reasons for the necessity of retreat. He then went to Kutuzov, ordering me to follow him. No one knew better than Barclay the varied ways of making war and which of them were most feasible at any moment. In order to win the war, it was imperative for us to gain time, and, to that end, abandon Moscow.

Listening attentively, Kutuzov could not conceal his excitement that the idea for retreat would not be attributed to him, and, to further avoid any blame, he summoned the army generals for a council of war at 8:00 pm.[279]

Kutuzov met the generals in his quarters in Fili. The council was formed of the following: Barclay de Tolly, Bennigsen, Dokhturov, Uvarov, Osterman- Tolstoy, Konovnitsyn and Rayevskii. The latter had just returned from the rearguard near Moscow and, for this reason, General Miloradovich could not leave

---

[279] Yermolov's note: It is probable that Kutuzov was unaware of Suvorov's observation about him, 'Even Ribas cannot deceive him.' Yet, nowadays many could read him. (Editor: Joseph Ribas y Boyons (1749-1800) a Spanish noble, served in Naples and entered Russian service in 1774. He quickly advanced through the ranks, becoming a rear admiral in 1791 and admiral in 1799. He was famous for his shrewd and devious character.)

it to attend. The minister of war began explaining the present state of affairs as follows:

> Our current position is very unfavourable and, if we wait here for the enemy, it will very dangerous; considering that the French have superior forces, it is more than doubtful that we would be able to defeat them. If, after a battle, we still manage to hold our ground, we would have suffered losses similar to those at Borodino and, thus, would be unable to defend a city as extensive as Moscow. The loss of Moscow might upset the sovereign, but it would not be unexpected, certainly it would not incline him to end the war and would reinforce his resolute will to fight on. By saving Moscow, Russia will not avoid this brutal, ruinous war; but having preserved our army, the hopes of our fatherland would be persevered, and the war, our only means to salvation, would be continued on better terms. Our reinforcements, gathered at various places behind Moscow, would have enough time to join us. All recruitment depots have been removed to those regions. A new foundry has been established in Kazan and a new weapons factory has been set up in Kiev; in Tula, additional guns have been completed. The Kiev Arsenal has been evacuated; gunpowder, produced in factories, is being turned into artillery munitions and musket cartridges and stored deep inside Russia.

The minister of war preferred to move on Vladimir in order to maintain communications with St Petersburg, where the imperial family resided. Prince Kutuzov ordered me, as junior in rank, to declare my opinion. Completely convinced by the minister's logic, I still dared to add that Vladimir was not practicalable in the present circumstances. The imperial family could leave St Petersburg and reside somewhere else,[280] without forcing the army to take such an

---

[280] Yermolov's note: I tried to assure Grand Duke Constantine Pavlovich that the imperial family could remain in St Petersburg. He said 'My sister Catherine Pavlovna is unsure where she can find peace for the birth of her child' and I dared to offer lightheartedly to bet that St Petersburg would be safe. As events

unfavourable direction, depriving us of the abundant supplies in the south, and greatly complicating our communication with the armies of Tormasov and Chichagov.

Since I was still relatively unknown, I did not dare give my consent to the surrender of Moscow, fearing the accusations of my compatriots; so without defending my hasty opinion, I proposed an attack. I argued that, after 900 verstas of continual retreat, the French would not be prepared for such an action; that this sudden move would force the French to take up defensive positions and undoubtedly spread confusion which His Excellency, as a talented commander, could exploit to our advantage.

Clearly displeased, Kutuzov told me that I had suggested that only because I did not fear the responsibility of taking such an action. He had vented his indignation too hastily as he should have known that there would be some cautious opinions to come. Lieutenant General Uvarov briefly expressed his consent to retreat. Lieutenant General Konovnitsyn supported attacking; he was an enterprising and undaunted officer, but inexperienced in taking extensive and complex decisions. General Dokhturov said that it would be good to march against the enemy, however, because of the loss of so many commanders at Borodino, who had been replaced by less familiar officers, success in the ensuing battle could not be guaranteed; therefore, he proposed to retreat. General Baron Bennigsen, known for his knowledge of the military art and being experienced in the wars against Napoleon, supported attacking. I was encouraged by his views since I was confident that he based them on the most correct calculations of the likelihood of success, or at least on the possibility of not being overwhelmed. However, there were certainly some at the council who were astonished by his proposal. Lieutenant General Count Osterman agreed to retreat, and, to criticize the proposed offensive, he asked Bennigsen if he could guarantee success? With his usual calm, Bennigsen responded that if the subject of our discussion were not in doubt, it would have been unnecessary to call a council and his opinion would not have been required. I was ordered to relay Barclay's observations and the opinions of each council member to Lieutenant General Rayevskii, who had arrived late. He soon expressed his consent to retreat. Everyone based their decisions on the minister's

---

showed she could have stayed in the city.

observations, without explaining their reasons or considerations, and certainly there could hardly be a more thorough reasoning than that of Barclay. Completely sharing his opinion, Kutuzov ordered plans drawn up for a retreat. He courteously listened to the opinions of his generals and could not hide his pleasure that the surrender of Moscow had been urged upon him whilst he had been committed to giving battle.

Around 10:00 pm, the army departed in two columns; one of them, under Uvarov, marched through the sentry gate and across the Dorogomilov bridge. Kutuzov accompanied it in person. Another column, under Dokhturov, moved through Zamoskvorechye towards the Kamennyi bridge. Both columns were directed through the Ryazansk gates. Junctions, narrow streets, large wagon trains (which had been moved closer in anticipation of a battle) trailing the army, reserve artillery and parks, and the fleeing residents of Moscow – all these factors so complicated our movement that the army was unable to leave the city before noon. Prince Kutuzov sent me to General Miloradovich to urge him to delay the enemy as long as possible or make a truce to gain time to evacuate the heavy transports. I found Lieutenant General Rayevskii[281] with part of the rearguard near the Dorogomilov bridge and informed him about Kutuzov's orders for Miloradovich.

Our rearguard had been constantly pursued and Miloradovich had to pull back as the enemy had brought troops against Baron Winzegorode's detachment, demonstrating their intention of breaking into the city and threatening our rearguard from behind. Miloradovich dispatched a messenger to the French general Sebastiani warning him that if he decided to pursue us into the streets of the city, he would face our most resolute resistance and that, defending each house, the Russians would set fire to the entire city. An agreement was made and the enemy entered without a fight and the army trains, together with the city's inhabitants, left the city without any difficulty.

I was eager to examine what effect the abandonment of Moscow had on the troops and was thrilled to notice that the

---

[281] Yermolov's note: We dismounted and spoke for some time; looking at Moscow, we shared our sorrow about its fate. We could see nothing comforting in the future. We did expect something from Kutuzov, but did not have much confidence.

soldiers were not disheartened and no grumbles were uttered; yet, their commanders were astonished by the loss of our ancient capital.[282] Only a few residents remained in Moscow, mostly those without any shelter. Houses were empty and locked; large squares now resembled the steppes; not a single man could be seen on some streets. Few churches were without a few praying victims, now at the mercy of the inhuman enemy. The laments of the wounded being abandoned to the enemy tore at my soul. In Gzhatsk, Prince Kutuzov had given the unwise order of gathering all the sick and wounded in Moscow, which had never seen such victims before, and so more than 20,000 of them were sent there. The troops were outraged by this whole affair. A soldier might see his comrades in arms abandoned on the battlefield but he understood it was being done because there was no alternative. However, here, in Moscow, there were many ways to attend the wounded soldier who has defended his fatherland with his life. Here the wealthy reposed in sweet bliss behind the protection of the soldier's firm chest and where their proud halls rose to the clouds, the poor soldier shed his last drop of blood on their staircases or exhausted his powers on the stone courtyards of their houses. Yet, Moscow's insulting indifference towards the soldier's dreadful labour had not cooled the zeal and dedication of the troops.

Thus, the army passed through Moscow. I found Kutuzov beyond the city and informed him that I had delivered his orders to Miloradovich. Soon, two explosions were heard in Moscow and large fires were observed. I recalled the words Count Rostopchin had uttered the day before; indeed, Moscow would cover the shame of profanation under its ruins and ashes! The flames devouring our ancient capital were started with our own hands. There is no reason to blame our enemy for this or to express regret for something that raises the honour of our nation. Each Russian and the entire city in particular generously sacrificed themselves for the common good. In the deliberate destruction of Moscow, the enemy could perceive an omen of future calamity. No other nation of those that remained

---

[282] Yermolov's note: The lower ranks of the Moscow Garrison Regiment, or Arkharov's, were mostly married and with families; long engaged in commerce and other trades like the Janissaries. They left Moscow in order, with singers leading the way.

subservient to Napoleon for more than 15 years demonstrated such an example. Providence saved this honour for the glory of the Russians! Conquering all for 15 years, Napoleon had triumphantly entered capital after capital. Yet, the road through Moscow led to the downfall of his glory and power! For the first time frightened Europe could dare to see he was a mere mortal!

Our army bivouacked for the night and then had a rest on 3 [15] September some 15 verstas from Moscow. After marching peacefully through the Ryazan gates, our rearguard deployed its outposts three verstas from the city and spend the night near the army.

The crossing of the Moscow River near Borov was accomplished with great difficulty and in incredible confusion because of the vehicles belonging to the fleeing residents of Moscow. Gunfire could be heard but the enemy did not attack. The minister of war's suggestion to head to Vladimir had been overturned and it was decided to move down the Tula road.[283] This idea originated with Bennigsen and this daring and decisive flanking movement, quite risky because of the proximity of the enemy, was completed without any difficulty and the army, despite the most appalling weather and dreadful country roads, quickly reached Podolsk. Kutuzov wasted two days there. However, whilst we made one error, the enemy made two serious mistakes. Held in Moscow by robbery, alcoholism and plunder, the French merely watched our retreating army and worried about nothing else. Because of our slow movement from Moscow, they could have advanced along the right bank of the Moscow River and beaten us to the crossing or at least driven us to Ryazan, barring all other routes. Moreover, confusing a small Cossack detachment under brave Colonel Efremov for our rearguard, the French pursued it to Bronnitsa; realizing their mistake only too late, they hastily returned to Moscow, but our army was already near Krasnaia Pakhra on the Kaluga road.

Rayevskii's corps covered our flank movement to Podolsk; Dorokhov's detachment was deployed ahead of him and the Cossacks under Colonel Ilovaisky (II) routed part of the French

---

[283] Yermolov's note: Later, many claimed they made this suggestion, but it belonged to General Bennigsen alone, and I am aware of all the details that surrounded it.

cavalry, pursued it to the local village and surrounded it there, killing many and capturing some.

Our army marched peacefully to the village of Krasnaia Pakhra but, finding the position unfavourable, we proceeded further to Voronovo and then to Tarutino. Our rearguard deployed at Krasnaia Pakhra and was pursued by weak enemy forces; as a result, our outposts were deployed rather clumsily and no patrols were sent out. Near our camp, isolated by an impassable ravine, there was a beautiful estate with a garden and Miloradovich, who commanded the rearguard, visited it, barely escaping capture.[284]

Soon afterwards, in a skirmish, our Life Guard Dragoons routed two dragoon squadrons of Napoleon's Guard. Meanwhile, our rearguard was hard pressed by the enemy forces near Mocha; a difficult crossing near the village of Voronovo causing serious confusion among the troops, and the right flank was in danger of being isolated. The deployment of the rearguard troops was so strange and perplexing that Rayevskii, believing he had only our cavalry ahead of him, spent the night with an entire infantry corps and all his battery artillery deployed. The cavalry had not considered it necessary to cover this corps and, if nothing happened that night, it was only because our luck held.

On 21 September [3 October], the army arrived at Tarutino. After an intense combat at Chirikov, the enemy forced our rearguard to fall back to the heights some three verstas in front of Tarutino.

On 22 September [4 October], the army began constructing earthworks to reinforce a position near Tarutino. The enemy resumed its fierce attacks, but Miloradovich gallantly fought them off. It was impossible to yield a single yard of ground since, in front of our camp, there was a continuous slope leading into the creek and, had they captured the heights, the enemy could clearly observe any motion in our camp and deploy picquets along the creek to prevent our access to water. Our troops maintained outstanding

---

[284] Yermolov's note: Dissatisfied with a hut, Miloradovich decided to indulge himself in luxury and occupied a beautiful mansion, inviting generals to lunch, hoping to rest and amuse himself. Just then, an enemy squadron entered the garden and approached the mansion, while another squadron was in reserve. Our sentries in the court managed to mount their horses and repulse the closest enemy squadron while the other enemy squadron avoided fighting. Captured enemy soldiers revealed that these were Prussian squadrons.

order during the battle. Changing the direction of their attacks, the French were always opposed by equal Russian forces, which acted with extraordinary rapidity and did not allow the French to gain any advantage; the reserves were not committed. Major General Shevich, commanding our cavalry on the right, even gained some ground; the French cuirassiers could not repulse a vigorous attack of several squadrons of our Guard Uhlans, whose lances were blunted against their armour. The 1st Jäger Regiment under Colonel Karpenko cleared its way to success with bayonets; our artillery was simply superb; two battery companies under Lieutenant Colonel Gulevich, operating without cover, shielded the movement of our troops and the enemy could do nothing against them. In the evening, the enemy retreated and camped nearby. Up until now, circumstances had burdened us with the bitter necessity of retreat and allowed the French to reach their objectives. However, now their efforts proved fruitless for the first time.

After the battle, the vanguard returned to the army, leaving a strong cavalry force with a few horse artillery batteries. The following day, the quiet in the enemy camp made us believe that they were expecting the arrival of large reinforcements. Yet, against expectation and without any agreement, no action took place and not a single shot was fired. Generals and officers on both sides frequently met each other chivalrously at the advance posts and this led many to conclude that an armistice would be concluded.[285]

Our camp at Tarutino was thoroughly reinforced. Strong batteries protected its front and the forest on its left was intersected with abatises while, beyond the right, there was an open plain convenient for cavalry. Yet, some disadvantages were clearly discernible; the camp was very small and crowded and the

---

[285] Yermolov's note: Our czar was displeased with this and, in a letter to Kutuzov, he noted how improper such meetings between generals were and specifically ordered Bennigsen that it was especially unacceptable for him. Miloradovich met Murat, King of Naples, on more than one occasion. It was easy to notice that the French were not always first to boast. If it were possible to forget we were enemies, the meetings would have seemed like an entertainment at a local fair. Murat appeared either dressed in the Spanish fashion or in unbelievably ridiculous costumes, with a velvet hat and flashy pantaloons; Miloradovich – on a Cossack horse, with a whip in his hand, and three bright scarves, which did not match, wrapped around his neck and flapping in the winds. There was no third man like them in either army.

movement of troops inside it was complicated by numerous earthen huts; the heights to our left favoured the enemy, while a steep-banked creek, which separated us from these heights, also complicated any cavalry action on the opposite side and would deprive us of a convenient retreat. If the French attacked our position and were forced to retreat, they would still be able to halt our pursuits using the fire of their batteries located on the elevated bank of the creek that dominated the entire valley and could meet us with canister at 300 sazhens. On our side, we had no place to deploy batteries in front of our position. Nothing could impel the enemy to attack our strongly fortified positions, especially the right where many expected an enemy attack. Yet, as soon as the enemy forces appeared on the Kaluga road, which we had weakly protected, we abandoned Tarutino.

Completing its flanking march, the army arrived at Podolsk, where Bennigsen considered taking up a position either near Borovsk or at a fortified camp near Maloyaroslavets. There was no doubt that such an action would disturb the enemy, especially since their cavalry was exhausted by the lack of forage and by the numerous partisans who inflicted much damage. Nevertheless, it seemed proper to reject this idea since the enemy would tolerate our presence at Tarutino more than at Maloyaroslavets or Borovsk. The French disregarded a weak detachment under Major General Dorokhov, deploying only small forces against him at Vereya, and giving us enough time for respite and the chance to rally our armies, to rest our fatigued cavalry and to establish an efficient supply system. In a word, the French revived our hopes and our ability to resume the fight and achieve final victory. Had we remained at Borovsk with the forces we had at Moscow, without adding reinforcements, including 26 regiments arriving from the Don Cossack Host, and with our disordered cavalry and exhausted troops, the French would have attacked us at once in order to drive us from their lines of communication and from the rebellious provinces where peasants were already incensed by pillages and other transgressions.

Soon after leaving Moscow, I informed Prince Kutuzov that Artillery Captain Figner had offered to gather intelligence on the French army in Moscow and on any preparations it was making;[286]

---

[286] Alexander Figner was fluent in French and Italian and often disguised himself

the prince agreed to this mission. In order to conceal his intentions, I gave him official orders to travel to Kazan since our main headquarters was a foe of any secrecy. Returning from Moscow, Figner arrived at Podolsk, where he met Lieutenant General Rayevskii, who served with him against the Turks and knew Figner as a courageous and enterprising officer;[287] I had ordered Figner to ask the first commander he encountered for a small cavalry detachment to operate against the enemy communications. Receiving the troops, Figner moved on to the road between Mozhaisk and Moscow. He soon reached the main army at Tarutino. Prince Kutuzov was very pleased with his first guerrilla actions and increased the number of his troops. Guard horse artillery Captain Seslavin was the second officer after Figner to lead a similar detachment and Guard Colonel Prince Kudashev followed him.[288] The advantages gained by them soon became apparent. Prisoners were brought back in large numbers; no transports or artillery parks could travel without a strong escort; the French now foraged with infantry and guns and never returned without loss. Our guerrilla forces appeared along all their lines of

---

as a French officer and gathered intelligence on the French deployment. He even attempted to assassinate Napoleon in the Kremlin, but barely escaped after an Imperial Guard sentry suspected his intentions. Figner demonstrated fanatical hatred of the French and, on some occasions, executed prisoners of war. Yet, his daring raids on the French supply and communication lines caused great distress to Napoleon, who called him 'A True Tartar'. Figner quickly advanced through the ranks, becoming captain, lieutenant colonel and colonel within a couple of months in late 1812. In 1813, he formed a special detachment from Italian and German deserters and harassed the French throughout Saxony. He was surrounded by the French near Dessau on 13 October 1813 and drowned attempting to swim a river.

[287] Yermolov's note: Upon departing Moscow, Figner obtained a passport from the French saying he was a peasant from Vyazma. Dressed in peasant clothes, he was taken as a guide by one of the French detachments marching from Mozhaisk. He followed the French for a march, observed that the detachment comprised of recovering soldiers from hospitals and was accompanied by six guns from the Italian artillery from Pavia. At night, Figner escaped the camp to join his detachment waiting for him near the road and attacked the French. Almost the entire camp was captured without resistance. Among the captured was a colonel from Hanover and I witnessed his meeting with Bennigsen, whom he had known in his youth and had family in common.

[288] The first guerilla detachments were organized in the summer and were actually commanded by Winzegorode and Davidov.

communication; local inhabitants served as loyal guides to them, providing important news and, taking up weapons themselves, they often joined the bands. Figner should be justly credited as the first to incite the local population to fight the enemy and his call had such dire consequences for the French.

The French found only scant supplies in Moscow and their troops were soon receiving less than half their rations, no special arrangements were made to address this problem and this complete idleness exposed Napoleon's hopes of peace, in which he imagined himself dictating conditions. I do not know for certain what his conditions were, but everybody easily understood that General Lauriston, former ambassador to our court whom Napoleon sent now to negotiate, was certainly instructed to declare his desire to end the war. Moscow, our ancient capital, turned into ashes by our hands, proved that there were no heavy sacrifices that the Russian people were not prepared to make and revealed our readiness to respond to this unjust attack with ruthless war. General Lauriston arrived several days after the army reached Tarutino. At that moment, I was in Kutuzov's quarters, but he ordered all of us to leave. Afterwards, rumour had it that the prince promised Lauriston he would inform our sovereign about Napoleon's desire to end the war, which, meanwhile, was about to flare up still further. Ever cunning, Kutuzov immediately grasped the gullibility of the French envoy, who left with the expectation of a favourable outcome. Time was gained to rest our exhausted troops, to receive and train reinforcements, restore and reinforce our cavalry and prepare our artillery.

Whilst at Tarutino, Lieutenant General Konovnitsyn was appointed duty general to Kutuzov. He had rightly acquired the reputation of being a gallant and steadfast officer, but many, expecting commensurate abilities and efficiency from him, were disappointed. During the reign of Catherine II, he had served as a colonel and commanded a regiment, then lived in retirement before returning again to service. Modern war presented new pastures, where, even with excessive ambition and indomitable desire, it was impossible to rise through the ranks with bravery alone. Yet as a clever and even cunning individual, he knew how to exploit Kutuzov's weaknesses and was assisted in this by Toll, who wielded great influence over Kutuzov.[289]

After being promoted to General Field Marshal for Borodino, Kutuzov found it necessary to appoint a duty general with the intention – which is so easy to guess – of reducing Bennigsen's role in military matters. They had a hostile relationship but Bennigsen's rank kept him close to Kutuzov.

We soon received news of the death of our most admirable and memorable Prince Bagration.[290] In his memory, the designation of the 2nd Army was kept intact for some time, although in reality it had ceased to exist.

On 22 September [4 October], Barclay de Tolly left the army, travelling through Kaluga. His patience had gone by now: he had angrily observed the continuous disorder in the army and was indignant about the lack of trust or care shown to his reports.[291] I was aware about his decision to depart and, shortly before, I wrote a report saying that, feeling myself incapable of performing my duties, I requested my dismissal and my return to the army. The field marshal left my report without answer. Barclay was accompanied by the director of his chancellery, Guard Colonel Zakrevskii, an officer of noble traits, with whom I enjoyed friendly relations, sharing both the misfortunes and pleasant minutes of this unsuccessful war. Only one person remained close to me, Flügel Adjutant Colonel Kikin, serving as a duty general, whom I genuinely respected for his noble character. I was hardly liked by anyone else, being a meticulous executor of the will of our demanding commander-in-chief and did not chance upon friendly faces, but only those of the spiteful around me. In his new position, Konovnitsyn suddenly had to deal with matters completely beyond

---

[289] Yermolov's note: I now observed a very different man from the one I remembered from the celebrated retreat from Bavaria. Age, a serious wound and scores of insults significantly reduced his powers. His previous enterprise was now replaced by timid caution. It was easy to gain his confidence with open flattery and it was as easy to lose his trust through outside influence. His associates, having studied his character, could even direct his will. Among these were some with limited abilities who, through shrewdness and intrigues, managed to become indispensable and get appointments. There was constant intrigue, men rose quickly and their fall was hardly discernible.

[290] Bagration had died on 24 September from complications of the wound he received at Borodino.

[291] Yermolov's note: The day after Borodino, Barclay told me, 'I sought death yesterday and failed to find it.' I was very surprised to see tears in his eyes. He must have suffered greatly.

him and he helped himself by forwarding them to me in enormous heaps so I had to take the relevant course of action. I fulfilled his requests for some time out of my respect towards him and notwithstanding his great incompetence. At the same time, he did not hide his regret that he was unable to serve capably in such an extensive and complex position. Konovnitsyn, with his innate cunning, which he made seem it were innocence, told everyone that no matter how much he had tried to avoid his new position, he was still appointed. Yet, in reality, he was very excited about the appointment.

Until now, I had submitted reports to the field marshal and issued orders in his name, but, under the new arrangement, I personally reported to him only in extraordinary cases and soon noted how much he changed towards me.[292] I had never tried to court favour and took advantage of the situation to move out of headquarters and to meet with the field marshal only if he desired it. I often ran into Konovnitsyn, but was mostly corresponding with him, declining assignments which I was not obliged to carry out and, of course, in this correspondence, he never managed to outwit me. I believe, without doubt, that he was secretly trying to harm me. Nature rarely creates men with such a calm and impenetrable appearance. Konovnitsyn had the same expression for emotion or passion, equally displaying treacherous indifference or a smile of deceiving simplicity. Yet, there was something he could not control – the feeling of envy, which was easily readable on his pale features.

Thus, I enjoyed complex relations with Konovnitsyn, who managed to sway Colonel Toll against me, whose friendship I hitherto had no reason to doubt. Both of them sought influence over Kutuzov and together they managed to sow the seeds of hostility between him and Bennigsen. My reduced responsibilities forced me to ask for my dismissal, but to no avail; I remained to

---

[292] Yermolov's note: The czar had sent Prince Volkonsky to Krasnaya Pakhra to gather information on the state of our armies. I learned from him that, before sending Kutuzov to take command, the czar gave him some of my letters so he could learn something of the armies whilst travelling. This explained to me a change in Kutuzov's disposition towards me, although he tried to conceal it. Before leaving, Volkonsky told me that the czar, wanting to know why Moscow was surrendered without a fight, told him 'Ask Yermolov, he certainly knows why'.

witness the swagger of so many, their hauteur, intrigue and machinations.

According to intelligence delivered by partisans, it emerged that the enemy vanguard under Murat had no reinforcements closer than Moscow and therefore it could not hope to receive support in time. The field marshal decided to attack. It was impossible to remove Bennigsen, the chief of staff of all armies, from the drafting of the orders, yet his plan, in which we would certainly achieve victory through superiority of force, was undesirable to Kutuzov; furthermore, he also wanted to lead the forces intended for the first wave. The terrain was thoroughly examined and dispositions were made accordingly; the first troops, committed to battle, quit the camp on the night of 6 [18] October, while the rest crossed the Nara at dawn and prepared for combat; the latter included the 1st Cavalry Corps under Baron Müller-Zakomelsky, with Count Orlov-Denisov's Don Cossacks to the fore. These would turn the French left and act against their rear; at the same time, Lieutenant General Baggovut's 2nd Infantry Corps was dispatched to the far wing of this flank, followed by 4th Corps under Count Osterman-Tolstoy. Their reserves consisted of the 3rd Infantry Corps under Count Stroganov. The 6th Corps of General Dokhturov was deployed in the centre whilst the left, under General Miloradovich, included the 7th Corps of Lieutenant General Rayevskii and the troops of the vanguard. Our entire Guard and the cuirassier regiments were placed in reserve and the field marshal was with them.

Sporadic gunfire was heard at dawn. The French, peacefully encamped without any precautions, were thrown by the unexpected attack of the Cossacks and, unable to rally, they but faintly resisted our assault; the 2nd Corps moved out of the forest without difficulty and fell upon them. Cossacks, led by the courageous Colonel Sisoev, rushed at the guns and captured several pieces. However, Lieutenant General Baggovut was killed by a cannonball as the battle opened.[293] The 4th Corps under Count Osterman-

---

[293] Yermolov's note: He was well known for his exceptional courage and enterprise, respected for his outstanding nobility of character. The field marshal ordered Konovnitsyn to go to the battlefield and report on the situation. I was also told to go. On several occasions, I had to act in the name of the field marshal: I saw what was happening and what had to be done. General Baron Bennigsen, having determined the objective of the troops on the right, did not assume command of them thinking that the field marshal, to whom he had

Tolstoy did not arrive at its destination on time due to the count's inefficiency and barely participated in the fighting. The battle could have been better but there was little communication between our forces. The field marshal, confident in our success, remained with the Guard, and thus saw nothing of the battle; the commanders on the ground acted on their own. An enormous cavalry force in the centre and on the left seemed to have been assembled for a parade, showing off its orderly deployment instead of attacking. It would have been possible to prevent the French from gathering their scattered infantry, surround them and cut off their retreat since there was a considerable distance between their camp and the woods. Yet the enemy was given time to rally, bring up some artillery from other directions, reach the woods without any difficulty and retreat along the road through Voronovo. The French lost 22 guns, up to 2,000 prisoners, their entire baggage and Murat's carriages. The baggage was bursting with riches and was a tasty treat for our Cossacks, who busied themselves robbing it, got drunk and never thought of interfering with the enemy's retreat.

Two days before, the enemy had received information about our intention to attack; the troops had been battle ready and alert throughout the night, but the waiting had been in vain. However, the French had ordered their artillery and transports to retreat. An adjutant, sent with orders to the commander of their artillery, found him asleep and hesitated before waking him, unaware of the importance of the orders he was carrying. That is why the French troops were sleeping and our troops found them half asleep, without picquets and their horses unsaddled. Our first offensive operation during this campaign had a very encouraging effect on the troops and demoralized an enemy who were thereby punished for the impudence of resisting us with such weak and isolated forces.

I rode alongside the field marshal's carriage from the battlefield to our camp and, listening to him, I easily understood how he would embellish this event in his report to the czar.[294] The

---

explained everything, would lead them.

[294] Yermolov's note: His conversation with me usually began with 'My dear', especially when he hoped to mask his genuine ideas and one could discern the level of his pretence only by the changing tone of his voice. Now it was late and darkness concealed any changes in his features and so he felt uninhibited, 'What a glorious day the Lord has given us! The enemy suffered enormously. Many guns

following day, without waiting for General Bennigsen's report, who, according to the plan he drafted, commanded the troops in the action and opened the battle. Without consulting him, Kutuzov sent his report to the czar. The hostility between Kutuzov and Bennigsen increased from now on. Bennigsen was probably not given due credit for the battle and none of us, his subordinates, were mentioned in Kutuzov's report.

Major General Dorokhov, with a detachment on our left, reported that he had taken Vereya, seizing a redoubt and its entire garrison, while enemy reinforcements withdrew. The guerrilla leaders Seslavin and Figner, observing the enemy near Fominskoe, turned for help to Major General Dorokhov, requesting him to support their attack with his detachment. Encouraged by his promise, they engaged the enemy but, Dorokhov arrived alone without his troops only to witness their failed attacks and, considering the disproportion in forces, some losses on our side. Figner explained this affair to Konovnitsyn, but Major General Dorokhov not only escaped without reprimand but, hoping to get permission to capture Fominskoe on his own, he informed headquarters on 9 [21] October, that the French were occupying the villages of Fominskoe and Kotovo and moving some of their forces to Borovsk. He added that they had no more than 8,000 men and that he would easily defeat them if he were given two infantry regiments and artillery. Because of their friendship, Konovnitsyn was ready to oblige Dorokhov and reported to the field marshal. However, ever careful Konovnitsyn thought it better to have this mission entrusted to General of Infantry Dokhturov.[295] The 6th Infantry Corps, the 1st Cavalry Corps of Müller-Zakomelsky, Colonel Nikitin's horse artillery company and several Cossack regiments were committed to this affair. I was ordered to accompany General Dokhturov.[296] Seslavin and Figner were sent

---

are captured and, it is said, there are even more scattered in the woods, and what about the prisoners – they are gathered in large groups!' I never saw any guns or prisoners. The enemy was not pursued and thus could not have been forced to abandon guns. Hearing his tale, I was sure the report would be written without exaggeration.

[295] In the original, Yermolov mistakenly refers to Dorokhov instead of Dokhturov.

[296] Yermolov's note: Having summoned me, the Field Marshal met me with his usual empty greeting of 'My dear' and told me that he greatly desired the capture

forward to see whether the enemy had reinforcements around Fominskoe which could arrive in support.

Our troops marched out on 10 [22] October. Drizzling autumnal rain further worsened the already terrible country road. The march proved to be an ordeal, our movement was delayed by an artillery battery which the infantry had to constantly free from the mud. General Dokhturov agreed to my proposal to leave it behind. Some light artillery pieces accompanied us.

Major General Dorokhov, who joined us with his detachment, reported that the French were pursuing Colonel Vlasov's three Cossack regiments from Borovsk with as many as 2,000 men. Another 4,000 Frenchmen were bivouacked near Kotovo. An enemy camp near Fominskoe was located in the woods and thus it was difficult to precisely determine their strength. Campfires were visible at night, and a battery was observed deployed on the bridge across the Nara.

Approaching Kotovo, our troops camped in such a manner as to attack at dawn and then immediately assault Fominskoe. All the troops were forbidden to light fires so that our position would not be revealed. The 1st Cavalry Corps and all the Cossacks were moved forwards. I was with Adjutant General Baron Müller.

Midnight quickly passed and it was time to move. Yet, there was no news from the guerrillas, who were supposed to meet me. The drumming of hooves was soon heard and Seslavin responded to our sentry's call. His news took us all by surprise and changed our plan of action.

Hiding in the woods near the road some four verstas from Fominskoe, Seslavin saw Napoleon with his enormous entourage, followed by his Guard and numerous troops. As they passed, he captured several prisoners and brought us the most intelligent of them, a non-commissioned officer in the Guard, who told us the following: 'We abandoned Moscow four days ago. Marshal Mortier and his detachment have blown up the Kremlin walls and joined the army. Heavy artillery, the cavalry, which has lost many horses, and many transports have been directed to the Mozhaisk road under the protection of the Polish Corps of General Prince

---

of Fominskoe, concluding, 'You will go with Dokhturov and I will be at ease, but keep me informed about events.'

Poniatowski. Tomorrow, Imperial headquarters will be in Borovsk, and then will head to Maloyaroslavets.'

General Dokhturov was immediately informed about this and the duty general staff officer of the corps was dispatched to the field marshal, calmly residing in Tarutino. He had no information from Baron Winzengorode, who was located near Moscow. Had Seslavin failed to inform us in time, the 6th Infantry Corps and the rest would have suffered a serious defeat at Fominskoe and Maloyaroslavets would have been occupied without any difficulty. General Dokhturov graciously accepted my suggestion: to march back at dawn and, after joining the battery artillery we had left on the road, hurry to Maloyaroslavets. He also agreed that Müller, with the 1st Cavalry Corps, Colonel Nikitin's horse artillery company and the Cossacks, were to scout towards Borovsk and return to the corps. I departed with Müller.

It was a foggy morning and little could be observed. Nevertheless, we managed to make out Borovsk, occupied by large enemy forces and artillery. Some enemy infantry left the city and stretched down the post road. Cavalry outposts were deployed along the River Protva and, although they were attacked, they received reinforcements which had hidden in the woods and increased their fire. Although unwilling to get involved in a major combat, General Baron Müller[297] was forced to commit troops and half of his artillery company to this skirmish. Galloping for about a verst through the young birch groves that still preserved their foliage, we reached the post road from Borovsk and observed the bivouacs of the army of the Italian viceroy, Eugene, and the corps of Davout. We immediately returned to the left bank of the Protva. I selected an enterprising officer from Sisoev's Don Cossacks and ordered him to lead several Cossacks along the enemy side of the river towards Maloyaroslavets to reconnoitre the town and then find a road back to General Dokhturov at night. The Cossack caught up with us long after midnight and reported that the bridge across the Luzha creek at Maloyaroslavets had been dismantled by local inhabitants and he had spoken to them across the creek. Platov dispatched a Cossack outpost to the place. Three enemy

---

[297] Yermolov's note: I had served with Baron Müller-Zakomelsky in the division of His Excellency Prince [Arkady] Suvorov, who drowned in the Rimnic, and we were always good friends and acted as one.

battalions were near the bridge. The municipal officials still remained at their posts at 9:00 am but then fled and chaos overtook the town.

Having marched the entire night, with just a few breaks, we joined the 4th Corps early in the morning. This corps was deployed near the town, on the road to Kaluga. Our artillery battery on the left was directed towards the bridge, which the enemy tried in every way possible to repair.

The first regiment sent in was the 33rd Jägers. It fought the enemy for a long time, taking advantage of a position atop a steep riverbank, but the part of the town by the bridge, was constantly occupied by the French and they managed to get two guns across the repaired bridge. Enemy troops quickly multiplied and they began to enter the streets. The opposite bank was covered by the troops of the Viceroy of Italy.

The 6th and 19th Jägers under Colonel Vuich were sent to aid the 33rd. General Dokhturov entrusted me with our troops in the town. These troops fought fearlessly, but were overwhelmed by enemy superiority and had to retreat; despite being pursued, they succeeded in removing the artillery and left only one gun in the town. The enemy occupied it with a few artillery pieces.

Just then, enemy infantry appeared to our right probably sent to probe our strength in this direction since they quickly withdrew under fire from our batteries. On General Dokhturov's orders, the Libavskii and Sofiiskii regiments arrived incredibly quickly. I ordered each regiment to deploy in columns, personally told the lower ranks not to load their muskets and, without shouting 'hurrah', attack with the bayonet. I assigned Major General Talyzin to lead the Libavsk and Colonel Khalyapon the Sofiisk, followed by all the Jäger regiments. Their attack was preceded by an intense bombardment from our guns. The enemy was driven back with heavy casualties and a large part of the town was reoccupied. Colonel Nikitin[298] seized a cemetery on a hill in the centre and deployed his battery guns there. For a long time, the enemy could

---

[298] Yermolov's note: My adjutants were placed at his disposal: Guard Lieutenant von Vizin was with our advance posts and observed the enemy; Artillery Lieutenant Pozdeev was sat in a nearby bell tower, directing the fire of our battery against enemy columns which were masked by houses.

not match us in artillery, probably to avoid complications in case of retreat.

Half of the day had passed. Masses of enemy troops were approaching Maloyaroslavets and were deploying across the Luzha; enemy artillery fire increased and their attacks became more and more persistent. I ordered the Wilmanstrandsk Infantry and the 2nd Jägers, our reserve, to enter the town. They greatly assisted us in holding our ground, but we were no longer secure and I ordered part of our artillery to be evacuated.

After receiving General Dokhturov's permission, I directed Adjutant General Count Orlov-Denisov to inform the field marshal on my behalf about our current position and about the need to hurry our main army to prevent the enemy from capturing the town. Our army was near Spaskoe on the Protva. The field marshal probably found my news unpleasant, especially as it was relayed to him in the presence of many generals. He sent Count Orlov-Denisov back without orders. My second messenger was received no better (the generals were still with the field marshal) and my importunate request for the most expedite arrival of the army was probably seen by Kutuzov as a criticism or reproach. Greatly annoyed, Kutuzov spat so closely to my messenger that the latter had to reach for his handkerchief for, according to witnesses, his face was greatly in need of it.

However, my persistence was not in vain since Rayevskii arrived with his corps around 3:00 pm.[299] Occupying a large part of the town on the right and establishing reserves there, he allowed my forces to push forward. The field marshal finally arrived with the main army[300] early in the evening and occupied a position astride the Kaluga road and on the heights two and half verstas from the

---

[299] Yermolov's note: He had been close but his corps could not march without the personal order of the field marshal. I saw him arriving alone to witness the scene and learned that his troops were close.

[300] Yermolov's note: General Dokhturov deemed it impossible to attack Fominskoe and turned back on 11 [23] October to Maloyaroslavets. The field marshal received a report on this matter early in the morning of the same day. Had the army quit Tarutino at once and marched without halting at Spaskoe on the Protva, it would have arrived at Maloyaroslavets at least three hours before the French and occupied the position on the Kaluga road. This would have saved many thousands of lives; furthermore, Napoleon, having the entire town in his possession and seeing our army retreating, made no effort to attack so it was obvious that he had no plan for an offensive.

town. He ordered Lieutenant General Borozdin (I) to replace the exhausted regiments that had been defending the town from the outset and I would never return there. Kutuzov also ordered the construction of several redoubts within range of the town and the earthworks were started at once.

The French fought with remarkable determination and Borozdin's corps was soon unable to repulse their vigorous attacks. Borozdin's troops were replaced by the grenadier regiments, who continued fighting almost to midnight. Konovnitsyn took over with his usual fearlessness but he had to abandon the town despite all his efforts. After the town had fallen, the French deployed artillery around the town and undertook no further actions.

On the morning of 13 [25] October, the army still remained in the same position although Platov had gathered substantial forces of Cossacks on the extreme left. He attacked the enemy cavalry. This sudden assault spread confusion and disorder among the enemy and the Cossacks took prisoners, 30 guns and one flag. They only retreated after the French directed superior forces against them. A Polish uhlan regiment suffered enormous casualties here. Platov left a few regiments behind, ordering them to operate against the enemy rear, if possible. On the field marshal's orders, the captured guns and flag were taken to our camp to display to the troops.

Having summoned me, Kutuzov told me about his intention to retreat towards Kaluga. Trying to convince him to remain in position if not for the entire day, then at least for a few hours, I explained that the enemy's artillery was not supported and nothing indicated the enemy might attack. How could one expect Napoleon to resolve upon such a reckless attack against our army in such a position, having the town with its narrow streets, the bridges under our artillery fire and inconvenient banks of the creek that could prove fatal in retreat. Our army outnumbered Napoleon's, especially as the French had sent the Poles and heavy artillery to Mozhaisk.[301] Our cavalry was fresh and in good condition, whilst the enemy lacked mounted troops. It seemed possible that the town was occupied by a mere vanguard as the bulk of the enemy were

---

[301] Yermolov's note: We later learned from captives that Poniatowski, with the Poles and some other cavalry, was with Napoleon and that the dismounted French cavalry had been dispatched from Moscow to Mozhaisk.

observed across the Luzha ravine. The field marshal stressed the advantages of retreat. He asked me for my opinion. I responded that it might be possible but only for a short distance towards Medyn. He continued, 'How could this be possible in front of the enemy?' I answered that Platov had seized guns on the far side of the Luzha ravine. Kutuzov then noted, 'I love to speak to you since you never see anything negative.'[302] But that is how things seemed to everyone else as well. I am confident that Kutuzov did not expect an attack from Napoleon; he did not contradict my thinking that it was impossible to move the French army and artillery through a town in a single day and that the French needed space to deploy their army. Nevertheless, our army moved back a march along the Kaluga road, where Kutuzov arrived very early on 14 [26] October. A rearguard was left behind under Miloradovich and it was composed of the 2nd Corps (of the late General Baggovut), the 4th Corps of Count Osterman, the cavalry corps of Baron Korf and several Don Cossack regiments under Karpov. On 14 [26] October, a small infantry detachment sortied from the town and its guns exchanged fire with the artillery of our rearguard. No other troops were involved in this skirmish and the day ended without consequence.[303]

I returned to the headquarters that night and, warming myself in my hut, I felt no need to attend to the field marshal. Unexpectedly, he called for me. His first words were, 'Miloradovich reports that the enemy has left Maloyaroslavets and it has been occupied by our troops. Napoleon, with the army, is five verstas away from the place.' I helpfully told him that my suggestion not to withdraw the army to Kaluga had been ignored. The field marshal

---

[302] Denis Davidov noted, 'After the battle, Kutuzov had a curious conversation with Yermolov, which I can only summarize as follows:
 The prince: 'My dear, are we to march back?'
 Yermolov: 'Of course, but only towards Medyn.'
 The prince: 'How can we move in plain view of the enemy.'
Yermolov: 'There is no danger at all. Ataman Platov captured several guns on the other side of the creek without encountering any resistance. After this battle, which has proved we are ready to repulse all enemy attacks, we have nothing to fear from them.'
[303] Yermolov's note: Although one of the generals, commanding a division, hosted a dinner for his corps commander Count Osterman, which I attended. The fresh air led to multiple toasts. I later took a cart back to headquarters hoping to rest and even have some sleep.

continued, 'Only our advance Cossack posts are observing the enemy. Miloradovich has ordered Baron Korf to take a cavalry corps and the Don Cossacks under Karpov to follow the enemy once the bridges over the Luzha have been repaired, but he did not issue orders for the two infantry corps. You need to go to Miloradovich at once and tell him about my instructions. Report everything in detail and remain with Miloradovich until further word! My dear boy, you know that not everything can be written in reports so keep me informed via messenger as well! I will coordinate the army's movement with the actions of the vanguard.'

Before leaving, I informed the field marshal that since it was now obvious that Napoleon was retreating, the vanguard should be reinforced and asked him to give me Major General Paskevich, known for his courage, and his 26th Infantry Division; Paskevich was immediately ordered to follow me.

I found Miloradovich in Maloyaroslavets indulging in jovial conversation and supper with Baron Korf. The night was still young and there had been no changes in the dispositions. Napoleon's camp was still there, probably to give scattered detachments a chance to gather. Information from local residents was contradictory. It was said that a large enemy force had been observed towards Borovsk and Vereya. I informed the generals about the field marshal's orders to have the 2nd and 4th infantry corps moved towards Medyn at dawn. At break of day, General Baron Korf, with his cavalry corps and all the Don Cossacks, were busy observing the enemy. Napoleon had continued his retreat, leaving Vereya to his right, but it was not easy to guess his precise direction. Approaching Medyn, I received news that Platov was pursuing the French, had turned their flank and that the Cossacks he had dispatched under Adjutant General Count Orlov-Denisov had decisively defeated the Polish troops marching for Medyn.

General Miloradovich, having hurried forwards, passed through the villages of Odoevskoe and Kremenskoe on the Luzha and the village of Georgievskoe; this region was still undisturbed, the inhabitants had not left their houses and we wanted for nothing.

Meanwhile, Ataman Platov captured 25 guns without a fight near the Kolotsk Monastery on the road from Mozhaisk to Gzhatsk; everyday prisoners were taken en masse and it was apparent that the hastily retreating French army was in a bad way. Pursuing towards Gzhatsk, Platov approached Miloradovich's vanguard then heading for Nokolskoe on the road from Gzhatsk to Yukhnovo. Here we established contact with each other. At Georgievskoe I wrote to the field marshal informing him that the army could shorten its march by moving directly on Vyazma. He agreed to my suggestion but did not respond and all we knew was that the army had quit its camp near Dichin and was moving towards Medyn. According to Platov's intelligence and information from prisoners, Napoleon, accompanied by his Guard, was a day's march ahead of us; three other corps were also on the move but were in great disorder. The Italian viceroy, Eugene, commanding these troops, only saw Cossacks and failed to suspect that our infantry were busy observing his troops at close quarters from the road on his left. Lack of cavalry deprived the French of their ability to scout.

General Miloradovich concluded that it was not safe to cut the only line of retreat for the French and face their entire army with just his vanguard; instead, he decided to move to Czarevo Znaimische, where the position, well known to us, presented greater opportunities. Whilst marching to the village, the officers were told to conceal their campsites during the night and all fires were prohibited.

Never before had Miloradovich's presence been as necessary. Miloradovich had a very capable and brave colonel, Potemkin, performing the functions of the chief of staff. On that day, Potemkin was hosting a dinner for Miloradovich and everyone was complimenting his cook; some were admiring a stylish carriage, where a set of china and different tasty treats were stored. There was even a place for champagne. Regiments passed by singing and shouting

'hurrah'! The day passed very quickly and the time to camp was approaching. Then we suddenly heard musket shots. Galloping forwards, we arrived at our destination only to find ourselves in the midst of a firefight. The commander of the 4th Division, Prince Eugene of Württemberg, had not only failed to hide his troops' presence, but he had moved them so close to the road, along which the French were carelessly marching, that they had been obliged to send some tirailleurs and infantry against him. This reckless action of Prince Eugene – who was a fearless officer and beloved by his troops, but had no stomach for complex matters – forced Count Osterman to reinforce him with the 4th Corps and to get all the other troops battle ready. The French took advantage of the long night and continued their movement without pausing for a break. General Miloradovich, a very adroit courtier, quickly realized that Prince Eugene was a member of our imperial family and so he was very lenient towards him. However, I explained to him the likely consequences of this insubordination and could have told him that my rank required me to report it to the field marshal. I also knew that Prince Eugene was aware Kutuzov surpassed Miloradovich in his courtliness. If the French had not been alarmed by our unexpected appearance, they would have bivouacked for the night and would have been attacked the following day. Our vanguard could easily have intercepted part of their troops and destroyed it.

After departing early next day, we came across a very long defile behind Czarevo Znaimische. There was a high bank covered with enormous poplars and a twisting road cut through it. It was obvious that this had presented serious difficulties to the French as they passed through at night. In many places, heavy guns were abandoned in the mud, together with carriages, caissons and transports, some pushed off the road to allow the troops to pass. We spent more than two hours getting our vanguard through the defile.

After the message I sent to the field marshal from Georgievskoe, I wrote another letter urgently requesting his presence with the army at Vyazma on 22 October [4 November]. I soon received a letter from Colonel Toll, written on behalf of the field marshal, which expressed annoyance at the persistence of my requests and informed me that the prince would certainly have issued such an order if he had been informed more frequently about the actions of the vanguard. The letter finished by notifying me that the army would arrive at Vyazma on 21 October [3 November].

General Miloradovich received the field marshal's order to dispatch the 26th Infantry Division under Paskevich[304] and three cavalry regiments to Platov who was operating along the main road. He desired me to join him and I moved on 22 October.[305]

---

[304] Yermolov's note: The division was on its way to the vanguard.
[305] Yermolov's note: I was ready to go as I needed a rest from the disarray without which Miloradovich could not spend even a single minute. He was never at his headquarters. His officers, dispatched on mission, often ran into each other

The enemy retreated in a hurry that day, barely resisting us, and Platov established a camp some 27 verstas from Vyazma. Some prisoners told us that the enemy was determined to defend the city and that Napoleon was but a short march from it. Miloradovich and Platov, although they had wished to reward the hardships the troops had endured with success at Czarevo Znaimische, had not been successful and they therefore agreed to combine forces and coordinate their actions on 22 October [4 November]. Our vanguard, moving quickly along the country road, was to be ready to strike the right flank of the French as they approached Feodorovskoe. That day, Platov began his pursuit later than usual, thinking that the vanguard would not arrive at their objective before 11:00 am. He sent along two Cossack detachments with artillery under major generals Ilovayski (V) and Kuteynikov. He also sent for 300 men of the 5th Jägers from the 26th Infantry Division, which was still at some distance, mounting them on horses so they might arrive in time. Platov then broke camp at around 7:00 am The enemy had a weak rearguard. At 9:00 am, a cannonade was heard on our left, probably caused by Ilovayski and Kuteynikov. They, however, soon joined us and brought back news that large enemy forces had halted our vanguard. The Jägers mounted on horses arrived and Major General Paskevich, with his division, was hurrying along at a remarkable pace.

Platov placed some regular troops at my disposal, having reinforced them with a few Cossack regiments. The enemy doggedly protected some key heights. I moved the cavalry which had arrived with Colonel Prince Vadbolsky forward, and the cannonade began. The Courland Dragoons attacked the infantry and, despite canister fire, it scattered the enemy, inflicting heavy losses, although our regiments were then not only driven back but our battery was threatened as well. At that moment, the regiments of the 26th Division arrived in time to restore order and the enemy, considerably reinforced by now, was repulsed. Miloradovich's vanguard, facing weaker resistance, pushed forward. The Don Cossack regiments were dispatched with some artillery to envelop some enemy cavalry, which had rallied in a small group to the right. The enemy, supported by strong infantry, defeated our cavalry. One

---

on roads as they sought him out. Count Osterman and I shared Miloradovich's quarters.

of its columns bravely attacked and routed the Kargopol Dragoons. Platov's troops established contact with the vanguard, a fierce cannonade started along the entire front and the French, still fighting with determination, had to retreat at all points, pulling back to a much better position nearby, where they reformed. Our line was also reduced. Some of our troops had been victorious, although there were also less successful actions. It seemed that the enemy, aided by its position, would hold its ground until the night and would occupy Vyazma to ensure a convenient retreat. Therefore, we were completely astonished to see the enemy abandoning their position upon our approach. Our troops quickly pursued them further increasing the confusion in the enemy ranks and, without halting on the plain in front of the city, they soon linked with Miloradovich's vanguard. The approaches to the city were strongly occupied and, for a while, only our artillery was in action. On the extreme right, Platov personally led his Don Cossacks and artillery. We were aware that the field marshal was nearby but he did not advance. During the artillery barrage, an entire cuirassier division arrived with the Guard horse artillery which soon came into action inflicting, however, little damage on an enemy who had been retreating ever since observing the arrival of our cavalry. The cavalry commander, Uvarov, prudently avoided any unnecessary losses in the best of our regiments – the Chevalier Guard and Horse Guards. I soon met Bennigsen, who told me that the main army was not far off and that he was simply a curious spectator to the battle. Konovnitsyn also arrived but did not interfere. Night was fast approaching and General Bennigsen, feeling cold, told me that he would go back to headquarters to warm himself with hot tea.

It was noticed that the city suburbs were weakly defended and that therefore a general attack along the entire line was resolved upon. Miloradovich appointed the commander of the 11th Infantry Division, Major General Choglokov, to lead the attack and the Pernov and Kexholm regiments carried out a bayonet charge as they entered Vyazma. They encountered a column of grenadiers of the Army of Italy and pursued it through the streets. At the same time, the troops entrusted to me by Platov moved along another thoroughfare and Major General Paskevich with the 26th Division cleared a way with his bayonets through the bodies of the enemy and, without wasting a minute, he crossed the river to pursue them to the edge of Vyazma. Platov himself entered from the right and, having crossed the river, he occupied large sections of the city. Our troops descended on the place; my adjutant, Lieutenant Grabbe, attached to Miloradovich, led a detachment of tirailleurs with two horse artillery guns, while the guerrilla leaders Seslavin and Figner were on the far side of the city. The French were retreating everywhere and, in their hurry, they set several buildings on fire, including an artillery workshop; the fire quickly spread and engulfed a military hospital. That day we captured one general, numerous officers and over 2,000 soldiers, 2 flags and several guns. The prisoners told us that there had been three corps under Eugene, Davout and Ney, with a total strength of 40,000 men. Ney had been 17 verstas beyond Vyazma, when he heard a cannonade and returned to help his comrades. It was said, without proof, that Napoleon himself had been there when we approached, but later joined his Guard and the remaining troops retreating on Smolensk.

As they were abandoning Vyazma, the French had occupied a cemetery and established a battery there. Our infantry was deployed in the main square, where large numbers of Cossacks gathered around Platov, and I was with him too. Our campfires served as a target for the French and some of their cannonballs caused some damage. An artillery company was moved to the city outskirts and we had to abandon the square.[306] Had our army, located nearby, joined our vanguard, the enemy would have been thoroughly routed, its remaining forces would have been pursued and destroyed piecemeal and we would have captured the city by late afternoon. Considering our superiority of numbers, it would not have been difficult to drive the French towards the Dukhovshina and to cut them off on their march to Smolensk.

Here at Vyazma we witnessed for the last time the actions of the enemy forces that had spread horror by their victories and earned our respect. We could still see the skill of their generals, the obedience of their subordinates and their energy. But, the very next day, there were no orderly enemy troops left; the experience and abilities of their generals were now of no use, discipline had

---

[306] Yermolov's note: After learning about Napoleon's departure from Maloyaroslavets, which was occupied by our troops, Kutuzov slowly advanced. He believed that the harsh climate, hunger and other hardships would doom the French army and so he had no intention of pursuit. Our Guard Cuirassier Division was at Vyazma and, naturally, the czar would assume that our entire army was there too! Anyone can perceive Kutuzov's hand in this.

disappeared and the soldiers seemed to have lost their last strength, each of them now a victim of hunger, exhaustion and the cruelty of the weather. Some four verstas from Vyazma, we found several abandoned guns on the crossing over a small ravine. This disorder was not caused by our vanguard's pursuit as they had been allowed to march all night without impediment.

On 23 October [5 November], our vanguard was being led by Miloradovich – I had orders to serve with him – and he pursued the enemy along the main road to Dorogobouzh. Platov with his Cossacks and horse artillery moved to the right of the main road. The field marshal, with the main army, was heading for Yelna. The weather was unusually cold.

Our vanguard reached Semlevo without having fired a single shot. It captured over 1,000 soldiers and several officers, all completely exhausted and sick. There were numerous guns, caissons and carriages abandoned all along the road. Horsemeat was being used as food and even that was scarce since all the fit horses had been taken for the artillery. The French retreated in a hurry, briefly resting in the daytime out of reach of our vanguard, but continuing their retreat during the night despite the Cossacks harassing them. Their progress demonstrated the gradual destruction of a fleeing army.

Eight verstas from Dorogobouzh, the enemy crossed the Osma and bivouacked there; the bridge was preserved so that the stragglers could cross. Our troops fell on it so suddenly that the enemy became disorganized, surged on to the bridge and threw their guns into the water while our guns bombarded their camp. However, a strong enemy infantry column quickly crossed back over the bridge and menaced our batteries.

Platov quit Vyazma for Dukhovshina after receiving news that a heavy artillery park, which Napoleon had dispatched from Moscow to Mozhaisk, was there. It was moving slowly due to the vast numbers of vehicles belonging to different staffs and numerous civilians and was protected by the troops of the Italian viceroy and other allied soldiers. Not being on the main road, they considered themselves out of danger and maintained lax discipline. The sudden appearance of a cloud of Cossacks led by Platov spread confusion everywhere; no one thought of fighting and everyone sought refuge. The Cossacks captured one general, who occupied an important position in the army, numerous officials and lower ranks as well as a copious collection of maps and plans.[307]

Suffering insignificant losses, the Cossacks seized 36 guns and rich booty. Platov then moved to the right bank of the Dniepr and halted close to the suburbs of Smolensk. Napoleon, with his Guard and army, occupied the city.

At Dorogobouzh, Miloradovich was ordered to march to join the army, while I was instructed to return to headquarters. Major General Yurkovskii, with two Jäger regiments and some light cavalry pursued the enemy rearguard from the river Osma to Dorogobouzh, capturing several guns. Having defeated it at the Solovyev bridge, he seized even more guns and rejoined the vanguard. Before our army reached Yelna, Count Orlov-Denisov had sent a detachment to capture the French depots scattered throughout the region, some of which were already being observed by Davidov, Figner and Seslavin.

Major General Prince Iashvili, who commanded the militia in the Kaluga region, was at Yelna. Learning about a force under General Augereau, he left the city, but was attacked and forced to accept an unequal battle against superior enemy troops from one such depot. However, Orlov-Denisov suddenly arrived to rescue the militia and pursued General Augereau who threw himself into a nearby village. Three other guerrilla leaders [Denisov, Seslavin and Figner] assisted Orlov-Denisov. Our artillery fire destroyed some enemy munition wagons and the French general had to surrender. We captured more than 1,500 men. General Charpentier, who was rushing to the rescue with his cavalry, had to retreat, after some of his troops were driven into the swamps. Magazines with numerous provisions were burnt at Klementino. General Baraguay d'Hillers, learning about the surrender of General Augereau, hastily retreated after exchanging several volleys.

Between Smolensk and Moscow, the enemy had organized a series of military posts to maintain communications, which were located in well- fortified churches and other buildings, and where provisions and other supplies could have been stockpiled. However,

---

[307] Yermolov's note: I later saw one of these, an enormous map of the greater part of Germany with exquisite detail, in possession of Prince Volkonsky, chief of the imperial general staff. Our cartography department was certainly enriched by such maps.

because of incredible negligence, no supplies were actually stored anywhere.

The locals around Moscow took up arms only after Napoleon's occupation of our capital. The rapid advance of his army had left no time to harass the villages on both sides of the main road and people had remained in their homes, continued working in the fields and suffered no discomfort. Thus, the French could have taken advantage of the villages to their rear, had the disordered throngs of lewd allied scoundrels that followed in their wake been prevented from pillaging and other crimes. Regular payments to the peaceful population would have, if not prevented an uprising, then at least greatly mitigated against one and there was no doubt that there were some ready to support the French.

Seeing our army retreating after the terrible battle of Borodino and then observing Moscow being abandoned and deliberately doomed to destruction in the flames, Napoleon should have understood that the war would inevitably continue, especially after he had waited in vain for our offers of peace and after sending General Lauriston[308] with proposals to our main headquarters at Tarutino.

It might have been possible that he could have reinforced his army with fresh troops and called in his numerous reserves located not far from our borders. Thus, nobody dared think that he would begin to retreat so soon and at such an unfavourable time of year.

The field marshal's main headquarters was at Yelna; Count Osterman's 4th Corps was ordered forwards. There were rumours that enormous supplies had been gathered in Smolensk and the field marshal found it plausible that Napoleon could rest his army there and restore order; he certainly found absurd the prevalent talk in the headquarters that if our army approached Krasnyi, Napoleon would move from Smolensk through Mstislavl, and, having joined the Polish troops of General Dombrowski at Moghilev, he would then advance through the undamaged provinces towards Lithuania. At Smolensk, Napoleon found nothing had been readied and even his Guard lacked full rations. He then moved to Krasnyi, occupying it with his Guard and the weak corps of Davout while his main body slowly moved along the main road, with each corps in

---

[308] Yermolov's note: He was an ambassador at our court, universally respected for his gracious and reverential attitude.

isolation, without coordination or provision for mutual defence, acting in complete disorder, with thousands of people too weak to hold their weapons and starved to exhaustion.

I informed the field marshal that Count Osterman had reported that based on information gathered from the local population and the residents of Smolensk, Napoleon had left for Krasnyi more than 24 hours ago. There could not have been pleasanter news for the field marshal, who considered the Guard the strongest troops and die-hard supporters of Napoleon who were determined on taking any desperate action. After listening to my report, he suggested to Bennigsen that they continue their breakfast and, after placing his cutlet on the plate, he, with his usual courtesy, offered it to me together with a glass of wine. I took them and went closer to the window since the room was so small there was no place for me to sit. Bennigsen argued for an immediate march on Krasnyi. He was surprised by Napoleon's blunder of wasting three days in Smolensk instead of crossing over to the right bank of the Dniepr via the bridge constructed at Dubrovno. He could have done this not only without any interference but completely unnoticed by our armies.[309]

Kutuzov ordered that a vanguard be organized under Miloradovich, and that it should comprise the 1st and 2nd cavalry corps, 2nd and 4th infantry corps, strong artillery and several Cossack regiments. I was assigned to this vanguard.

Asking that the reader tolerate a little smugness on my part, I must explain that this stemmed from Bennigsen's flattering approval of my suggestion for the forthcoming action. I believed that it would have been more advantageous for Napoleon to have left Smolensk down the right bank of the Dniepr. The freezing weather had frozen the swamps that now became just as convenient for movement as any postal road. Marching on Smolyani meant passing through the towns of Orsha and Dubrovno, reducing the distance and hastening the union with the forces of Marshal Oudinot. Napoleon was still unaware that Polotsk was already in our hands and had no information about the fate of the troops that

---

[309] Yermolov's note: After breakfast, I asked General Bennigsen to explain himself. He responded, 'If I had not known you since your childhood, and your long service under me, I would have thought that you desired the opposite since all my suggestions are largely carried out improperly. You may not know this.'

protected this city. Besides, there were many other reasons to force him to hurry.

Count Orlov-Denisov soon reported that because of his illness, he was unable to command his detachment and asked for a transfer. He openly expressed his indignation and was insulted when the defeat of General Augereau's troops was attributed to the assistance of the three guerrilla commanders, and not to him alone. Major General Borozdin took over command of his detachment. Another unit was organized from the 19th Jäger Regiment, six artillery pieces and a considerable number of Cossacks under the command of Adjutant General Count Ozharovskii. Approaching Krasnyi, he did act with the proper caution, assuming that the retreating enemy would not attempt anything. Yet, during the night, Napoleon's Guard swiftly attacked Ozharovskii; the gallant Jägers suffered heavy casualties, our artillery miraculously survived and, in the general confusion, the darkness proved to be a blessing. As the rumours about this failure spread, our superiors tried to gloss over them but the details still leaked out. Nevertheless, the czar was told about this incident in a most flattering way and everyone was satisfied! The enemy, meanwhile, also celebrated victory in its own camp. Thus, the renowned leader Napoleon now had an open road to continue his exploits.

CHAPTER VII
THE PATRIOTIC WAR
NOVEMBER – DECEMBER 1812

General Miloradovich's vanguard was ordered to Krasnyi. Platov, following the capture of Vyazma and the brilliant raid on Dukhovshina, where he seized the extensive artillery park and other important objectives, appeared before the fortified suburbs of Smolensk on the right bank of the Dniepr while Napoleon was still in the city. Following the river, he hoped to intercept Napoleon at Dubrovno or Orsha, obstruct his passage and slow him down as much as possible, but he soon learned the Napoleon had crossed the Dniepr and had already reached Orsha. Platov could not have imagined that our army, knowing the state of the retreating enemy, would not even pursue them.

On 3 [15] November General Miloradovich's vanguard was some 10 verstas from Krasnyi, approaching the main road from Smolensk. General Rayevskii's 6th Corps[310] had replaced the 4th Corps. Part of the vanguard's cavalry had engaged the enemy, but the French soon faded away into the woods. Many prisoners were taken, in addition to a train loaded with rich loot from Moscow.[311]

Our infantry was little used that day and the vanguard fell back to bivouac for the night in a nearby ruined village which had been abandoned by residents. Our advance posts observed the road.

On 4 [16] November, the Viceroy of Italy quit Smolensk with the remnants of his army which had been reinforced by other units and, having passed the right flank of our vanguard, moved off the road and vigorously attacked our

6th Corps. General Rayevskii met the enemy with his characteristic steadfastness; the canister fire of our artillery,

---

[310] Rayevskii commanded the 7th Corps.
[311] By 14 November, Kutuzov's main body was at Yurovo, some 19 miles from Krasnyi. Major General Ozharovskii briefly captured Krasnyi but was driven out by the division of General Claparède and retreated to Kutkovo, two miles to the south. On 15 November, Napoleon arrived at Krasnyi, the French dislodged Ozharovskii from Kutkovo and cleared the route to Orsha. Meanwhile Osterman-Tolstoy, with the 11th Division and 2nd Reserve Cavalry Corps, attacked the Poles near Kobyzev.

which was far superior in numbers, inflicted appalling losses on the French but Rayevskii also suffered significant losses. An enemy column, which had earlier marched to Krasnyi, turned back at the sound of the gunfire and attacked the rear of the weak 4th Infantry Division of the gallant Prince Eugene of Württemberg and threatened to overwhelm the superb Belozersk Regiment. A vicious fight took place there, but the regiments of the 1st Cavalry Corps of Adjutant General Baron Müller- Zakomelsky arrived in time and the enemy column was routed.

Whilst the attack of the Italian viceroy was being contained and repulsed, the Moscow Dragoons under the command of the fearless Colonel (Nikolai Vladimirovich) Davidov fell on an isolated enemy infantry column of some 2,000 men. Our horses were so tired that we could barely penetrate the enemy column but as the enemy infantry was exhausted to such a degree that they were not only unable to defend themselves, but even to move, they lay down their weapons and surrendered. An eagle, belonging to one of the most famous French units, was captured.[312] The success of our troops on that day could have had far-reaching consequences, but night was quickly approaching and our troops had to fall back to rest, which was essential to everyone. Our Cossack advance posts soon notified us that the Italian viceroy and his troops had passed through Krasnyi during the night.

At dawn on 5 [17] November, the vanguard approached the main road near Krasnyi and took up a position parallel to it. Our troops were reinforced that day: we received the Grenadier Division and the 3rd Infantry Division, several regiments of light cavalry and cuirassiers. The Guard protected Kutuzov's headquarters. Two Guard infantry regiments with artillery, two cuirassier units and Cossacks formed a detachment under Major General Baron Rosen (commander of the Life Guard Preobrazhensk Regiment). He also commanded Adjutant General Count Ozharovskii's and Major General Borozdin's detachments. These troops were termed a vanguard and positioned themselves at Dobroe not far from Krasnyi.

The enemy forces, which we observed in the distance, spent most of the day marching in isolated bands rarely more than 2,000-

---

[312] This was at Merlino, where the French 35th Line lost its flag and some 2,000 men.

men strong. Coming under fire from our batteries, they often abandoned their guns and vehicles and scattered with enormous losses, finding refuge in the forest. Some courageously moved forward, but they fell to the bayonets of the Grenadier Division of Count Stroganov and the 3rd Infantry Division.

General Baron Rosen was the closest to Krasnyi and the enemy columns soon encountered him. Yet, they fought briefly and with little stamina, abandoning their guns and fleeing. Parts of Napoleon's Young Guard and the corps of Davout fought resolutely,[313] but they could not withstand a vigorous attack by the Life Guard Jägers. When Rosen finally broke into the town, he captured many abandoned guns and heavy wagons, including the personal baggage of Davout, his secret correspondence and his marshal's baton. Our troops had rich booty.

The 5 November ended with this exploit. Our Guard entered Krasnyi. The main army was coming up and bivouacked near the town. Baron Rosen was reinforced and could have followed the French to observe their movements, but he was ordered not to leave the town.

Early on the morning of 6 [18] November, we observed enemy forces marching up from Smolensk. For a while dense fog prevented us from determining their strength, but prisoners soon told us that it was Marshal Ney with his rearguard. It was composed of survivors from all the corps, had considerable artillery and some 900 cavalrymen from eleven different regiments of various nationalities. In all there were some 15,000 men, of whom only Ney's own corps, now significantly reduced in strength, maintained order and discipline.

General Miloradovich with the 7th infantry and the 1st cavalry corps occupied a position astride the main road, some four verstas from Krasnyi. He had reserves behind him and deployed strong batteries to cover his lines not far from the descent into the valley where the bridge was located. Approaching this place, Ney deployed a battery on the opposite height, but our artillery quickly

---

[313] Denis Davidov wrote, 'Finally, the Guard arrived… and seeing us, the soldiers levelled their muskets and proudly kept moving… In tall bearskin hats, blue uniforms, white belts, red plumes and epaulettes, they seemed as poppies in the middle of snow fields… The Guard advanced through our ranks like a hundred-gun warship through fishing boats.'

silenced it. Then, after sending out a large number of tirailleurs, he forced our own skirmishers to retreat, repaired the bridge and decided to break through. For a long time dense fog covered the ground and, as they moved through this haze, the three French columns marched silently with incredible determination under our murderous canister fire, without making a single musket shot.[314] Our batteries were moved and it was now up to our infantry to check the French advance. Brave Major General Paskevich, who commanded a division in the 7th Corps, swiftly attacked one of the columns with two regiments, routed it and scattered its feeble survivors. The Pavlovsk Grenadier Regiment charged the second column and routed it and scattered it with equally heavy losses. The third French column had five artillery pieces, but the Life Guard Uhlans quickly attacked it; the guns did not fire, but the enemy musket fire reduced the impact of our cavalry attack and the column escaped destruction.[315] Marshal Ney commanded these troops in person and, after realizing the impossibility of breaking through to join the main French army, he retreated into the woods. Yet, he still had enough troops and enough artillery. Napoleon, who was still not far from Krasnyi, made no attempt to help Ney. Nothing could have told us more about the grave position

---

[314] The Russian officer, Sherbinin, recalled, 'On a misty and freezing morning, Ney's corps was moving from Smolensk and came against Miloradovich's batteries. This was not a battle, but the annihilation of enemy columns with artillery fire. It was assumed that Ney's remaining troops would surrender; therefore, the cannonade was ceased before nightfall, and many enemy guns were captured.'

[315] Wilson left an interesting account of this engagement: 'The Russians courageously repulsed these enemy attacks and finally, the Guard Uhlans promptly attacked and destroyed three enemy columns and captured one general, six guns and three colours.... The remnants of the enemy, exploiting a dense fog, turned to our right and reached the forest near the Dniepr; yet, some 3,500 men did surrender by evening, and even more were captured this morning during the pursuit. Marshal Ney with some 3,000 men reached the ford on the Dniepr river that everyone had forgotten, and it seems the enemy corps crossed the river here, leaving some 20 guns.... Numerous prisoners are still arriving... many of them simply appear from the woods and silently join the Russians around the fire. Several colours and other trophies were sent to His Majesty in St Petersburg as examples of the patriotism and courage of the Russians. It is difficult to describe enemy losses. But at the present moment there are 17 captured generals, more than 400 guns, including 112 left on the Smolensk road...' Sir Robert Wilson to Sir Cartwright, 7 (19) November 1812.

Napoleon was in, but it did not excite a reaction from our army. Our field marshal remained unwavering in his decision and our army therefore concentrated on these few survivors of Ney's dying corps.

During the battle, Miloradovich ordered Baron Korf[316] to move his cavalry corps forward in order to divert the enemy but the latter reported that he was protecting the right wing of the vanguard. Some other troops carried out this order without difficulty. Having instructions to observe the action against Ney in the woods, I personally noted how inconvenient it is to advance deep into a forest along mere tracks; so I ordered an end to this useless skirmish and prepared to act with artillery if necessary. I soon reported that enemy columns had appeared on the left edge of the woods and, having come together, they were moving towards our position, stopping not far from our batteries and sending an officer to negotiate. He declared that the column, comprised of more than 6,000 men, was ready to surrender. They had far fewer muskets than men and not a single gun. They presented a terrible sight and it was possible to save only some of them.

The field marshal consented to General Rosen's idea of using his detachment to observe enemy forces and he was given the Guard infantry regiments, two cuirassier regiments and three Don Cossack regiments.

Following the surrender of a substantial part of his troops, Ney recognized his perilous position and decided to attempt a desperate enterprise: he believed the crossing of the Dniepr was his only means of escape. Miloradovich, having dispatched some of his troops to collect surviving enemy troops scattered in the woods, returned to Krasnyi and I accompanied him.

---

[316] Yermolov's note: I often heard sarcastic jokes about Baron Korf: for instance that during an offensive he found roads difficult and inconvenient, and yet, the same roads seemed quite easy when the enemy advanced. General Baron Korf was known for his courtesy, loyalty in friendship and enjoyed the high respect of his comrades in arms.

Editor: Some Russian officers blamed Korf for letting Ney escape. Thus, Creitz noted in his memoirs, 'Baron Korf was to be blamed for Ney's crossing of the Dniepr. It seems it was the only mistake Miloradovich made when he ordered this general to pursue the remnants of the corps. Korf, together with General Sablukov, was preoccupied with the prisoners.'

On 7 [19] November, I suggested to the field marshal that General Rosen's detachment should be strengthened and that the order should be given to advance, giving overall command to me. Kutuzov generously listened to me, expressed his consent and immediately ordered the necessary changes in the composition of the detachment. Following his orders, the Life Guard Jägers and Finland regiments, His and Her Majesty's Cuirassier regiments, the Guard field artillery and a battery company of horse artillery were assigned to the detachment. The twelve infantry battalions had their own field artillery guns as well.

Although I had been unable to see any of the people who wielded significant influence at headquarters, I was still aware that Toll persisted in arguing about the necessity of deploying troops to observe the Dniepr and the village of Syrokorenye, but Konovnitsyn, far inferior in his ability to make far-reaching and complex decisions, turned down his suggestion; so Ney owed his escape to him.[317] Reaching Syrokorenye without any difficulty, Ney attempted the desperate enterprise of crossing the Dniepr on ice. The frost had not been sufficiently severe and the ice cracked under their feet. After abandoning ten guns and a few heavy wagons, Ney made the crossing accompanied by some 1,500 men and his sole surviving horse.

In his report to the czar, Kutuzov portrayed the indecisive and sluggish action of our army at Krasnyi as being a series of major battles fought over several days, whereas the engagements had been fought in isolation and none of these battles had been fought according to any general plan. Yet, our timid actions had to be presented in a positive light and what could have been better than describing them as battles? But, in reality, they were carried out randomly. At the same time, the enemy losses and complete disorder of their army were reported, but no attention was paid to ensuring the complete destruction of the enemy as they crossed the Berezina, to where Admiral Chichagov was directing all his troops.

---

[317] Sherbinin observed, 'Only one general at headquarters perceived where Ney would break through. It was Oppermann. On 7 November, Oppermann arrived at a small hut where General Konovnitsyn occupied, and where I was also billeted. He named a place on the Dniepr some twelve verstas from Krasnyi, where Ney would certainly cross the river; he advised Konovnitsyn to occupy this location at once. Konovnitsyn initially agreed with him... and went to Kutuzov to inform him about Oppermann's views, but no decision was made.'

Departing for my detachment, I received the following instructions from the field marshal: 'My dear boy, be careful, avoid any situation where you might sustain losses in men!' I replied, 'Having seen the condition of the enemy, who are driven away by whoever so wishes, I do not think that I will distinguish myself like Ozharovskii.' His Excellency forbade the crossing of the Dniepr, but allowed the dispatch of some infantry if Platov found it necessary.

Promising to precisely execute my orders, I soon broke my oath and, I must confess, decided to do things differently. Kutuzov's desire was that we should assume that Napoleon was nearby and that he was going to pursue him. Platov had intended to bar the enemy crossing of the Dniepr at Dubrovno or Orsha, but the French had already crossed without any difficulty.

My detachment arrived at Dubrovno but Major General Borozdin, who had been dispatched ahead of us, crossed the Dniepr without bothering to repair the bridge. Learning that the bridge had been built under the direction of a French officer, now residing in the town, I forced him to repair the bridge as well as possible. He was given chains and ropes from the artillery and the ropes from the regimental trains; the bridge's structure was solid and reliable. During the next day and a half, I was absent from the repair works for only a very short period of time and everything was duly completed.

The infantry crossed unhindered and the artillery was manhandled over the thick planks laid over the bridge. Horses presented a greater problem and, although some precautions were taken, the bridge shook and seemed on the verge of collapse. The only way to get the horses of the two cuirassier regiments across was to tie their legs, lay them down on planks and drag them by the tail over the bridge. The Don Cossack horses simply swam across the river. I hurried to join Platov, who was on the opposite bank requesting more infantry. Two small boats served as the means of communication between us. He sent two captured officials to me, and I forwarded one of them with a letter to the field marshal.[318]

---

[318] Yermolov's note: In the letter, I asked Kutuzov to grant an audience to this officer since he was with Napoleon's army in Smolensk and had precise information on its condition. I later saw a book written by M. Puibusque, chevalier of the Order of St Anna of the 2nd class, which he received while

However, the ice strengthened on the Dniepr and soon destroyed the bridge, stranding all the wagons, part of our caissons and supply train on that shore.[319]

The field marshal ordered Count Ozharovskii's and Borozdin's detachments to proceed to Moghilev, assuming that the Poles of General Dombrowski were still there. As for the partisans, Davidov swam across the Dniepr and captured a cuirassier depot while Seslavin was left at the disposal of Platov. The main army moved from Krasnyi to Kopys in order to procure better supplies.

My detachment bivouacked at the village belonging to one of the monasteries in Orsha. Platov informed me that after quitting Smolensk while Napoleon and his army were still there, he had received no new intelligence on the French. He was extremely surprised when a prisoner described in detail how Marshal Ney, with a few troops, had crossed the Dniepr, had learned from the peasants about the appearance of Cossacks in force and took cover in the woods not far from Dubrovno until additional French troops had been dispatched from Orsha to his rescue and helped him to proceed in complete safety. I submitted a report to the field marshal about my crossing of the Dniepr and received the order to halt at the village of Tolochno until the arrival of Miloradovich's vanguard.

At my first bivouac, a certain Jew arrived with Count Wittgenstein's report to Prince Kutuzov, informing him that Marshal Victor and his corps were at Chereya, probably covering the troops of Oudinot, and that his cavalry greatly complicated any observation of the enemy movement. After reading the report, I added a note with my observation that the French could be deploying part of their troops in front of Wittgenstein to cover their movement and be directing their forces to Lake Dolgoe, opposite the Berezina, thereby drawing closer to Napoleon by at least one march.[320]

---

serving Field Marshal Kutuzov. (Yermolov refers to Viscount L.G. Puibusque, Lettres sur la guerre de Russie en 1812, sur la ville de Saint Petersbourg, les moers et les usages des habitants de la Russie et de la Pologne, Paris, 1816-1817.)

[319] Yermolov's note: I disclosed some details of the crossing only because it was made in such a way as to demonstrate what can be done with the incomparable Russian soldier.

[320] Yermolov's note: During my absence from headquarters, I was given permission by Kutuzov to open dispatches addressed to him, add information or simply mark them, 'Read by the chief of staff'.

My detachment briefly entered Orsha, where Murat had been with part of his cavalry shortly before, and I then hurried to join Platov. The latter agreed to support my report to the field marshal and would say that I only received his order to wait for the vanguard at Tolochna after I had already passed it (although in reality I was still one march away); he also informed Kutuzov that since he was entering the immense woods of the Minsk province he needed additional infantry and therefore he had invited me to follow him or keep as close as possible. On the march, we found abandoned artillery everywhere and some of the guns were thrown into the water with such haste that no attempt was made to conceal them! The loss of life greatly exceeded everything. There were thousands of dead and freezing people. There was no refuge or shelter; villages and settlements were all reduced to ash and an increasing number of prisoners, all wounded and sick and many non-combatants, were all doomed to an inevitable death. The never-ending sight of suffering humans exhausted compassion and dulled the very feeling of remorse. Each of these unfortunate men had seemed to cease to be human in the eyes of others. Everyone suffered and the calamity was beyond any imagination! Without any means to help them, we saw them as victims fated to perish.

Platov was soon informed about the order I received to cooperate with him and to follow his orders as much as possible.

Count Ozharovskii advanced on Moghilev, occupying the town and capturing the few remaining Poles and local hospitals. Meanwhile, General Borozdin carefully observed those regions from which the enemy had long ago departed![321] Borozdin owed his appointment to the patronage of Konovnitsyn, who could not resist a man who had the ability to flatter in a very adroit manner. Yet, he made sure that the abilities of others were never given prominence.

Napoleon retreated with incredible haste, fearing to be overtaken by our army before crossing the Berezina. But he had nothing to fear since, despite the precise intelligence on the enemy forces, the field marshal refused to move, believing that the prolonged retreat, worsening winter weather, raging hunger and the

---

[321] Yermolov's note: General Dombrowski's division of Polish troops had left Moghilev ahead of time but the last two or three thousand men from various units departed later. Borozdin was sending his dispatches directly to headquarters. His main talent was flattery!

forthcoming combat on the Berezina would bring the French army to the verge of destruction without the involvement of the main army. Had the main headquarters informed Platov in time about the departure of 3,000 Polish troops from Moghilev, they would have all been captured since my detachment was marching in their wake. Platov could not comprehend the indifference with which important goals, such as the union with the army of Admiral Chichagov and the need to reinforce it, were addressed.

After completing a march late in the evening of 15 [27] November, I bivouacked near Lozhnitsy, the last post station before Borisov. Admiral Chichagov's adjutant, Lieutenant Lisanevich, soon arrived with an offer to join him in Borisov. The adjutant described to me in detail how Platov, having approached Borisov, had the brave partisan Seslavin move ahead of him and break into the city under cover of darkness. The surprise factor and thousands of attacking Cossacks produced general confusion among the enemy. The weak French infantry division of General Partonneaux hastily retreated towards the forces deployed near the crossing, but Count Wittgenstein's troops intercepted them and the division was forced, together with two cavalry regiments of the Rhine Confederation, to surrender, while the town remained in our hands and communications were soon restored with the opposite bank.

As I sent the adjutant back, I gave him a report to the admiral and asked that he be informed that my troops, although having just completed an arduous march, were ready to make another one although I thought it necessary to give them four hours to prepare porridge, repair their shoes and rest, after which I would march without delay. The troops marched quickly, burning with the desire to fight, and they entered Borisov long before noon, without halting, and immediately began work on the crossing.

While marching at night from Loshnitsa, some horses from three Cossack regiments were captured by enemy soldiers hiding in the woods; but scores more enemy soldiers preferred to surrender to avoid dying of hunger.

After reaching Borisov in the morning, I met Platov, who told me that the admiral was asking me to hurry to join him and begin construction of the crossing over the Berezina. Several temporary bridges were built, covered with straw and drenched with water which froze in the cold. The infantry passed over without difficulty, and the artillery and ammunition caissons were also transported across without problems. The exceptional ability and adroitness of the Cossacks overcame all hurdles; fords were discovered and two cuirassier regiments crossed the river at once.

The vague and alarming rumours that reached us earlier were clarified upon our arrival at Borisov. Admiral Chichagov's considerable forces had just recently occupied the town and the vanguard under General Count Pahlen (a relative of the famous Peter Petrovich) had been dispatched towards Loshnitsy. The French, taking advantage of the wooded terrain, routed the cavalry that had moved ahead of us and as it retreated, they trampled our nearby infantry sent to support it. Without warning, the vanguard suddenly appeared in great disorder near Borisov, pursued by enemy forces which broke into the town. The admiral withdrew with his troops across the bridge, which was burnt down on his orders. Entire convoys with horses were lost, including the admiral's personal carriages with his possessions and precious baggage and a silver dining set prepared for lunch. Reconnaissance on the left shore of the Berezina was interrupted.

As he passed through Bobr, Napoleon received the fresh corps of Victor, the troops of Marshal Oudinot which had earlier defended Polotsk (excluding the Bavarian corps, which General Prince Wrede took directly from Polotsk to Lithuania) and the Polish troops of General Dombrowski.

Count Wittgenstein established his headquarters at Borisov. His main forces were nearby and he had only part of his troops at his disposal and these were prevented from reaching the crossing by Victor's rearguard.

As an old acquaintance,[322] Wittgenstein received me with particular attention and I found in him all the traits of a knight, not the least of which was pride. It was evident in the discussion about the plans and actions he had carried out, about the many battles he had won and the courage of his troops. He told me that Admiral Chichagov, although having the means to prevent the enemy crossing or decisively defeat the army of Napoleon, had only left a

---

[322] Yermolov's note: We served together under Prince Repnin, commander-in-chief of the army in Lithuania, in 1794. In 1796, while I served under Count Zubov, operating against Muhammed Agha Shah, Wittgenstein delivered the news of the death of the Czarina Catherine II.

weak detachment under General Chaplitz and moved his remaining troops a considerable distance away. I told the count that I was aware of the general plan of action drafted by the czar, which had been delivered to the field marshal by Colonel Chernishev at the village of Krasnaya Pakhra six days after Napoleon had occupied Moscow while our army was making that memorable flanking movement from Podolsk along the right bank of the Moscow River towards the Kaluga road. No one anticipated that after a brief stay in Moscow Napoleon would be forced to retreat; therefore, the czar's plan to direct significant forces against the enemy lines of communications, where the enormous supply magazines, depots, reinforcements and various kinds of supplies were located, seemed most sensible. The field marshal had entrusted this mission to Admiral Chichagov, thinking that the latter would march with no less than 60,000 men.

Admiral Chichagov received this order while still facing General Prince Schwarzenberg, who commanded the Austrian troops, and the Saxon corps under the command of the French general Reynier, a zealous executor of Napoleon's commands, who persistently demanded more decisive action from Prince Schwarzenberg. Chichagov left Lieutenant General Baron Osten-Sacken with 26,000 men to keep them at bay and led his remaining troops through Minsk to Borisov, the main line of enemy operations. He was to establish communication with our forces around Polotsk which was expected to fall soon after the arrival of the St Petersburg and Novgorod militias, Adjutant General Kutuzov's detachment and the large reinforcement of Lieutenant General Steingell which had been recalled from Finland. Thus, considerable forces were being gathered in the rear of the army of Napoleon and these threatened him with dire consequences. Wittgenstein was already aware that the main reason why the Admiral had marched on Igumen was because of the field marshal as he had heard unsubstantiated information about Napoleon seeking a crossing site there. Before departing, I told the count that Platov and his Cossacks and my detachment would join the admiral's army during the night of 16 [28] November.[323]

---

[323] Yermolov's note: I found Major General Begichev (Ivan Matveyevich) serving as duty general at headquarters. During Suvorov's capture of Praga, the suburb of Warsaw, in 1794, he commanded the artillery. Many of us, serving in the same

A day later Platov joined forces with Admiral Chichagov. We soon learned, that on his advance through Minsk, the admiral had captured enormous stores with provisions and supplies, hospital and medical supplies and had left a small detachment to protect them. Further along the way, his vanguard under the courageous Adjutant General Count Lambert found an enemy fortification near Borisov, which we had earlier constructed to defend the bridges; almost one verst long, it was built across the swamps through which the Berezina and its tributaries flowed.

Count Lambert had ordered his infantry to form columns and immediately attacked the fortification, taking it by assault. The enemy defended resolutely, but suffered heavy casualties. General Dombrowski retreated across the river, without halting in the town. The victors captured six guns and up to 2,000 prisoners.[324] The admiral finally reached the Berezina with less than 30,000 men, that is, less than half the strength the field marshal had initially assumed.

Chichagov lacked intelligence on our forces and had virtually no information on Napoleon's troops. The enemy was in Borisov on the left bank and, based on the resolute resistance and good condition of General Dombrowski's troops, Chichagov assumed that the rest of the enemy were in similar condition.

I arrived and saw the admiral at dawn on 17 [29] November. He kindly received me and told me that, hearing about the appearance of enemy cavalry on the left bank of the Berezina some 23 verstas from Borisov, he left General Chaplitz to defend the Zembinskoe defile and marched on Igumen, bypassing Borisov; however he quickly returned after learning that the enemy had arrived in large numbers at Vytcha, organized enormous batteries on the heights on the left bank of the Berezina, bombarded the valley, constructed bridges and moved part of its infantry and guns across the river. Unable to contain the enemy, Major General Chaplitz had to destroy the bridge across the Goina, expose the

---

ranks, found him a strict and demanding superior. To my question, 'What are you doing around here?', he responded, 'We are acting like children who ought to be whipped with birches. We know that the vanguard is close; the first and second lines operate separately and we do not know if they will arrive in time! Our main players are the artillery Lieutenant General Prince Iashvili and Major General Baron Diebitsch of the Quartermaster Service.'

[324] Yermolov's note: Count Lambert was seriously wounded and the admiral's army lost one of its most distinguished and efficient generals.

Zembin defile and retreat into the woods, which were immediately occupied by the enemy. The admiral invited Platov to dispatch Cossacks up the Goina, where they could cross the river and destroy the bridges and paths along the Zembin defile. I dared to suggest to the admiral that 'if Napoleon were to find it difficult to march towards Zembin, the only solution for him would be to seize the road to Minsk, where he would have abundant supplies (which would have supplied our army and other troops), could rest his army, call in reinforcements from Lithuania and restore order.' The admiral responded that, by defending the Zembin defile, he was simply carrying out the orders of the field marshal.

I told him, 'As the chief of staff of the 1st Army, I am aware of His Excellency's orders. You can easily discern how much the current circumstances differ from them and how different the means are at your disposal, especially after Napoleon has just joined Victor's corps and that of Oudinot. A few of these troops were captured yesterday, which means Count Wittgenstein failed to prevent their junction with Napoleon.'[325]

Early on the morning of 17 November, a skirmish had begun and gradually intensified. Our infantry, scattered as tirailleurs, was under Lieutenant General Sabaneev, the chief of staff of the admiral's army, a gallant officer with outstanding abilities. The army was mobilized and the grenadier battalions, which constituted our reserve, were still on the march from Igumen. The cavalry, preserved in perfect order, was useless because of the wooded terrain; only part of our artillery could be used, deployed on the post road in the forest: light guns, equal in numbers to the enemy guns, were deployed to the fore, while battery guns, placed behind, fired at the enemy infantry massed in the clearings. My detachment formed the reserve.[326] It was soon noted that the enemy forces were

---

[325] Yermolov's note: Lieutenant General Ertel, deployed with 15,000 men near Mozyr, was ordered to join the admiral's army; yet precious time was wasted waiting for replies to his meaningless questions and he remained where he was. Ertel had distinguished himself by his efficiency and agility; while serving as ober-policemeister of Moscow, he earned notoriety for his low, obsequious character. Konovnitsyn, knowing about Kutuzov's animosity towards Chichagov, found a way to excuse Ertel from responsibility for his insubordination.

[326] Yermolov's note: The appearance of the Life Guard Jäger and Finland regiments, the Guard artillery and His and Her Majesty's Cuirassier regiments had a good influence on the spirit of the army.

increasing, exhausted troops being replaced with fresher units and our troops driven back. Attacks were resumed frequently and with increasing vigour. There was not a clearing in the woods where small enemy cuirassier detachments did not attack and disorganize our infantry, even inflicting some losses. Prisoners explained the reason for such fierce fighting informing us that Napoleon had crossed the Berezina and was personally commanding the troops.

The infantry on the left bank moved across the bridges, leaving numerous heavy guns, wagons and private carriages blocking access to the river. The advance forces of Count Wittgenstein arrived before 10:00 am but limited their actions to exchanging artillery fire. Around 1:00 pm, his entire corps had finally concentrated; the enemy withstood the devastating fire of his batteries for a brief period and, sweeping all obstacles aside, Wittgenstein's troops occupied the elevated ground on the right bank, inflicting terrible losses on the enemy troops fleeing into a depression. Everyone was gripped by desperation and confusion reigned everywhere. Everyone suddenly rushed to the bridges, where thousands of unarmed people tried to clear their way, dumping transports into the water. The bridges could not withstand such weight and collapsed.

Around 10:00 am on the same day Napoleon had entered the Zembin defile. His infantry swiftly followed him, driven out of the woods with heavy casualties by the admiral's troops. These captured many officials and officers.[327]

Confusion on the bridges was already visible as people feared capture at our hands and our troops occupied the banks. Platov informed Chichagov about the return of the detachment that had earlier been dispatched to destroy the bridges to Zembin. They had had to cross the Goina, which was not frozen yet and, although the creek was shallow everywhere, it was impossible to approach it to within less than 30 sazhens because of the impassable swamps, in which horses got stuck. So, the enemy army was in complete retreat. All the complex and difficult plans for operations on the Berezina finally ended.

---

[327] Yermolov's note: One French officer – old, seriously wounded, commanding a light infantry regiment – lived with me until we crossed the borders and told me that no less than 15,000 military men died here as well as thousands of other people of various nations, standing and professions.

Prince Kutuzov had precise information about the condition of the enemy army; with his characteristic foresight, he had seen these inevitable calamities, which continuously increased and threatened the enemy army. The French still had a long way ahead to the frontiers of our empire, yet harsh winter was setting in and the enemy would have to retreat rapidly despite complete exhaustion. It was obvious from the thousands of corpses covering the road that the enemy army could not escape destruction. Yet, our army would be preserved without sacrifice.

Kutuzov dwelt upon what Napoleon might attempt in such a desperate and extreme situation, for there was no enterprise too dangerous or reckless which Napoleon's supporters, his Guard and the army might attempt when he commanded them and when there was only one way to save him for the glory of France and the hope of seeing the fatherland! But our goal was achieved. Several thousand more prisoners and even some captured marshals could not have increased the glory and celebration of the Russians.

Chichagov's weak army could not have stopped Napoleon. Heading for Minsk would have been better for the French but they needed to take the shortest route; could Napoleon have supposed that our entire army was close by and, having united with the Admiral's army, completely destroy him? After leaving numerous prisoners, virtually everyone unarmed and sick, Napoleon marched on Zembin. Major General Chaplitz was soon dispatched after him, but since his vanguard was too weak, the admiral suggested that I support him with my troops. I did so enthusiastically, allowing Chaplitz, although junior in rank, complete command over the troops. The French tried to slow us down as much as possible, destroying bridges over the valleys and the ravines and burning settlements. On many occasions, our artillery fire dispersed them. Occupying Molodechno, we seized officers' uniforms, which the fleeing enemy had no time to take with them. Here, Chichagov allowed us to halt, rest and then advance at our discretion. His entire army moved behind the vanguard.

I cannot leave out a description of the scene on the Berezina when we quit it and which I had personally witnessed. The bridges had collapsed in places and guns and various heavy transports had fallen into the river. Crowds of people, many of them women with infants and children, had come down to the ice-covered river. Nobody escaped the severity of the frost. No one will ever witness such horrific scenes. Blessed were those who ended their misery by dying. They left behind many who envied their lot. Others would be even more miserable after preserving their lives only to be deprived of them from the cruelty of cold in the most terrible tortures. Fate, our avenger, presented us with scenes of all kinds of desperation and all forms of death. The river was covered with ice transparent as glass: there were numerous dead corpses visible underneath it for the entire width of the river. The enemy had abandoned enormous numbers of artillery and wagons. The riches of ransacked Moscow did not make it across the Berezina. The enemy suffered the shame of flight and the life expectancy of the surviving remnants of the army was already determined. Platov operated independently, destroying all resources that the enemy could have used along the road.

Wittgenstein did not march with Admiral Chichagov, who as the commander-in-chief would have been the superior officer; instead, he moved to the right, arguing that he intended to pursue General Wrede, who commanded the Bavarian troops. Soon after having departed from Polotsk, these troops had retreated into Lithuania and were probably already far ahead of Wittgenstein.

So, as a witness to the events on the Berezina, I present my observations without any partiality or prejudice. There are no compelling reasons as to why I might speak unfavourably about Wittgenstein, who is noted for his chivalrous character and his love of speed! Any mishaps probably stemmed from foreign influence.

In our first conversation, Chichagov proved to be of excellent intelligence and I feel with indignation how powerless my evidence is against the charges made against him.

Whilst on the march along the main road to Vilna, Kutuzov suddenly arrived at our bivouac and stayed for the night. I immediately went to see him and he questioned me rigorously about the battle along the Berezina. I managed to explain to him that Chichagov had not been as guilty as many had desired to portray him. I did not justify his erroneous movement on Igumen, but similarly I did not hide the mistakes committed by Wittgenstein. I easily perceived the depth of Kutuzov's antipathy towards the admiral. He was not pleased that I dared defend him. However, it was difficult to disregard my testimony considering my high rank and Kutuzov was reluctant to sway me away from the facts I had seen with my own eyes. He pretended to be extremely satisfied to learn the truth and assured me (although I was not reassured) that he would now look upon the admiral in a different light and that up to now he had been determined to treat him unfavourably. He ordered me to draw up a secret report on the operations on the Berezina.

Not far from the regional capital of Oshmyani (49 verstas from the provincial capital of Vilna), Platov overtook the vanguard of the admiral's army and continued marching at night without halting. Seslavin's detachment was moving independently ahead of him: his guide was a captured Jew, a town resident, who was aware that Napoleon himself had stayed there but knew nothing about the house that he had occupied. This Jew had guided the detachment down a path covered with deep snow and which was hardly discernible. The city was quiet and completely carefree.

Seslavin first targeted the house that stood apart from the rest due to its appearance: there were crowds of people in its extensive court. The sudden appearance of Cossacks produced widespread confusion, many fled but there was some weak resistance that the Cossacks took advantage of to scatter the enemy.[328] However, the alarm had woken up enormous crowds and the Cossacks were forced to retreat. The house, which Seslavin attacked, was thought to be Napoleon's lodgings because of the number of troops deployed there, but it was the house of the city commandant and the troops were detachments from various army units, which were being hastily sent to Vilna. Napoleon's house was in a distant suburb of the city and he had quit the town with an escort of his guards for Vilna, from where he continued his journey unbeknown to anyone. A division of 10,000 fresh infantrymen, which was sent from Vilna to join the retreating French army, could not reinforce it since Chichagov's vanguard and the Cossacks of Platov were already approaching. The division was from the reserve, comprised of new conscripts, and so it could not endure the fatigue of the march and fell victim to the fierce cold between Oshmyani and Vilna; only a few survivors managing to return to Vilna. The frozen corpses were scattered in increasingly large groups in the fields

---

[328] Yermolov's note: Seslavin encountered no opposition. According to some prisoners, a messenger with dispatches from the rearguard could not find Napoleon, was captured by the Cossacks and delivered to Platov. He had confirmed that Napoleon was at Oshmyani.

adjacent to the road; the bones of the devoured horses lay everywhere, new artillery was abandoned without having been used and clothing was scavenged by those still strong enough to walk.

Seslavin was the first to enter Vilna with his detachment, but he had to yield to superior enemy numbers. Platov and Chaplitz's vanguard soon arrived and the enemy hastily abandoned the town. The admiral's army appeared, followed by that of the field marshal. On 29 November (the thermometer showed 27 degrees of cold), I reached Vilna with my detachment and immediately met Kutuzov. He ordered me to deploy sentries on all food, ammunition and supply stores.[329]

I found Chichagov in the city, but his army was being dispatched towards the borders of Prussia and as it had only slightly more than 15,000 men under arms other troops were ordered to join it at once. Wittgenstein, who had begun his alleged pursuit of the Bavarians from the Berezina but had never even seen them, arrived at Nemenchina not far from Vilna, from where he dispatched Tettenborn[330] with a detachment to assist in the occupation of the town and later halted in one of the suburbs.

Prior to Napoleon's passage, and one might even say his flight, through Vilna, the vigilant French police had concealed French defeats and spread rumours of Napoleon's victories. There the capture of Riga and the conquest of Kiev had been celebrated. The city was brightly illuminated, beautiful paintings were displayed, music thundered in the squares and speeches, remarkable for their insolent audacity, were given. After Austerlitz in 1805, Kutuzov had been appointed the governor of Lithuania with only two battalions of internal guard at his disposal. High society had been charmed by his charismatic and very gracious manners. Polish women, who possess a gift to captivate with their kindness and vivacity, played an important role in his court. Now, here again was Prince Kutuzov of

---

[329] Yermolov's note: The supplies were stored in enormous quantities. Nothing was overlooked or destroyed by the enemy. The value of state property exceeded many millions and many private magazines with abundant supplies were captured as well.

[330] Yermolov's note: Prior to this war, Prince Schwarzenberg, former ambassador to the Russian court, had Tettenborn as his adjutant. He was later accepted into our service, and distinguished himself as a very courageous and capable officer, rendering good service on many occasions.

Smolensk, this time a field marshal and conqueror of Napoleon, whom he had banished beyond the borders of our fatherland.

I found the field marshal with Chichagov and Wittgenstein and the latter was describing several battles he had won in such a bragging tone that it seemed the main army's role had only consisted of winning some small, insignificant actions. Even Kutuzov's finesse was not enough to hide his indignation and he showed it, although he treated the admiral with more attention and he was content with such respect. The relationship between Chichagov and Kutuzov seemed courteous, but that did not prevent Kutuzov from doing harm to the admiral, something which was subsequently noted by many. Kutuzov acted this way because of his belief that Chichagov had intended to steal the glory of concluding peace with the Ottoman Porte following Kutuzov's famous victory over the Grand Vizier at Ruse.

Wittgenstein frequently, but always very eloquently, hinted that St Petersburg owed its salvation to him and that the road to Lithuania was thrown open by his victories. Serving as a major general in Kutuzov's army during the celebrated retreat from Bavaria in 1805, he was known to the commander-in-chief as a courageous chef of a hussar regiment.[331] Finding him elevated to the status of a leading public figure, Kutuzov now found it necessary to gain a thorough understanding of the abilities and knowledge such a commander might need to possess if he was to be trusted with extensive and complex responsibilities. Discussing various incidents that had taken place, as well as talking about the forthcoming campaign abroad, Kutuzov gave Wittgenstein a chance to express his opinion. A quarter of an hour was enough for the shrewd Kutuzov to see through and understand Wittgenstein.[332] Although praised by his many admirers as the saviour of St Petersburg, I am still certain that Wittgenstein was not so intoxicated by this flattery so as to try to compare himself to Kutuzov, who could employ him as an assistant.

---

[331] Wittgenstein was chef of the Mariupol Hussar Regiment between 1802 and 1807.

[332] Yermolov's note: Wittgenstein did not bother to think and left others to do the dirty work. Those serving close to him influenced him, although they did not always belong to the class of decent men.

The main army arrived at Vilna several days later and was given a much needed rest. The field marshal rested on his laurels, ready to pursue his idleness. Generals gathered at headquarters where it was pleasant to find all the comforts and pleasures and to be able to put aside official duties after such an arduous campaign.

The field marshal soon received the decorations for the battles, including Borodino, based on the nominations he made earlier. The confirmation process for these nominations was delayed because many commanders of the 2nd Western Army had been killed or wounded; their replacements submitted reports separately and it had been necessary to examine the merit of the reported deeds individually and to select the appropriate awards.[333]

The enemy continued fleeing over our frontiers. The Austrian corps of Prince Schwarzenberg abandoned the Grodno province. General Reynier, with the Saxon corps, retreated in the direction of the Narev, while the Polish forces of the Grand Duchy of Warsaw moved towards Warsaw. Marshal Macdonald's corps and the Prussian troops fell back from Courland to Tilsit. The survivors of the great Napoleonic army were on the verge of complete destruction[334] while the remnants of the allied forces were marching back to Prussia. Almost no enemy soldiers were left on Russian soil.

Our army was deployed in the following order. Chichagov's army was at Ezdna on the Niemen. Osten-Sacken's large corps, earlier detached to prevent the Austrian and Saxon troops from seizing extensive territory in rich provinces, was also moving in that direction. Wittgenstein's 1st Corps reached the vicinities of Kovno

---

[333] Yermolov's note: As he left the army in September, Barclay de Tolly had instructed Flügel Adjutant Colonel Zakrevskii, the director of the ministerial chancellery, to show me his report to the field marshal nominating me for the Order of St George (2nd class). Of course, it was not appropriate to nominate me for an award that the commander-in-chief himself had been nominated to, but it was equally unsuitable to suggest awarding me with the Order of St Anna which was given to brigade commanders and regimental chiefs and was often awarded for reviews and parades.

[334] Yermolov's note: When Napoleon rushed to cross the Berezina, he was joined at Bobr by the French corps of Marshal Victor and only one division took part in the battle at Chashniki. Also, Marshal Oudinot's troops, that had defended Polotsk, were in relatively good condition. They watched in horror the disastrous state of the main army and the troops of the Confederation of Rhine, could not recognize the once glittering Guard, which was now destined for inevitable destruction!

on the Niemen without trouble and watched the retreat of Macdonald. Kutuzov enjoyed complete rest. Nothing was allowed to reach his ears except the servile praise of flatterers, those inescapable companions of might. We were reminded about the war only by the disorder that reigned absolutely everywhere and which was, evidently, just as widespread among our enemies.

In Vilna, all suitable buildings and the refectories of monasteries had been transformed into hospitals by the French. In some of them, there was no firewood despite the severity of the winter; and a few bundles of scattered straw made do for beds. A few patients were given clothing, but they had no plates or dishes. One of the senior physicians, who accompanied me, showed me an enormous hospital and, after pushing open the door with his foot, we were afflicted by a suffocating stench. He told me that these hospitals had been abandoned by their doctors since there were no means to save the patients and communication with them only exposed the doctors to the risk of infection. In his opinion, it was necessary to take advantage of the strong cold, which prevented the decomposition of the bodies, to clear the town and safely remove all the corpses. Many thousands of corpses were taken out of the town, some of them were burnt, others thrown into the ditches and covered with lime. The field marshal issued orders to carry out these measures.

There were still enormous supplies of various kinds of provisions in Vilna, which, under the orders of the field marshal, were protected until Quartermaster General Kankrin arrived. There were also equally large stores of ammunition, hospital clothing, linen, dishes, expensive medicines and sets of the best surgical instruments, numerous barrels filled with quinine, camphor and other substances. Grand Duke Constantine Pavlovich was permitted to take the necessary resources for the lower ranks of the Guards from the ammunition stores and Major General Baron Rosen of the Guard Infantry Division was ordered to submit a detailed report on this matter.[335]

---

[335] Yermolov's note: I was present during this conversation and easily noticed how pleased the field marshal was when the grand duke did not pursue other issues with equal persistence. I assume the goal was to preserve as much state property as possible.

Soon rumours began to spread about the arrival of the czar. We had to make arrangements for his coming and the field marshal's luxurious recreation was now concealed beneath a veneer of activity. In Vilna, we also found private magazines with abundant supplies of golden and silver accessories for officers, which were appropriated by various people.

The czar arrived and, in appreciation of the great services of His Excellency Prince Kutuzov, decorated him with the Order of St George (1st class).[336] Decorations were lavishly distributed according to Kutuzov's nominations, which were not always impartial and had often been made without serious deliberation. Soon, the court was organized, with its inseparable factions and gossip; so there was an extensive field for intrigue, where Kutuzov, well known for his cunning, was constantly in the lead. Here at least he was an invincible opponent.

Among such important events, I want to mention something else, less important in itself but original in the way it ended. The Austrian corps, having mostly left our frontiers, still had a few of its remaining troops at Grodno. Count Ozharovskii soon arrived with his detachment and presented the enemy with an offer of surrender, which they rejected. Meanwhile, the guerilla leader Davidov, with a much smaller Cossack detachment, approached the enemy outposts and, without the verbose speeches of a courtier or political debate, he threatened to take the town by assault with the main army following him if the town was not immediately surrendered. Soon, the sound of clinking glasses was heard among the Hungarian hussars, and, amid praises to the national beverage, hands were shaken in a sign of friendship. Conditions were then discussed with their commander and Grodno was soon in our hands![337] Thus, the field marshal received Count Ozharovskii's report that the Austrian commander refused to surrender the town at exactly the same time that he received Davidov's message that it had fallen!

After his arrival, the czar announced his intention to take the army over the border. Showing great respect to the field marshal, he

---

[336] Yermolov's note: This order was abolished by Paul I but restored by Alexander; Prince Kutuzov was the first chevalier of the order (1st class) during Alexander's reign.

[337] Yermolov's note: The staff officer was allowed to return to his troops. Order and discipline were restored in the town and its vicinities. Davidov's detachment now awaited further instructions.

noted at the council that the age, serious wounds, labours and anxiety of the last campaign had weakened Kutuzov's abilities. The sovereign, wanting to give him some peace of mind, let him keep the title of commander-in-chief and the external show of some authority. In reality, he personally took charge of the armies and ordered those persons enjoying his particular confidence, to report on the state of the armies and the means of supplying them.

Prince Kutuzov thought it necessary to present Konovnitsyn and Quartermaster General of the 1st Army Toll as his most important associates and praised them above all. Before the war, the czar had often singled out Konovnitsyn's 3rd Infantry Division as being exemplary for its order and parade ground skills with the lower ranks being given exceptional monetary rewards. The czar received Konovnitsyn very kindly, thanked him for his zeal and the courage he had demonstrated on so many occasions. I do not know if he was equally satisfied with the general's knowledge of the military art or tested his opinion on the forthcoming campaign.[338]

In his dealings with Konovnitsyn, Count Arakcheyev had never been able to obtain thorough explanations on many issues. Prince Volkonsky also did not benefit from his discussions with Konovnitsyn and, on matters regarding the most convenient ways to unite the armies, Konovnitsyn seemed to rely on the knowledge of General Toll, reporting his words back to the sovereign, getting attention from the czar, who thus noted his abilities. Konovnitsyn soon had to attend to his family for some personal reasons and the czar granted him leave for his efforts. His absence from the army was felt, but soon he was not remembered. Prince Volkonsky was appointed the chief of staff of all armies under the field marshal.[339] Thereafter, the czar himself issued all the orders and supervised

---

[338] Yermolov's note: During the reign of Catherine II, Konovnitsyn was a colonel of an infantry regiment. His father, a prominent official, had connections to many powerful personalities and, by various means, managed to promote his son within a remarkably short time. When Konovnitsyn returned to military service he revealed his actual knowledge of military art. His fearlessness was dazzling indeed, but could not replace his lack of education.

[339] Yermolov's note: The czar needed a man whom he had known for long time and completely trusted. Prince Volkonsky was absolutely loyal to him. (Editor: According to some contemporaries, after the creation of the General Staff and the position of the chief of staff, Yermolov commented that thereafter the minister of war could be simply referred to as the minister of supply and commissariat forces.)

their execution. General Baron Bennigsen attended His Imperial Majesty and the czar consulted his renowned experience and knowledge on all those occasions when the importance of circumstances required accurate considerations.

Before the czar's arrival, I presented the field marshal with my secret report on the actions of Chichagov on the Berezina. He told me that he was ready to look on Chichagov without hard feelings. In the opinion of many, Chichagov's fault consisted of the fact that he managed to see through and completely understand Kutuzov! The field marshal could not ignore my report (coming from the chief of staff of the 1st Army), in which I described myself as an actual witness, whose troops comprised the reserves and had not fired a single shot.[340]

Chichagov was marching towards the imperial border when the czar arrived. It is more than likely that Kutuzov took advantage of the admiral's absence to describe Chichagov's actions on the Berezina to the czar, no doubt defending him against all those unwarranted accusations. I am not aware if the czar met Chichagov, but the latter soon left his post and retired. Kutuzov's interests were not at risk in this matter so his indifference is understandable.[341] The army was to cross the imperial borders on 1 [12] January 1813. The general plan of action was kept secret. The preliminary disposition of the army was as follows: Miloradovich, with the vanguard, was in Grodno and towards Belostock. Chichagov was at Ezdna and in the direction of Olita. Osten-Saken's corps, detached from Chichagov's army, had halted on the border and was busy observing the retreat of the Austrian and Saxon troops. Dokhturov, with the 6th Corps and other detachments, was also near the frontier. Tormasov, with the entire Guard, the Guard cavalry, the 1st Grenadier Division and numerous artillery, occupied Merech and its environs. The general headquarters of the czar and the field marshal was also established there. Wittgenstein's 1st Corps was not far from Kovno, watching the retreat of the Prussian forces from

---

[340] Yermolov's note: The field marshal did not wish to have Bennigsen around him because the latter often disagreed with him. Toll took advantage of every chance to provoke disagreement between them and thus prudently sought to increase his influence over the frail Kutuzov.

[341] Chichagov was officially relieved of his command because of 'poor health', but, in reality, he was harshly criticized and blamed for mishandling the operation on the Berezina.

Riga.³⁴² Platov, with most of the Don Cossack regiments, was near Merech; all the other forces were ready to cross the border. Winzegorode was offered the chance to lead a detachment.³⁴³

After the headquarters of the 1st Army was abolished, I was appointed commander of the artillery of all the armies. I appealed to the field marshal to overturn this appointment but he told me to explain my request to the czar. This flattering position was given to me despite my rank since, in the circumstances, the czar was reluctant to offer it to anyone else; so I was ordered to accept it and had to obey! My new position involved extensive responsibilities and there were matters which required quick correction. Our means had been exhausted by the campaign while many essentials were unavailable. Until now, each army had had its own artillery commander; all of them were now subordinated to one commander. The czar, having listened to me kindly, confirmed my appointment.

To ease some of my concerns and to accelerate the orders of the Artillery Department, the czar ordered me to prepare reports and to present them to Count Arakcheyev, who would ensure their immediate completion by announcing his intentions to the

---

³⁴² Yermolov's note: The Prussian commander General Yorck is one of the best commanders. He halted military operations and opened negotiations, as desired by the troops loyal to him. French garrisons were still in the fortresses of Prussia and so the Prussian king could not approve such an obvious breach of the alliance with Napoleon.

³⁴³ Yermolov's note: Winzegorode knew from local residents that Napoleon had quit Moscow and only a few troops remained in the city. Captured prisoners confirmed that Marshal Mortier, left behind with a few forces, was ordered to blow up the Kremlin, leave Moscow and follow the main army. Accompanied by a small convoy and some of his suite, Winzegorode approached the city gates with the intention of frightening the enemy and forcing them to surrender Moscow. Yet, his weak party was routed and he was captured because he made no sign of being sent to negotiate. A weak convoy of gendarmes escorted him along remote roads; Winzegorode was already on the other bank the Berezina, when he was suddenly liberated by a Cossack outpost from the detachment of Flügel Adjutant Colonel Chernishev, who was being sent from St Petersburg to the field marshal's headquarters with instructions to Admiral Chichagov. Unaware of his whereabouts, Chernishev was surprised to see Winzegorode. They shared a common sorrow and, without a doubt, both these prominent men would have gladly given up all their exploits to be the one to have liberated Moscow; but it was Don Cossack Major General Ilovaisky (IV) who was the first in.

Inspector of All Artillery, Müller-Zakomelsky. This measure was essential given the large number of officers, lower ranks and horses that needed to be assigned to the artillery for the campaign abroad. Around Vilna some 600 guns and trained cadres were gathered to organize 50 horse and field companies, which, as soon as they were properly trained, would follow the main army. The inexperienced companies were ordered to Vilna.

The czar arrived to Merech at the same time as the field marshal. Our armies marked the first day of 1813 by crossing the border. In the course of seven months, having lost no less than eight provinces to the enemy, after being deprived of the capital that was turned into ashes, having more than 500,000 enemy troops in the heart of our land, Russia had triumphed! The czar showed an example of determination and revived everyone's hopes for the salvation of the fatherland. No one spared efforts to win this war. Inspired by the feeling of self-sacrifice, the brave militias of Russia marched against the enemy; the hour of liberation arrived and the Lord, defender of the righteous, broke our haughty enemies, and none of them remained on the soil of our beloved fatherland!

Having described the events taking place in the course of the Patriotic War and the pursuit of the fleeing enemy to our borders, I now come to close of my account of this campaign.

Made in the USA
Lexington, KY
05 April 2013